Mat 10:5 These twelve Jesus sent forth, and commanded them, saying, Go not into the way of the Gentiles, and into any city of the Samaritans enter ye not:

6 But go rather to the lost sheep of the house of Israel.

7 And as ye go, preach, saying, The kingdom of heaven is at hand.

8 Heal the sick, cleanse the lepers, raise the dead, cast out devils: freely ye have received, freely give.

WARNING:

THIS BOOK WILL CHALLENGE CHRISTIANS WHO ARE SECURE IN THEIR RELIGIOUS CONCEPT OF CHRISTIANITY, AND WHO ARE COMFORTABLE WITH "DOING CHURCH" AS USUAL.

Going On To Perfection:

A Disciple's Guide To Ministry

Advancing the Kingdom of God In Today's World Like Jesus Did.

Going On To Perfection:
A Disciple's Guide To Ministry

Advancing the Kingdom of God In Today's World Like Jesus Did.

Lance Rowe

Cross Country Publishing

Dutton, Al 35744

Definitions for the Greek and Hebrew words contained herein are from Strong's Exhaustive Concordance of the Bible, Thayer's Greek Definitions, and Brown - Driver - Briggs' Hebrew definitions.

Commentaries used and quoted from in this work are:
Adam Clarke's Commentary
Jameson, Faucett and Brown
Keil and Delitz
F B Meyer

ISBN: 978-0-692-76160-1

Library of Congress Control Number: 2016912379

© 7/27/2016

"It is the great business of every Christian to save souls. People complain that they do not know how to take hold of this matter. Why, the reason is plain enough; they have never studied it. They have never taken the proper pains to qualify themselves for the work. If you do not make it a matter of study, how you may successfully act in building up the kingdom of Christ, you are acting a very wicked and absurd part as a Christian."

— Charles Grandison Finney

Contents

'Not called!' did you say? 'Not heard the call,' I think you should say. Put your ear down to the Bible, and hear him bid you go and pull sinners out of the fire of sin. Put your ear down to the burdened, agonized heart of humanity, and listen to its pitiful wail for help. Go stand by the gates of hell, and hear the damned entreat you to go to their father's house and bid their brothers and sisters, and servants and masters not to come there. And then look Christ in the face, whose mercy you have professed to obey, and tell him whether you will join heart and soul and body and circumstances in the march to publish his mercy to the world."

--William Booth

Notes:

_____
_____
_____
_____
_____
_____
_____
_____
_____
_____
_____
_____
_____
_____
_____
_____
_____
_____
_____
_____
_____
_____

Introduction

**Mat 28:16 Then the eleven disciples went away into Galilee, into a mountain where Jesus had appointed them.
17 And when they saw him, they worshipped him: but some doubted.
18 And Jesus came and spake unto them, saying, All power is given unto me in heaven and in earth.
19 Go ye therefore, and teach all nations, baptizing them in the name of the Father, and of the Son, and of the Holy Ghost:
20 Teaching them to observe all things whatsoever I have commanded you: and, lo, I am with you alway,** *even* **unto the end of the world. Amen.**

IT WAS A Sunday in 1988. We lived in Chino Valley, Arizona, and had two children, ages one and two. My wife and I had been Christians since 1983, and we both had a mindset to live for the Lord in whatever capacity He called us to live for Him.

We were house sitting my in-law's house at the time. Michelle's parents had gone on vacation to visit family in Minnesota, and we temporarily moved from our little one bedroom mobile home into their spacious modular home to take care of it while they were gone.

On this particular Sunday I was sitting at the dining room table immersed in my morning study of the Word of God, when I read these words:

Heb 11:6 But without faith *it is* **impossible to please** *him:* **for he that cometh to God must believe that he is, and** *that* **he is a rewarder of them that diligently seek him.**

I had been working for a construction company the past year and a half, doing concrete work, carpentry and steel building construction. We were comfortable and secure in our present circumstance, and life was good.

As I read that passage in Hebrews 11:6, my mind took me back to our first year of walking with the Lord.

I remembered when we lived in an efficiency apartment in Salt Lake City, and how every day seemed like an adventure as we lived out our new found faith in Jesus Christ.

I had originally gone to Salt Lake City in September of 1983 to sign the books at the IBEW local union hall in the hopes of getting hired on a high line construction job that was supposed to start in the near future.

It was on the way to Utah, that I surrendered my life to Jesus in a motel room in Fairbault Minnesota[1]. By the time I got to Salt Lake City, I'd been a Christian for less than a week.

Things didn't go as I planned in Salt Lake, and I ended up getting temporary work out of a day labor employment agency.

For the next six months, Michelle and I lived from week to week, sometimes from day to day, working at whatever came our way, from crushing cars in a salvage yard, cleaning mortar off of used bricks, doing residential and commercial roofing, and finding temporary employment at a graphic design company, always managing to have enough money to pay the rent by the end of the month for our small apartment, and to have food for the table.

But in February or March of 1984 we couldn't make the rent, because our 1973 Chevy Vega had quit running and had been towed away, and I had no transportation to get to and from work. Also, the demand for laborers at that time of year was almost non-existent.

We ended up leaving Salt Lake City with a back pack and a duffle bag filled with what we deemed to be our most important possessions, and hitchhiked west toward warmer country. We had no plan, no destination. But we had faith in God, which was a good thing, because my pride wouldn't allow me to ask anyone for help.

The next three months were filled with seeing God at work in our lives every day, as He brought people our way who we would witness to about our faith in God. We never went hungry, and each day we would let Him know our needs, and each day we would end up rejoicing because we saw His Hand at work in every situation.

We had opportunities to minister to people that we met, even though we didn't know that we were ministering to them. We were just living what we thought was a normal life of total dependence on Jesus. Neither one of us had been raised in Christianity, so it was all new for us, and we had the Bible to let us know how we should live.

Eventually we settled down in Arizona and spent our first year living near Show Low, and after that moved to Chino Valley. Now, four years later I was sitting at my in-law's table reading Hebrews 11:6. "Without Faith, it is impossible to please God." As I read those words, I remembered our three month adventure of living by Faith on the road.

I was a pretty good worker, and the job I had with that construction company paid relatively well for us. But now I had a thought come to me:

Do I have faith in my ability as a construction worker, or do I have faith in God?

Then I had another thought. I had the image of a school bus flash through my mind, and I looked up from the Bible and said to my wife, "Remember when we were hitch hiking and we had to depend on God for everything?" When she answered in the affirmative, I asked her "What if we just sold everything and bought a bus, and learned about faith? What if we just travelled until the Lord planted us where He wants us to be?"

She didn't hesitate. "If that is what the Lord wants, then that is what we should do," she answered.

It was settled. What I really thought it would be a six month journey became a lifestyle of dependence on God. At that time I didn't know that I was called to be an evangelist, or a minister of the Gospel. But as the Lord guided us on our way, it became more and more evident that He had gifted me with the Calling of an evangelist. You can read more about the history of the development of our ministry in the appendix [2].

In the years that I have been involved in ministry since 1988, I have met many Christians who have *had a desire* to serve the Lord in reaching out to their neighbors or their community, but they did not know how to do it. Many in the "church world" think that ministry is the exclusive responsibility of those who hold a title or stand behind a pulpit. But nothing could be farther from the truth.

Every Christian is called to do the work of the ministry. It is not a suggestion or an option, or a vocational pursuit; it is an obligation. Some will balk at that statement, but while the Bible says that we are not saved by our works, we are saved to do good works

Eph 2:8 For by grace are ye saved through faith; and that not of yourselves: *it is* **the gift of God:**
9 Not of works, lest any man should boast.

10 For we are his workmanship, created in Christ Jesus unto good works, which God hath before ordained that we should walk in them.

God's Purpose for you is that you should do the Work He has ordained for you personally. Another way of putting that is God has ordained that you should walk in your Calling.

Yes, you are called to ministry. You are called to serve God. Religion has substituted the Truth that is in Christ for a spectator mentality that most of the Body of Christ has bought into. Whether it is actually admitted or not, most "lay people" in the church think that the man up front is the minister who is specially anointed by God to do the "spiritual" work.

The rest of the people in the pews are supposed to work so they can support that man of God. The word "Anointed" in religious circles is synonymous with "talented". Some preachers who travel from church venue to church venue are called "anointed" preachers because they can really preach! Christians flock to hear this preacher or that preacher in much the same way the people of the world go from one concert to another concert in order to hear the talented singers and musicians. The majority of "church going" Christians have become hearers of the Word, and not doers of the Word.

It is easier to put in a couple hours a week attending "church" than it is to actually respond to and walk in the Calling that the Lord has for them. The average Christian thinks "I have a family. My duty in life is to provide for my family and to make sure my children are raised with Christian values. I take them to church and to VBS and revival meetings. I tithe from my income. The pastor or the guest speaker is the one who is called to ministry, not me".

What is passed off and accepted as "church" today is NOT the Biblical model of the Church that Christ founded.

In Matthew 28, the Lord commands His disciples to go and make disciples. He said that they were to teach those disciples to obey the things He had commanded them. And He had just commanded them to make disciples. Like the first disciples, we are all commissioned to make disciples, and in turn, to train them how to make disciples.

If you have given your heart to Jesus, you are to be equipped to be a minister. Another word for "ministry" is "service". You have been saved from the darkness of sin to serve in the Kingdom of God and to be a light to this world.

Most Christians I have met in my 30+ years in Christ are unaware that they have a Calling for ministry, and a responsibility to walk in that Calling. Why do they not know they have a calling? The blame chiefly lies on the leadership of the church they attend.

The Lord has set in place the five-fold ministry (*apostles, prophets, evangelists, pastors and teachers*) to equip Christians to do the work of the ministry.

Unfortunately, too often the five-fold ministry has become more of an income producing vocation with men seeking positions of honor and prestige in the sacred halls of Christendom, rather than a disciple making, ministry equipping lifestyle.

Men with titles before their names may preach a good message, telling the congregation they need to be bold about their faith to others, but they rarely equip the congregation to do so. Once the plate is passed and the honorarium is paid, the title holders are on their way to their next speaking engagement, leaving the congregation just as unequipped and unprepared for ministry as they were before they came.

But the blame isn't *only* on the professional pulpiteers.

While all Christians are called to be disciples, not everyone who professes a belief in Christ understands what a disciple is, or cares to apply themselves to *be* a disciple.

Christians who have been "saved" for 30 years still desire to be fed the milk of the Word of God, instead of maturing into their Calling.

They are much more comfortable with a religious outlook of Christianity which consists in doing the minimum "requirements", such as weekly attendance of "church" and giving something in the offering plate, rather than a *commitment* to Christ. Too many professing Christians think faithful attendance of weekly services as members of a given congregation is the essence of what Christianity is, and they resist any call to ministry.

Short term mission trips and occasional "Church outreaches" and "special offerings" may not have

Mat 25:31 When the Son of man shall come in his glory, and all the holy angels with him, then shall he sit upon the throne of his glory:
32 And before him shall be gathered all nations: and he shall separate them one from another, as a shepherd divideth *his* sheep from the goats:
33 And he shall set the sheep on his right hand, but the goats on the left.
34 Then shall the King say unto them on his right hand, Come, ye blessed of my Father, inherit the kingdom prepared for you from the foundation of the world:
35 For I was an hungred, and ye gave me meat: I was thirsty, and ye gave me drink: I was a stranger, and ye took me in:
36 Naked, and ye clothed me: I was sick, and ye visited me: I was in prison, and ye came unto me.
37 Then shall the righteous answer him, saying, Lord, when saw we thee an hungred, and fed *thee?* or thirsty, and gave *thee* drink?
38 When saw we thee a stranger, and took *thee* in? or naked, and clothed *thee?*
39 Or when saw we thee sick, or in prison, and came unto thee?
40 And the King shall answer and say unto them, Verily I say unto you, Inasmuch as ye have done *it* unto one of the least of these my brethren, ye have done *it* unto me.
41 Then shall he say also unto them on the left hand, Depart from me, ye cursed, into everlasting fire, prepared for the devil and his angels:
42 For I was an hungred, and ye gave me no meat: I was thirsty, and ye gave me no drink:
43 I was a stranger, and ye

been intentionally designed to help the Christian feel good about the bulk of the year that he spends neglecting his or her role in furthering the Kingdom of God in his or her sphere of influence, but often times that is what they succeed in doing.

That is why Jesus said "Many are called, but few are chosen." A person has to respond to the Call of God first in order to be chosen. Then once you respond, you must be trained or discipled to be an able minister.

In the military, a company typically consists of somewhere between 80-250 soldiers and it is usually commanded by a major or a captain, who is known as the "company commander". The soldiers in the company will generally assemble in an orderly fashion each morning to get their instructions for the day. During the morning assembly, the Company Commander may make a call for volunteers to perform a specific task. Generally there are only a few who will volunteer for the job. The call went out to everyone, *but only a few* were chosen.

The truth is, a lot of professing Christians choose to ignore the Call that God has on their lives because they are too preoccupied with living for what the world has to offer them, instead of living for the One Who has offered them eternal life. All of that will be settled in the Day of Judgment.

It is important to understand this: *while we are not saved by our works, we **are** saved to do good works.*

Jas 2:14 What *doth it* profit, my brethren, though a man say he hath faith, and have not works? can faith save him?
15 If a brother or sister be naked, and destitute of daily food,
16 And one of you say unto them, Depart in peace, be *ye* warmed and filled; notwithstanding ye give them not those things which are needful to the body; what *doth it* profit?
17 Even so faith, if it hath not works, is dead, being alone.

took me not in: naked, and ye clothed me not: sick, and in prison, and ye visited me not.

44 Then shall they also answer him, saying, Lord, when saw we thee an hungred, or athirst, or a stranger, or naked, or sick, or in prison, and did not minister unto thee?

45 Then shall he answer them, saying, Verily I say unto you, Inasmuch as ye did *it* not to one of the least of these, ye did *it* not to me.

46 And these shall go away into everlasting punishment: but the righteous into life eternal.

Notes:

_____

_____

_____

_____

_____

_____

_____

_____

_____

_____

_____

_____

_____

_____

_____

_____

_____

_____

_____

_____

_____

_____

_____

_____

_____

18 Yea, a man may say, Thou hast faith, and I have works: shew me thy faith without thy works, and I will shew thee my faith by my works.

19 Thou believest that there is one God; thou doest well: the devils also believe, and tremble.

20 But wilt thou know, O vain man, that faith without works is dead?

21 Was not Abraham our father justified by works, when he had offered Isaac his son upon the altar?

22 Seest thou how faith wrought with his works, and by works was faith made perfect?

23 And the scripture was fulfilled which saith, Abraham believed God, and it was imputed unto him for righteousness: and he was called the Friend of God.

24 Ye see then how that by works a man is justified, and not by faith only.

25 Likewise also was not Rahab the harlot justified by works, when she had received the messengers, and had sent *them* out another way?

26 For as the body without the spirit is dead, so faith without works is dead also.

Many times Christians are intimidated into *being silent about their faith* because of an inability to relate to others who do not hold similar beliefs as they do.

Many people cannot afford to go to a Bible college to become equipped for the Call to ministry that they know they have, and to tell you the truth, you don't have to go to a seminary to fulfill God's Calling for your life. You just need to have a willing heart to trust God to equip you to do what He has Called you to do.

This book is the by-product of 30+ years of living a surrendered (albeit not a perfect) life for the Almighty God Who created us for Himself and redeemed us through the Precious Blood of Jesus Christ.

We have been blessed with the privilege of being trained by our Lord in the area of faith, evangelism, and one on one ministry in pastoral roles, and we desire to share that knowledge and understanding with our brothers and sisters throughout the U.S. and the world, to encourage and equip the saints to be effective laborers for the furtherance of the Kingdom of God in their community or work place or wherever their sphere of influence may be.

I don't have all the answers, and many more qualified than I could have compiled a better book, but I haven't seen many, if any, that touches on this subject, and as such, I have undertaken the task of putting this book together.

This book is written for those true disciples who desire to get beyond the weekly milk of "doing church" as usual, and have understood their responsibility to respond to the Call to ministry. That is what "Going on to Perfection" means, getting to the point where you no longer need to be ministered to, or to be continually taught doctrine, but now as a mature Christian, you desire to *do the work of ministry*. In order to go on to perfection or maturity, we need to be able to comprehend the depth of our capabilities, our authority and our responsibilities as ministers of God in Christ.

My book "*The First Principles; A Course in Discipleship For Every Christian*" is based on Hebrews 6:1-2, which begins by saying *"leaving the principles of the doctrine of Christ, let us go on unto perfection;"* and then it lists those first principles as the doctrines of repentance from dead works, of faith toward God, of the doctrine of baptisms, of laying on of hands, of resurrection of the dead, and of eternal judgment. All of that is *milk*. No matter how many different creative ways a preacher may portray the Death, Burial and Resurrection of Jesus Christ over the years, or no matter how many times you may learn about the "soon return of Jesus Christ", or no matter how many "revival meetings you may have attended in your life; if you haven't yet stepped into ministry and making disciples yourself, you are still feeding off milk. Meat is to grow up and *do* the Will of God, like Jesus did.

I would recommend that the Christian who desires to step into ministry study The First Principles before they begin this book. Hebrews 5:12-14 tells us:

Heb 5:12 For when for the time ye ought to be teachers, _ye have need that one teach you again which be the first principles of the oracles of God_; and are become such as have need of milk, and not of strong meat. 13 For every one that useth milk *is* unskilful in the word of righteousness: for he is a babe.

Every minister needs to know these basic doctrines in order to effectively minister to others.

If you have not yet gotten a copy of that book, "The First Principles; A Course in Discipleship For Every Christian" can be ordered at:
https://www.createspace.com/5877934

Section 1

The Characteristics of a Minister of God

"The greatness of a man's power is the measure of his surrender." —
William Booth

Php 2:5 Let this mind be in you, which was also in Christ Jesus:
6 Who, being in the form of God, thought it not robbery to be equal with God:
7 But made himself of no reputation, and took upon him the form of a servant, and was made in the likeness of men:
8 And being found in fashion as a man, he humbled himself, and became obedient unto death, even the death of the cross.
9 Wherefore God also hath highly exalted him, and given him a name which is above every name:

In Christ we become God's
sons, man's servants and the
devil's masters.

John G. Lake

Notes:

_____
_____
_____
_____
_____
_____
_____
_____
_____
_____
_____
_____
_____
_____
_____
_____
_____
_____
_____
_____
_____
_____
_____
_____
_____
_____
_____
_____
_____
_____
_____
_____
_____
_____
_____

Chapter 1

First Things First

1Jn 3:1 Behold, what manner of love the Father hath bestowed upon us, that we should be called the sons of God: therefore the world knoweth us not, because it knew him not.

THE WORLD DOES NOT KNOW a true child of God. Are you a child of God? The word translated as "knoweth" is the same word that was used when we read that "Joseph knew her not", speaking of having intimacy with Mary until she gave birth to Jesus.

As a child of God, intimacy with the world should be a foreign concept just as intimacy with God is a foreign concept to the world.

Joh 15:19 If ye were of the world, the world would love his own: but because ye are not of the world, but I have chosen you out of the world, therefore the world hateth you.

Our passage in First John continues:

**1 Jn 3:2 Beloved, now are we the sons of God, and it doth not yet appear what we shall be: but we know that, when he shall appear, we shall be like him; for we shall see him as he is.
3 And every man that hath this hope in him purifieth himself, even as he is pure.**

But wait! Isn't this a contradiction of the message that we receive from so many in the pulpit today? Isn't it God who does the purifying? Yet here we read that those who have the Promise of being a reflection of Christ *purify themselves.*

And in Revelation we are told that the Bride has

1Pe 1:18 Forasmuch as ye know that ye were not redeemed with corruptible things, as silver and gold, from your vain conversation received by tradition from your fathers;
19 But with the precious blood of Christ, as of a lamb without blemish and without spot:
20 Who verily was foreordained before the foundation of the world, but was manifest in these last times for you,
21 Who by him do believe in God, that raised him up from the dead, and gave him glory; that your faith and hope might be in God.
22 Seeing ye have purified your souls in obeying the truth through the Spirit unto unfeigned love of the brethren, see that ye love one another with a pure heart fervently:
23 Being born again, not of corruptible seed, but of incorruptible, by the word of God, which liveth and abideth for ever.

Notes:

_____
_____
_____
_____
_____
_____
_____
_____
_____
_____
_____
_____
_____
_____

made herself ready, not that the Holy Spirit has made her ready.

Rev 19:7 Let us be glad and rejoice, and give honour to him: for the marriage of the Lamb is come, and his wife hath made herself ready.

How does the Bride of Christ make herself ready?

**Jas 4:7 Submit yourselves therefore to God. Resist the devil, and he will flee from you.
8 Draw nigh to God, and he will draw nigh to you. Cleanse *your* hands, *ye* sinners; and purify *your* hearts, *ye* double minded.
9 Be afflicted, and mourn, and weep: let your laughter be turned to mourning, and *your* joy to heaviness.
10 Humble yourselves in the sight of the Lord, and he shall lift you up.**

There is no getting around it. It is the individual's responsibility to purify himself or herself. But how is that done? You certainly cannot do it if you haven't been born from above, born of the Spirit of God.

In the Old Testament there were purification rituals that the priests had to engage in before they could minister in the presence of the Lord.

**Num 8:6 Take the Levites from among the children of Israel, and cleanse them.
7 And thus shalt thou do unto them, to cleanse them: Sprinkle water of purifying upon them, and let them shave all their flesh, and let them wash their clothes, and *so* make themselves clean.
8 Then let them take a young bullock with his meat offering, *even* fine flour mingled with oil, and another young bullock shalt thou take for a sin offering.
9 And thou shalt bring the Levites before the tabernacle of the congregation: and thou shalt gather the whole assembly of the children of Israel together:
10 And thou shalt bring the Levites before the LORD: and the children of Israel shall put their hands upon the Levites:**

11 And Aaron shall offer the Levites before the LORD *for* an offering of the children of Israel, that they may execute the service of the LORD.

12 And the Levites shall lay their hands upon the heads of the bullocks: and thou shalt offer the one *for* a sin offering, and the other *for* a burnt offering, unto the LORD, to make an atonement for the Levites.

13 And thou shalt set the Levites before Aaron, and before his sons, and offer them *for* an offering unto the LORD.

14 Thus shalt thou separate the Levites from among the children of Israel: and the Levites shall be mine.

15 And after that shall the Levites go in to do the service of the tabernacle of the congregation: and thou shalt cleanse them, and offer them *for* an offering.

16 For they *are* wholly given unto me from among the children of Israel; instead of such as open every womb, *even instead of* the firstborn of all the children of Israel, have I taken them unto me.

17 For all the firstborn of the children of Israel *are* mine, *both* man and beast: on the day that I smote every firstborn in the land of Egypt I sanctified them for myself.

18 And I have taken the Levites for all the firstborn of the children of Israel.

19 And I have given the Levites *as* a gift to Aaron and to his sons from among the children of Israel, to do the service of the children of Israel in the tabernacle of the congregation, and to make an atonement for the children of Israel: that there be no plague among the children of Israel, when the children of Israel come nigh unto the sanctuary.

20 And Moses, and Aaron, and all the congregation of the children of Israel, did to the Levites according unto all that the LORD commanded Moses concerning the Levites, so did the children of Israel unto them.

21 And the Levites were purified, and they washed their clothes; and Aaron offered them *as*

Mat 14:14 And Jesus went forth, and saw a great multitude, and was moved with compassion toward them, and he healed their sick.

Mat 20:30 And, behold, two blind men sitting by the way side, when they heard that Jesus passed by, cried out, saying, Have mercy on us, O Lord, *thou* Son of David.
31 And the multitude rebuked them, because they should hold their peace: but they cried the more, saying, Have mercy on us, O Lord, *thou* Son of David.
32 And Jesus stood still, and called them, and said, What will ye that I shall do unto you?
33 They say unto him, Lord, that our eyes may be opened.
34 So Jesus had compassion *on them,* and touched their eyes: and immediately their eyes received sight, and they followed him.

Mar 1:40 And there came a leper to him, beseeching him, and kneeling down to him, and saying unto him, If thou wilt, thou canst make me clean.
41 And Jesus, moved with compassion, put forth *his* hand, and touched him, and saith unto him, I will; be thou clean.

Notes

_____
_____
_____
_____
_____
_____
_____

an offering before the LORD; and Aaron made an atonement for them to cleanse them.
22 And after that went the Levites in to do their service in the tabernacle of the congregation before Aaron, and before his sons: as the LORD had commanded Moses concerning the Levites, so did they unto them.

According to Revelation 1:6, Christ has made each one of us (who have taken His Name as Christians) kings and priests. As such, we are also called to purify ourselves, but not with a ritual that has been laid before us by an ordinance written by man.

1 Peter 1:22 tells us how we are to purify ourselves:

1 Pet 1:22 Seeing ye have purified your souls in obeying the truth through the Spirit unto unfeigned love of the brethren, *see that ye* love one another with a pure heart fervently:

Walking in love toward one another in obedience to the Word of God through yielding to the Holy Spirit's Work inside us is what qualifies and sanctifies us to minister to others in the Name of Christ.

Eph 5:1 Be ye therefore followers of God, as dear children;
2 And walk in love, as Christ also hath loved us, and hath given himself for us an offering and a sacrifice to God for a sweetsmelling savour.

You can be a charismatic orator, a masterful preacher, an eloquent speaker with a dynamic personality, but if your primary motivation that compels you to minister to others isn't genuine love and compassion for those you encounter, you really will fail as a minister of the Gospel.

In the eyes of men, it may seem like you are a success by the crowds that may come to hear you preach. You may be skilled at wowing them by unveiling the mysteries of the Bible to them, but without the unadulterated Love of Christ working in you and through you, your ministry will be more beneficial to you than to those you encounter.

Compassion:

G4697 σπλαγχνίζομαι splagchnizomai splangkh-nid'-zom-ahee

Middle voice from G4698; to have the *bowels* yearn, that is, (figuratively) *feel sympathy*, to *pity:* - have (be moved with) compassion.

1Pe 3:8 Finally, *be ye* all of one mind, having compassion one of another, love as brethren, *be* pitiful, *be* courteous:

1Jn 3:16 Hereby perceive we the love *of God*, because he laid down his life for us: and we ought to lay down *our* lives for the brethren.
17 But whoso hath this world's good, and seeth his brother have need, and shutteth up his bowels *of compassion* from him, how dwelleth the love of God in him?
18 My little children, let us not love in word, neither in tongue; but in deed and in truth.
19 And hereby we know that we are of the truth, and shall assure our hearts before him.

Notes:

_____
_____
_____
_____
_____
_____
_____
_____
_____
_____
_____
_____

**1Co 13:1 Though I speak with the tongues of men and of angels, and have not charity, I am become *as* sounding brass, or a tinkling cymbal.
2 And though I have *the gift of* prophecy, and understand all mysteries, and all knowledge; and though I have all faith, so that I could remove mountains, and have not charity, I am nothing.
3 And though I bestow all my goods to feed *the poor*, and though I give my body to be burned, and have not charity, it profiteth me nothing.**

Genuine love is evidenced by compassion toward others. It was compassion that drove Jesus to heal those who came to Him, and as we walk in the Love of Christ, compassion will compel us to minister to those who we encounter like Jesus did.

1Jn 2:6 He that saith he abideth in him ought himself also so to walk, even as he walked.

**1Co 13:4 Charity suffereth long, *and* is kind; charity envieth not; charity vaunteth not itself, is not puffed up,
5 Doth not behave itself unseemly, seeketh not her own, is not easily provoked, thinketh no evil;
6 Rejoiceth not in iniquity, but rejoiceth in the truth;
7 Beareth all things, believeth all things, hopeth all things, endureth all things.**

Compassion for others should be the motivating force that compels one to ministry, not the prospect of a means of income, or because we are *supposed* to minister to others.

If we can't see others as Jesus sees them, then what we do in the name of Christ can bring more damage to the cause of Christ than Glory to His Name.

John the Baptist declared that he must decrease so that Christ would increase. Our prejudices, our perceptions, our personal agendas or our comfort have no place in genuine Christ centered ministry.

Some who step into ministry do so because they have a desire to preach before an audience or to be recognized by men for the men or women of God that they are. There are a large number of Christians I have met who believe they are called to ministry and who have said "I want to be a preacher". But ministry is so much more than going from speaking engagement to speaking engagement. It is more than "motivational speeches" given to crowds.

Jesus met the needs of those who He preached to, and all who came to Him regardless of the place or the time of day or night. His ministry was not scheduled by men, and the needs of others overrode His personal desires.

Jesus' ministry was motivated by a compassion for those He encountered, which came as a result of genuine unconditional Love for the multitudes who were held captive by the god of this age.

A minster of God should reflect nothing less than Christ's Love and Compassion toward others.

Most of His ministry was conducted outside of the synagogues or the four walls of the Church.

I've met "evangelists" who have never preached in the market place. Their itinerary is to travel from church to church. No matter what title they may go by, these are not evangelists. Motivational speakers, yes, but *not* evangelists in the Biblical sense. These professional speakers may draw crowds to hear them, but if most of their audience is the Church, and not the unsaved they are not evangelists. If the evangelist is in the house, he should be equipping and instructing the Church as to how to fulfill their Calling in Christ. One of the first qualifications of a minister of God is that he or she should have a desire to teach and equip the Body of Christ.

Paul's instruction to Timothy applies to *all* who will respond to the Call to ministry:

2Ti 2:24 And the servant of the Lord must not strive; but be gentle unto all *men*, apt to teach, patient,
25 In meekness instructing those that oppose themselves; if God peradventure will give them repentance to the acknowledging of the truth;
26 And *that* they may recover themselves out of the snare of the devil, who are taken captive by him at his will.

The word "*servant*" in verse 24 above is the Greek word translated *doulos,* which means a slave (whether involuntary or voluntary). The Bible is clear on this. All men are either servants of God or of sin.

Rom 6:16 Know ye not, that to whom ye yield yourselves servants to obey, his servants ye are to whom ye obey; whether of sin unto death, or of obedience unto righteousness?

> "You must be yielded to the Word of God. The Word will work out love in our hearts, and when practical love is in our hearts, there is no room to boast about ourselves. We see ourselves as nothing when we get lost in this divine love."
>
> Smith Wigglesworth

Notes:

_____
_____
_____
_____
_____
_____
_____
_____
_____
_____
_____
_____
_____
_____
_____
_____
_____
_____
_____
_____
_____
_____
_____
_____
_____
_____
_____
_____
_____
_____
_____
_____
_____
_____

17 But God be thanked, that ye were the servants of sin, but ye have obeyed from the heart that form of doctrine which was delivered you.
18 Being then made free from sin, ye became the servants of righteousness.

A minister of God is to reflect the Life of Christ in all aspects of his or her life, and the first step to accomplishing this is to walk in unfeigned love toward all those he or she encounters.

The primary place where we fail as the Church is in our love we have for one another. We may be familiar with Christ's Words:

Joh 13:35 By this shall all *men* know that ye are my disciples, if ye have love one to another.

And we may also be familiar with what Jesus identified as the two Greatest Commandments:

Mat 22:37 Jesus said unto him, Thou shalt love the Lord thy God with all thy heart, and with all thy soul, and with all thy mind.
38 This is the first and great commandment.
39 And the second *is* like unto it, Thou shalt love thy neighbour as thyself.
40 On these two commandments hang all the law and the prophets.

But what many Christians don't know is that Jesus gave a new commandment to us even greater than that second commandment in Matthew 22:39, and it precedes His Words in John 13:35:

Joh 13:34 A new commandment I give unto you, That ye love one another; as I have loved you, that ye also love one another.

In Matthew Jesus said we are to love our neighbor as ourselves. But here in John, we are told that we are to love one another just as Christ has loved us. That will put a whole new perspective on your walk as a Christian, if you allow it to.

The truth is a lot of people (yes, even Christians) don't love themselves. So the command to love your neighbor as yourself doesn't necessarily bring too high of a standard to live by. But to love someone as Christ loves us; now *that* is a different story!

If you were honest with yourself, you would have to admit that there are people you just would prefer not to deal with. But how does Christ deal with you?

There are people who have done you wrong, and who have taken advantage of your kindness. Have you ever taken advantage of God's Kindness toward you? Have you ever sinned against Him? How did He deal with you when you betrayed Him?

There are people who have lied to you. Have you ever lied to God? There are people who have cheated you. Have you ever cheated God? Have you ever stolen from God? Are you still His child? Does He still continue demonstrating His Love toward you?

Judas was a thief, and Jesus knew it from the beginning, yet He showed him the same care as He showed the other disciples.

True Compassion comes when you love people like Christ loves you. True ministry can only happen when it is born out of Love.

You cannot have the Character of Christ if you cannot walk in Love.

Faith Works by Love.

Love covers a multitude of sin.

Perfect Love casts out fear.

God is Love.

1. Try to fill in the blanks without looking up the answers:

1Co 13:4 Charity _____ long, *and* is _____; charity _____ not; charity _____ not itself, is not _____,

5 Doth not behave itself _____, seeketh not _____, is not easily _____, thinketh _____;

6 _____ not in iniquity, but _____ in the truth;

7 Beareth _____, _____ all things, _____ all things, _____ all things.

2) What is compassion? _____

_____
_____
_____
_____

3) Quote 1 John 1:6 _____
_____
_____

4) What is the five-fold ministry?
_____
_____

5) What is the purpose of the five-fold ministry?_____
_____
_____
_____

6) Who is called to ministry?_____
_____

7) Memorize 2nd Timothy 2:24-26 as a life verse. Write it down here:_____
_____
_____
_____
_____

8) Faith works by _____

We cannot exercise our faith beyond what we believe to be possible.
John G. Lake

What is a Disciple?

G3101 μαθητής mathētēs
Thayer Definition:
1) a learner, pupil, disciple

If you are in Christ, YOU are a disciple. Christians are expected to learn of Christ, to become His pupils with a heart to fulfill His Purpose in this life.

There are some teachers in Christendom that would categorize Christians into a class of those who are disciples and those who are not.

These maintain that there are only some who are called to be disciples, while there are others who are perpetually intended to be only part of the congregation in a setting that is not even like the early church. These would separate the Body of Christ into a clergy/laity division; those who are called to minister and those who are not.

The purpose of those who are actively in ministry is to train (disciple) those who are not yet in ministry how to minister. If we are in Christ, we are *all* His disciples, students who are intended to do the work of the ministry for the furtherance of the Kingdom of God in this world we live in.

Eph 4:11 And he gave some, apostles; and some, prophets; and some, evangelists; and some, pastors and teachers;
12 For the perfecting of the saints, *for the work of the ministry,* for the edifying of the body of Christ:
13 Till we all come in the unity of the faith, and of the knowledge of the Son of God, unto a perfect man, unto the measure of the stature of the fulness of Christ:

Chapter 2
Ministering From A Position of Poverty

1) A MINISTER OF GOD UNDERSTANDS HIS OR HER SPIRITUAL POVERTY IN THE LIGHT OF THE HOLINESS OF THE ALMIGHTY GOD.

Rev 3:17 Because thou sayest, I am rich, and increased with goods, and have need of nothing; and knowest not that thou art wretched, and miserable, and poor, and blind, and naked:

Mat 5:3 Blessed are the poor in spirit: for theirs is the kingdom of heaven.

WHILE IT CAN AND SHOULD BE applied to all who profess to be Christians, the "Sermon on the Mount" is principally a teaching of how a disciple is to conduct ministry.

All Christians are called to serve God, but unless they are discipled in the Way of Christ, they won't know how to properly serve God in the ministry that they are called to.

Notice that it is the disciples who He is talking to on the mountain, not the multitude:

Mat 5:1 And seeing the multitudes, he went up into a mountain: and when he was set, his disciples came unto him:
2 And he opened his mouth, and taught them, saying,

He saw the multitudes, and went away from them into a mountain. Once He was situated, the disciples came to Him, and He taught *them*, not the multitude.

Luk 6:20 And he lifted up his eyes on his disciples, and said, Blessed *be ye* poor: for yours is the kingdom of God.

If somebody writes a great poem, people don't run around applauding the pencil, saying 'Oh, what a great pencil," I'm a pencil in God's hands.
Keith Green

Let none expect to have the mastery over his inward corruption in any degree, without going in weakness again and again to the Lord for strength. Nor will prayer for others, or conversing with the brethren, make up for secret prayer.
George Muller

Mat 4:25 And there followed him great multitudes of people from Galilee, and from Decapolis, and from Jerusalem, and from Judaea, and from beyond Jordan....
Mat 5:1 And seeing the multitudes, he went up into a mountain: and when he was set, his disciples came unto him:
2 And he opened his mouth, and taught them, saying,

Notes

_____
_____
_____
_____
_____
_____
_____
_____
_____
_____
_____
_____

Jesus had just been tempted of the devil in the wilderness, and having passed the test, He went throughout Judea with power, casting out devils, and seeing the sick healed. During this time, He Called those who would be His Disciples into ministry (read the account in Matthew Chapter 4).

Contextually, it appears that they were being overwhelmed by the multitude, and Jesus and the disciples went up into a mountain where Jesus taught them in the Way of effective ministry.

If one reads the context of Matthew 5, 6, and 7, one can see that Jesus was teaching His disciples about how a minister of the Gospel should conduct himself or herself.

Jesus was preparing the disciples to minister effectively to the multitudes that they left at the foot of the mountain, and He gave them a crash course in the proper demeanor needed for a person who ministers as an ambassador of the Kingdom of God.

In Matthew 8:1, we see that when He was done instructing them, they came down from the mountain, and multitudes followed them.

He begins His teaching with what is commonly referred to as "the Beatitudes". The word "*Beatitude*" actually means "blessings", but as a minister of the Gospel, it would be appropriate to view these teachings of Jesus as the "*Be Attitudes*" for ministers.

When teaching about the identifiable marks of a Christian Minister, the first thing Jesus addressed here was the humility of the servant of God: *"Blessed are the poor in Spirit"*.

Some people have interpreted this to mean that if a person is financially poor, he or she is blessed. In fact, some translations of the Bible seem to indicate that (NLT, for example). But that is not what it means at all. Jesus said it was the one who was poor *in spirit* that was blessed.

G4434

πτωχός ptōchos

Thayer Definition:
1) reduced to beggary, begging, asking alms
2) destitute of wealth, influence, position, honour
2a) lowly, afflicted, destitute of the Christian virtues and eternal riches
2b) helpless, powerless to accomplish an end
2c) poor, needy
3) lacking in anything
3a) as respects their spirit
3a1) destitute of wealth of learning and intellectual culture which the schools afford (men of this class most readily give themselves up to Christ's teaching and proved them selves fitted to lay hold of the heavenly treasure)
Part of Speech: adjective

Joh 14:10 Believest thou not that I am in the Father, and the Father in me? the words that I speak unto you I speak not of myself: but the Father that dwelleth in me, he doeth the works.

Notes:

_____
_____
_____
_____
_____
_____
_____
_____
_____
_____
_____
_____
_____
_____
_____
_____
_____
_____
_____
_____

The word "*poor*" in the Greek here is the word "***Ptochos***", and it generally means a person who has been absolutely reduced to beggary, and who asks alms of others. This person is not a beggar because he chooses to be - those people are referred to as "bums"; people who are perfectly capable of making it on their own, yet don't, because they prefer to have a handout every time they turn around, rather than working for their living.

The person who is poor in spirit honestly understands that his or her ministry is entirely dependent upon the Work of the Holy Spirit in their lives. Other translations put this in perspective:

Mat 5:3 "Blessed are those who recognize they are spiritually helpless. The kingdom of heaven belongs to them. (God's Word)

Mat 5:3 God blesses those people who depend only on him. They belong to the kingdom of heaven! (Contemporary English Version)

This verse flies in the face of those who say "God helps those who help themselves". That is *not* a Biblical concept.

Mat 5:3 "Great blessings belong to those who know they are spiritually in need. God's kingdom belongs to them. (Easy To Read Version)

The minister described in Revelation 3:17 is the opposite of those who understand their spiritual poverty:

Rev 3:17 Because thou sayest, I am rich, and increased with goods, and have need of nothing; and knowest not that thou art wretched, and miserable, and poor, and blind, and naked:

A Little Insight In Revelation Chapters Two And Three:

Revelation 2 and 3 are *parenthetical* chapters, addressing those who are called as ministers to the seven Churches.

G32 ἄγγελος

aggelos

ang'-el-os

From ἀγγέλλω aggellō (probably derived from G71; compare G34; to *bring tidings*); a *messenger*; especially an *"angel"*; by implication a *pastor:* - angel, messenger.

Notes:

_____
_____
_____
_____
_____
_____
_____
_____
_____
_____
_____
_____
_____
_____
_____
_____
_____
_____
_____
_____
_____
_____
_____
_____
_____
_____

"Angel" is the Greek word "Angellos" and means *Messenger*. This messenger can be a pastor or some other minister who instructs the Body of Christ.

Here are a few instances where "angelos" is used in reference to a human messenger:

Mat 11:10 For this is *he,* of whom it is written, Behold, I send my messenger (angelos) before thy face, which shall prepare thy way before thee. (see also Mark 1:2, Luke 7:27)

Luk 7:24 And when the messengers (angelos) of John were departed, he began to speak unto the people concerning John, What went ye out into the wilderness for to see? A reed shaken with the wind?

**Luk 9:51 And it came to pass, when the time was come that he should be received up, he stedfastly set his face to go to Jerusalem,
52 And sent messengers (angelos) before his face: and they went, and entered into a village of the Samaritans, to make ready for him.**

The Luke-warm minister of Revelation 3:17 thinks he is alright, and successful in the ministry, but he doesn't realize he is truly in need of the Lord's sustainable Grace in all that he or she does. He's a good speaker, has a charismatic personality, is very popular, and uses those attributes for his personal benefit. He relies more on his ability to conduct his ministry than he does on the Spirit of God.

Those who are spiritually poor realize that they are Christ's Workmanship, created unto good works. Everything they are is dependent on Him.

The Spiritual Bum resists the idea of doing good works for the furtherance of the Kingdom of God; their motivation is to further their own success, using the "Kingdom of God" to advance their personal agenda. They may not realize that is what they are doing, but for these, the "Kingdom of God" is synonymous with their own church, or personal ministry. Their goal is to build a larger sanctuary, to have a larger congregation; to give the best speeches; to have the best clothes. The "poor" that Jesus refers to here are comparable to those people who are absolutely helpless to make it on their own, and all they can do is stretch out their hands and ask for help, or die.

We have all seen pictures of the beggars in third world countries where there are no social agencies to help them - people with no legs, or who are blind or physically disabled in some other way. These people are well aware that their survival is dependent on the benevolence of others who have the means to help them. A bum who doesn't get a hand-out for the day will figure out another way to survive. But the hapless beggar's very survival depends on the merciful generosity of others.

A bum can be filled with pride because he sees himself as a "survivor". A beggar has been stripped of all vestiges of pride because of his position of utter dependency on others in order to survive.

In the realm of Christianity there are spiritual bums and then there are spiritual beggars. We can see these two types of people illustrated in Jesus' parable of the Pharisee and the publican:

Luk 18:10 Two men went up into the temple to pray; the one a Pharisee, and the other a publican.
11 The Pharisee stood and prayed thus with himself, God, I thank thee, that I am not as other men are, extortioners, unjust, adulterers, or even as this publican.
12 I fast twice in the week, I give tithes of all that I possess.
13 And the publican, standing afar off, would not lift up so much as his eyes unto heaven, but smote upon his breast, saying, God be merciful to me a sinner.
14 I tell you, this man went down to his house justified rather than the other: for every one that exalteth himself shall be abased; and he that humbleth himself shall be exalted.

The Pharisee is a picture of the spiritual bum. He attributes his goodness to God, but stands upright and is proud of his position in comparison to others who "have not arrived" to the place he is at. His conversation to God is centered around his works and his abilities. Notice how his "I" is at the center of his prayer: "*I* am not like other men"; "*I* fast twice a week"; "*I* am diligent to give my tithes".

HAVE YOU EVER NOTICED THAT "I" IS IN THE MIDDLE OF SIN?

The spiritual bum prays to God in his uprightness, having an "*I*" centered prayer life. "*I* am a King's kid, and *I* am reminding you, Father, that because *I*

Notes:

am a King's kid, you are obligated to bless *me*." "*I* want a new car." "*I* want a big house." "*I* want this, *I* want that." The spiritual bum's prayers are rarely prayed on behalf of others, or in simple reverence toward God. Ultimately his prayers end up asking God for "things", and if God doesn't respond the way he thinks He should, he gets upset at Him, and brags to others in his testimonies how he got mad at God, and demanded that God honored his prayer. There is no fear of God or dependence on God for the spiritual bum.

His faith is mainly in his ability to convince others to support His ministry instead of relying on God to open doors and to shut doors. His dependence is primarily on the support of men, rather than Provision from God.

Heb 13:5 *Let your* **conversation** *be* **without covetousness;** *and be* **content with such things as ye have: for he hath said, I will never leave thee, nor forsake thee.**

Mat 6:24 No man can serve two masters: for either he will hate the one, and love the other; or else he will hold to the one, and despise the other. Ye cannot serve God and mammon.
25 Therefore I say unto you, Take no thought for your life, what ye shall eat, or what ye shall drink; nor yet for your body, what ye shall put on. Is not the life more than meat, and the body than raiment?

Php 4:11 Not that I speak in respect of want: for I have learned, in whatsoever state I am, *therewith* **to be content.**
12 I know both how to be abased, and I know how to abound: every where and in all things I am instructed both to be full and to be hungry, both to abound and to suffer need.
13 I can do all things through Christ which strengtheneth me.

The bum is never content. He always wants more. There are preachers who teach the congregation not to be content with their 12 foot boat when they can have a yacht.

**1Ti 6:3 If any man teach otherwise, and consent not to wholesome words,
even the words of our Lord Jesus Christ, and to the doctrine which is
according to godliness;
4 He is proud, knowing nothing, but doting about questions and strifes of
words, whereof cometh envy, strife, railings, evil surmisings,
5 Perverse disputings of men of corrupt minds, and destitute of the
truth, supposing that gain is godliness: from such withdraw thyself.
6 But godliness with contentment is great gain.
7 For we brought nothing into *this* world, *and it is* certain we can carry
nothing out.
8 And having food and raiment let us be therewith content.
9 But they that will be rich fall into temptation and a snare, and *into*
many foolish and hurtful lusts, which drown men in destruction and
perdition.
10 For the love of money is the root of all evil: which while some coveted
after, they have erred from the faith, and pierced themselves through
with many sorrows.
11 But thou, O man of God, flee these things; and follow after
righteousness, godliness, faith, love, patience, meekness.
12 Fight the good fight of faith, lay hold on eternal life, whereunto thou
art also called, and hast professed a good profession before many
witnesses.**

**2Pe 2:1 But there were false prophets also among the people, even as
there shall be false teachers among you, who privily shall bring in
damnable heresies, even denying the Lord that bought them, and bring
upon themselves swift destruction.
2 And many shall follow their pernicious ways; by reason of whom the
way of truth shall be evil spoken of.
3 And through covetousness shall they with feigned words make
merchandise of you: whose judgment now of a long time lingereth not,
and their damnation slumbereth not.**

There was a time when I was living in Salt Lake City as a young Christian. My
wife, my dad, and I would go to a local "Denny's" restaurant almost on a daily
basis, and have coffee and fellowship.

My father had deserted my mother, my sister, and I when I was 9 years old,
and now at 27, I had been reunited with my dad, who had recently given his
life to Jesus, and we were "redeeming the time", and getting to know one
another. Those times at Denny's were some special times.

One day we were walking out of Denny's, and a man came up to me and
humbly asked me if I had some spare change. I had just spent almost all I had
on our coffee and our breakfast. But I wanted to help this guy out anyway I

could, so I reached into my pockets, and grabbed all the money I had at the moment. It was 11 cents. I apologized that I couldn't give him more, but explained to him that it was all I had, said "I pray the Lord will bless you with more." When he took my change and saw that it was only 11 cents, he blew up at me. "*WHAT!?*" He shouted indignantly. "*ELEVEN CENTS? THAT'S ALL YOU GIVE TO ME? DON'T YOU KNOW THAT I HAVE SOME DIGNITY?*" He then let loose with a string of profanities that let me know without a doubt that he wasn't happy with my meager offering. I just shrugged my shoulders, and said, "Man, I gave you everything I have. If that's not good enough, I don't know what to tell you."

The spiritual bum is like this man. He still has his "dignity". He stretches out his hand in a time of trouble, and asks Jesus to come into his life. Jesus gives him everything that pertains to life and godliness. But the spiritual bum clings to his "dignity". In his own eyes, he deserves more than what he gets from God. He compares himself to others, and prides himself on his "spiritual" accomplishments.

The minister who is a spiritual bum will resort to shaming the congregation into supporting him with their "best offerings." This is not the Way of Jesus, and when they stand before God, I am afraid that they may hear the words: "You had your reward while you walked on earth and you profaned My Name while you ministered for your personal gain in My Name".

The bum sits under the overpass with his buddies and his cheap Thunderbird wine, and brags about the "take" he made today. He might even brag about the man he told off for giving him 11 cents. The conversation may go something like this: "Man, right in Denny's parking lot, when the church crowd was coming in for lunch, I ask this guy for some spare change, and he gives me eleven cents, and tells me 'God Bless you!' I see these well dressed people getting out of a new Lincoln Continental, and I see my chance. I put that man on the spot right in front of all them religious people. 'What?!' I says, *'ELEVEN CENTS? That's all you give to me? Don't you know I have some DIGNITY?'* The guy is embarrassed, shrugs his shoulders, and gets into his car. But I play this thing up good. Man, I let those tears come out, and start shouting to God about how me and my wife who's sick at home are just trying to make ends meet, and some guy degrades me by giving me eleven cents. Them church people are getting closer to me. 'Lord, help me!' I cry. And then I look this lady with her expensive fur coat in the eye, and said, 'ma'am, in Jesus' Name, won't you help me?' She gave me twenty bucks! There are three couples with her, and one gave me 5 dollars, and another one gave me a ten. Man, did I make a haul today!"

Just like this scheming con man who preys on the emotions and the sense of decency of others, and who is so puffed up with pride that he thinks he deserves accolades from his peers for his ingenuity that helps him to survive, professional pulpiteers have crept into the Church, and the Church needs to wake up and get out of its' man-centered infatuation with the spiritual hucksters that are out there, fleecing the flock in the Name of Ministry.

The spiritual bum is wrapped up in pride and his accomplishments in life, although in God's sight, that pride and his accomplishments are mere filthy rags. He brags to his fellow Christians about how he got mad at God and demanded that God would give him what he asked for. As I said earlier, he has no fear of God.

One type of spiritual bum conducts what he calls a "revival", and plays on the emotions and the sense of decency that true children of God have concerning their walk with Jesus Christ.

He talks about how people generally give God their "second best" (which is true). He equates "giving God your best" with how a person dresses, the car he drives, the house he lives in, and the offering he gives. He may not say it with words, but he portrays himself as being God's gift to the church world. He has deep revelations that no one else has. He explains how expensive it is to put on such a revival. There are travel expenses, lodging expenses, food expenses, not to mention the wear and tear on his equipment. When I hear that, I always think "You should have thought about that before you ventured out".

If God calls you to a Work, He will finance that work. I have personally conducted many extended tent meetings and never have made an appeal for finances to help me cover the expenses, yet God knows how to speak to those who can hear Him to come along side the ministry He has entrusted to me without my persuasive words that are designed to convince others to "sow into my ministry". The spiritual bum puts on a semblance of humility, and quotes the scriptures, twisting them ever so subtly so he can manipulate the hearers. Most Christians today neglect the study of the Word of God, so they lack the ability to discern whether what is being preached is true or not. If it sounds good and he quotes the Bible, then it must be true.

Some spiritual bums sell their "anointing". Their spiel generally is a variation of this:

"This gift God has given me doesn't come cheap. I have had to forsake all that was dear to me in order to obtain it. The thing most people hold dear to them is their finances. If you are really serious about your loved ones coming to a saving knowledge of the Lord Jesus Christ, you have to get rid of that which stands in the way. For a lot of you, that is your money. Do you love your possessions more than you love God? Leave your best at the altar, and expect God to do a miracle in the lives of your loved one. Maybe you need a personal healing touch. Give your best today, and expect God to give His best to you!" God can't be bribed.

Others offer a tremendous return on your gift. Their pitch goes something like this: "If God is speaking to you to give a love offering of 100.00 or more, don't hesitate - bring it and lay it on the altar, believing God to give you a hundred fold return! If you want to get big results, you have to think big in your sowing. If you only sow eleven cents (or a dollar or five, or ten dollars), don't expect too much in return. God wants you to give in a HUGE way!" These bums are more like used car salesmen or professional auctioneers than ministers of the Gospel. God isn't in the numbers racket. There are principles in His Kingdom economy that we are to live by, but that isn't one of them.

Mat 19:21 Jesus said unto him, If thou wilt be perfect, go and sell that thou hast, and give to the poor, and thou shalt have treasure in heaven: and come and follow me.

**Mat 6:1 Take heed that ye do not your alms before men, to be seen of them: otherwise ye have no reward of your Father which is in heaven.
2 Therefore when thou doest thine alms, do not sound a trumpet before thee, as the hypocrites do in the synagogues and in the streets, that they may have glory of men. Verily I say unto you, They have their reward.
3 But when thou doest alms, let not thy left hand know what thy right hand doeth:
4 That thine alms may be in secret: and thy Father which seeth in secret himself shall reward thee openly.**

**Luk 12:29 And seek not ye what ye shall eat, or what ye shall drink, neither be ye of doubtful mind.
30 For all these things do the nations of the world seek after: and your Father knoweth that ye have need of these things.
31 But rather seek ye the kingdom of God; and all these things shall be added unto you.
32 Fear not, little flock; for it is your Father's good pleasure to give you the kingdom.
33 Sell that ye have, and give alms; provide yourselves bags which wax not old, a treasure in the heavens that faileth not, where no thief approacheth, neither moth corrupteth.
34 For where your treasure is, there will your heart be also.**

Pro 19:17 He that hath pity upon the poor lendeth unto the LORD; and that which he hath given will he pay him again.

Notes:

Please don't misunderstand. It is not wrong for a ministry to receive funds from their brothers and sisters in Christ to help them with the expenses of ministry. In fact, they should.

If a person is in full time ministry, their funds need to come from somewhere! The attitude of the Body of Christ should be that the possessions they have are not their own, but the Lord's. It is my personal conviction and experience that a minister of the gospel who is called by God to do the work of the ministry should never have to make appeals for funds for the ministry that God has called him to.

IF THE LORD CALLS YOU TO A WORK, HE WILL FINANCE THAT WORK. You don't need to convince or coerce people to support you.

True Christians will *give*, out of a pure motive, expecting nothing in return. If the Lord is calling you to go to India to evangelize, you can trust that He will provide your finances. He will speak to someone to sow into your ministry. Or He will bring you a job that will pay you generously, or you will get a bonus at work. You don't have to put people on a guilt trip for being tight with their money, or try to sell them ia piece of cloth that you touched and that is now blessed with your "anointing"!

That is akin to operating the way Simon the sorcerer did, and NOT Jesus or the disciples.

If you are calling yourself to India because you think it might be a good idea, you will have to figure out ways to finance your trip. The simple fact of the matter is that you are not God's gift to the world. Jesus is. The spiritual bum, like the Pharisee, will think that he is God's Gift to the Church and will try to persuade others to sow into his ministry. If God is calling you to build a building where the church can meet, He can speak to a millionaire to sow into the ministry He has entrusted to you. Or, He will speak individually to the hearts of those you minister to, telling them to give to the ministry toward the building. You don't have to make *ANYTHING* happen.

Notes:

How many ministries today are dependent upon the resources of those who sow into their ministries? What would happen to their ministry if they stopped sending out appeals for finances, and simply submitted all their requests before God and left them there?

THE WORD OF GOD SAYS:

**Jer 17:5 Thus saith the LORD; Cursed be the man that trusteth in man, and maketh flesh his arm, and whose heart departeth from the LORD.
6 For he shall be like the heath in the desert, and shall not see when good cometh; but shall inhabit the parched places in the wilderness, in a salt land and not inhabited.
7 Blessed is the man that trusteth in the LORD, and whose hope the LORD is.
8 For he shall be as a tree planted by the waters, and that spreadeth out her roots by the river, and shall not see when heat cometh, but her leaf shall be green; and shall not be careful in the year of drought, neither shall cease from yielding fruit.
9 The heart is deceitful above all things, and desperately wicked: who can know it?
10 I the LORD search the heart, I try the reins, even to give every man according to his ways, and according to the fruit of his doings.**

The T.V. ministry or the radio ministry that makes appeals to the Body of Christ to sustain their ministry may just be an *Ishmael* - something that a man's "good ideas" contrived, but that turned out not to be a GOD idea. Jesus, when He made the call to ministry said that His *Yoke* was easy, and His *Burden* light.

The God we serve, our Heavenly Father, our Redeemer, our Savior, our Friend is a *giving* God. He is a good Father. Those who serve Him in Truth should reflect Who He is in their lives. But too often Christians in ministry take more on themselves than what the Lord Himself has intended, and find themselves in a situation where they have to rely more on men than they do on God.

G3623
οἰκονόμος oikonomos
Thayer Definition:
1) the manager of household or of household affairs
1a) especially a steward, manager, superintendent (whether free-born as was usually the case, a freed-man or a slave) to whom the head of the house or proprietor has intrusted the management of his affairs, the care of receipts and expenditures, and the duty of dealing out the proper portion to every servant and even to the children not yet of age
1b) the manager of a farm or landed estate, an overseer
1c) the superintendent of the city's finances, the treasurer of a city (or of treasurers or quaestors of kings)
2) metaphorically the apostles and other Christian teachers and bishops and overseers

Notes:
_____
_____
_____
_____
_____
_____
_____
_____
_____
_____
_____
_____
_____
_____
_____
_____
_____
_____

This comes from a desire to be seen as "spiritual" or "successful in ministry". To have the attitude that people will be "blessed" if they become a "part of our ministry" is a self centered, self righteous Pharisaical viewpoint that needs to be repented of.

It is a privilege to be entrusted with the ministry (*or service - that's what the word "ministry" means. The minister of God is to serve others, not to expect to be served*) that God has given us. As *stewards* of the Grace of God, we need to understand that we are just that: *Stewards of a position that God has bestowed upon us.*

AGAIN, please try to hear what I am trying to convey here. God *expects* His children to be givers. A person will be blessed as they bless others in the work of the gospel.

But to present ourselves as the channel through which a person may be blessed is hypocrisy, and is the equivalent of being a spiritual bum.

Look at Paul's first letter to the Corinthians. In chapter 9, he mentions the fact that the workman is worthy of his hire.

He reminds the Corinthians that they should be free in their giving to those who sow into their lives the spiritual things. But then he makes it clear that the reason he is explaining this to them is not that he should receive finances for himself (verse 15), *but that the Church understands that the workman is worthy of his hire, and Christians should give accordingly and willingly to those who give of themselves for their spiritual well being.*

1Co 9:3 Mine answer to them that do examine me is this,
4 Have we not power to eat and to drink?
5 Have we not power to lead about a sister, a wife, as well as other apostles, and *as* the brethren of the Lord, and Cephas?
6 Or I only and Barnabas, have not we power to forbear working?
7 Who goeth a warfare any time at his own charges? who planteth a vineyard, and eateth not

Notes:

of the fruit thereof? or who feedeth a flock, and eateth not of the milk of the flock?

8 Say I these things as a man? or saith not the law the same also?

9 For it is written in the law of Moses, Thou shalt not muzzle the mouth of the ox that treadeth out the corn. Doth God take care for oxen?

10 Or saith he *it* altogether for our sakes? For our sakes, no doubt, *this* is written: that he that ploweth should plow in hope; and that he that thresheth in hope should be partaker of his hope.

11 If we have sown unto you spiritual things, *is it* a great thing if we shall reap your carnal things?

12 If others be partakers of *this* power over you, *are* not we rather? Nevertheless we have not used this power; but suffer all things, lest we should hinder the gospel of Christ.

13 Do ye not know that they which minister about holy things live *of the things* of the temple? and they which wait at the altar are partakers with the altar?

14 Even so hath the Lord ordained that they which preach the gospel should live of the gospel.

15 But I have used none of these things: neither have I written these things, that it should be so done unto me: for *it were* better for me to die, than that any man should make my glorying void.

16 For though I preach the gospel, I have nothing to glory of: for necessity is laid upon me; yea, woe is unto me, if I preach not the gospel!

17 For if I do this thing willingly, I have a reward: but if against my will, a dispensation *of the gospel* is committed unto me.

18 What is my reward then? *Verily* that, when I preach the gospel, I may make the gospel of Christ without charge, that I abuse not my power in the gospel.

19 For though I be free from all *men,* yet have I made myself servant unto all, that I might gain the more.

The spiritual bum preys off of the emotions and the desires of the Body of Christ. His attitude is "I

Notes:

deserve your financial help because of the wonderful work I do for you in the Name of Jesus Christ."

Mat 7:21 Not every one that saith unto me, Lord, Lord, shall enter into the kingdom of heaven; but he that doeth the will of my Father which is in heaven.
22 Many will say to me in that day, Lord, Lord, have we not prophesied in thy name and in thy name have cast out devils? and in thy name done many wonderful works?
23 And then will I profess unto them, I never knew you: depart from me, ye that work iniquity.

The prospective minister of the Gospel needs to understand this:

Covetousness of any form does not have a place in the Kingdom of God.

We are told to flee our desire (love) for money.

1Ti 6:10 For the love of money is the root of all evil: which while some coveted after, they have erred from the faith, and pierced themselves through with many sorrows.
11 But thou, O man of God, flee these things; and follow after righteousness, godliness, faith, love, patience, meekness.

Another type of spiritual bum is the person who prays to ask Jesus into his or her heart to get them out of trouble, and then when they are delivered from their distress, they turn away from Him and go back into the world until the next time they need Him.

The one Jesus referred to as "spiritually poor" is the one who has been stripped of all vestiges of self-sufficiency. He understands that his pride has gotten him nowhere. Actually, if the truth was known, it is his pride that got him in the trouble he is in, and he will readily admit it!

The spiritual beggar knows that anything that could be called "good" in his or her life is because of the

Mercy and Grace of the God they serve. He understands that if left to his own devices, he will fail every time. He is in need of the Provision and Grace of God in his life to be able to fulfill the Will of God for his life, and to function successfully as a servant of the Living God.

Rom 7:18 For I know that in me (that is, in my flesh,) dwelleth no good thing: for to will is present with me; but how to perform that which is good I find not.

Isa 64:6 But we are all as an unclean thing, and all our righteousnesses are as filthy rags; and we all do fade as a leaf; and our iniquities, like the wind, have taken us away.
7 And there is none that calleth upon thy name, that stirreth up himself to take hold of thee: for thou hast hid thy face from us, and hast consumed us, because of our iniquities.

Eph 2:1 And you hath he quickened, who were dead in trespasses and sins 2 Wherein in time past ye walked according to the course of this world, according to the prince of the power of the air, the spirit that now worketh in the children of disobedience: 3 Among whom also we all had our conversation in times past in the lusts of our flesh, fulfilling the desires of the flesh and of the mind; and were by nature the children of wrath, even as others.
4 But God, who is rich in mercy, for his great love wherewith he loved us,
5 Even when we were dead in sins, hath quickened us together with Christ, (by grace ye are saved;)

The one who is poor in spirit will know that any ability they may have is because of the Presence of God in their lives. They understand that the crumbs from the Master's table are good enough for them. They learn to be content with what the Lord has provided for them. They understand that as long as He is their Provider, they will never lack for any good thing.

2Co 3:5 Not that we are sufficient of ourselves to think any thing as of ourselves; but our sufficiency is of God;
6 Who also hath made us able ministers of the new testament; not of the letter, but of the spirit: for the letter killeth, but the spirit giveth life.

The prideful ones in the world have a favorite catch-phrase they like to use when referring to true Christians: "You just use Jesus (or Christianity) as a crutch." The one who is truly poor in spirit will confess that this is true. Unabashedly, he or she will freely confess:

"Yes, you are probably right. If I was to be honest with myself, I would have to admit that I really need a hand from God on a daily basis to make it in this world. Personally, I am glad that I have Jesus to help me through it all."

2Co 11:29 Who is weak, and I am not weak? who is offended, and I burn not?
30 If I must needs glory, I will glory of the things which concern mine infirmities.

It is significant that Jesus mentioned the Poor in Spirit before He mentioned any other characteristics in a Christian's life, because before a person can possess any of the other attributes we will be studying, we need to understand our own absolute personal dependence on our Lord for everything.

Mat 5:3 "Blessed are those who recognize they are spiritually helpless. The kingdom of heaven belongs to them. (God's Word)

What does it mean that the Kingdom of Heaven belongs to them? When you know that you are totally dependent on God for all that concerns your ministry and life, then you have an open door for the resources that are needed for the Work God has called you to. The person who is poor in spirit won't go to the internet to get his or her messages. They will be dependent on the Holy Spirit to give them fresh manna for their hearers.

Impromptu preaching in the public square is a wonderful way to learn how to give Holy Spirit led messages, and teaches the minister of the Gospel how to rely on God for their messages rather than their notes.

A Christian can buy an affordable portable sound system they can carry on their shoulder or wear on their belt to amplify their voice if need be, on a street corner. Check with your local city council to see what, if any, ordinances they may have concerning amplified sound. Then again, Jesus, the apostles, their disciples and the early revivalists like George Whitfield, Jonathan Edwards and John and Charles Wesley never used amplified sound, and they did great without it while they impacted the world for the Kingdom of God.

Another thing to consider is that in those days, there was never a distinction between "street preachers" and "church evangelists". All who ministered in the Name of Jesus were given to speaking in the public forum as well as in the "church buildings", and they were completely dependent on the Holy Spirit to give them the message appropriate for the moment at hand, and to lead them in any given circumstance.

Resolve in your heart to be dependent on God, and on God alone for all aspects of your ministry.

In your own words, describe the areas that you personally have recognized where you are spiritually impoverished. _____
_____
_____
_____
_____

_____
_____
_____
_____
_____
_____
_____
_____
_____
_____
_____

Where, if any are the areas in which you have become lukewarm in your walk in the light of Revelation 3:17 & 18?

_____
_____
_____
_____
_____
_____
_____
_____
_____
_____
_____
_____
_____
_____
_____
_____
_____

At the beginning of this chapter in the sidebar, we can see a quote from John G Lake: "**We cannot exercise our faith beyond what we believe to be possible." Discuss how this lesson on being spiritually impoverished pertains to this quote.**_____

_____
_____
_____
_____
_____
_____
_____
_____
_____

"I now ask you, my dear reader, a few questions in all love, because I do seek your welfare, and I do not wish to put these questions to you without putting them first to my own heart. Do you make it your primary business, your first great concern, to seek the kingdom of God and his righteousness? Are the things of God, the honor of his name, the welfare of his church, the conversion of sinners, and the profit of your own soul, your chief aim?"

George Muller

G3996

πενθέω pentheō *pen-theh'-o*

From G3997; to *grieve* (*the feeling or the act*): - mourn, (be-) wail.

Notes:

Chapter 3
Ministering in the Mourning

Mat 5:4 BLESSED ARE THEY THAT MOURN: FOR THEY SHALL BE COMFORTED

WE USUALLY ASSOCIATE mourning with the loss of a loved one. When we lose a loved one, it is a natural process to mourn for that loss. It is like a tangible part of our life has been stripped from us. There is a deep grieving in our souls, the depth of which no human comforter can know.

There is another kind of mourning that our God would have us to know.

Those who are **Poor in Spirit** will understand his or her own moral failure, when viewed in the Light of the Holy God, and will be grieved over that moral failure, their spiritual bankruptcy before the Lord.

The individual who is poor in Spirit will be grieved over the state of the church when it moves away from the initial Purpose of God through compromise with the world.

He will be grieved over the moral failure of humanity in the world. Instead of being quick to condemn and find fault with his brothers and sisters in Christ, he will be grieved over their moral failure, because he has seen his own lack clearly in the reflection of the Holiness of the Almighty God. It is only the one who has truly realized how much he is in need of the Lord's Involvement in all aspects of his life who will mourn before God concerning the spiritual state of the Body of Christ.

Several passages in the Bible touch on this type of mourning that a genuine Christian will experience.

Ezra mourned because of the transgression of his people.

His mourning was so great that it drove him to fast on behalf of his people.

2Co 5:14 For the love of Christ constraineth us; because we thus judge, that if one died for all, then were all dead: 15 And *that* **he died for all, that they which live should not henceforth live unto themselves, but unto him which died for them, and rose again**

Notes:

_____
_____
_____
_____
_____
_____
_____
_____
_____
_____
_____
_____
_____
_____
_____
_____
_____
_____
_____
_____
_____
_____
_____
_____
_____
_____
_____
_____
_____

**Ezr 10:5 Then arose Ezra, and made the chief priests, the Levites, and all Israel, to swear that they should do according to this word. And they swore.
6 Then Ezra rose up from before the house of God, and went into the chamber of Johanan the son of Eliashib: and when he came thither, he did eat no bread, nor drink water: for he mourned because of the transgression of them that had been carried away.**

Here we see that the Word of God says that Ezra mourned "because of the transgression of them that had been carried away". Israel had been carried away into captivity by a foreign nation because of their sin before God. Ezra did not walk in self righteous indignation toward those sinful Israelites. He didn't say "Well, I knew that sooner or later it would catch up to them." He didn't shout "I knew they weren't really children of God!"

Ezra mourned because of their captivity.

Christians on a daily basis fall into sin and are taken captive by Satan's crafty devices (2Ti 2:26).

When this happens, many Christians today do not mourn over this situation...they merely point their fingers and say "Aha! It serves them right!" The genuine Christian will be grieved that their brother or sister has fallen, and will try all they can do to see them restored.

**2Ti 2:24 And the servant of the Lord must not strive; but be gentle unto all men, apt to teach, patient,
25 In meekness instructing those that oppose themselves; if God peradventure will give them repentance to the acknowledging of the truth;
26 And that they may recover themselves out of the snare of the devil, who are taken captive by him at his will.**

Paul defines the ministry which is committed to the disciple of Christ:

2Co 5:18 And all things _are_ of God, who hath reconciled us to himself by Jesus Christ, and hath given to us the ministry of reconciliation; 19 To wit, that God was in Christ, reconciling the world unto himself, not imputing their trespasses unto them; and hath committed unto us the word of reconciliation.

If we have the mind of Christ, and if we are walking in the Light and the Love of Christ, our desire will be to see those who have strayed from the Truth to be reconciled to God.

Gal 6:1 Brethren, if a man be overtaken in a fault, ye which are spiritual, restore such an one in the spirit of meekness; considering thyself, lest thou also be tempted. 2 Bear ye one another's burdens, and so fulfil the law of Christ. 3 For if a man think himself to be something, when he is nothing, he deceiveth himself.

The truth of the matter is this: the state of the church in America is NOT good. The Bride of Christ has left her first love and has fallen in many ways into spiritual adultery. There are many self-appointed watchmen that point their fingers and call the Church in America names and point out all its wrongs, while accusing and condemning its' obvious sin.

We need to call sin what it is, and we need to proclaim the Standard of Holiness that is required of the Bride of Christ. We cannot compromise the Word of God. But finger pointing and calling names is not the way to see the Church restored.

Christians are being taken captive by the god of this world, and we should not tolerate that. If we are not spiritual enough to restore our brothers and sisters in a spirit of meekness (_Gal 6:1_), we should at least be driven by a deep sense of mourning to fast and pray on their behalf. The way of the world and the god it serves is to point fingers, to accuse, and to condemn.

The Way of Christ is to restore.

2Ch 7:14 If my people, which are called by my name, shall humble themselves, and pray, and seek my face, and turn from their wicked ways; then will I hear from heaven, and will forgive their sin, and will heal their land.

It's not only "them" that need to turn from their wicked ways, oh "righteous man or woman of God"! If you are pointing your fingers and accusing and condemning others for their spiritual lack, _that_ is wickedness itself, and needs to be repented of as well. You ought rather to mourn over their captivity, as well as your own. In his first letter to the church at Corinth, Paul addressed

_____
_____
_____
_____
_____
_____
_____
_____
_____
_____
_____
_____
_____
_____
_____
_____
_____
_____
_____
_____
_____
_____
_____
_____

1Co 3:16 Know ye not that ye are the temple of God, and *that* the Spirit of God dwelleth in you?
17 If any man defile the temple of God, him shall God destroy; for the temple of God is holy, which *temple* ye are.

the need of the church to be mourning over a particular situation that was taking place in the Body of Christ in Corinth:

1Co 5:1 It is reported commonly that there is fornication among you, and such fornication as is not so much as named among the Gentiles, that one should have his father's wife.
2 And ye are puffed up, and have not rather mourned, that he that hath done this deed might be taken away from among you.

While they were whispering to one another over the juicy bit of gossip that this scandal in the church had generated, their attitude should have been one of mourning for a couple of reasons.

First, the Name of God was being blasphemed because of this sin. The unbelievers that learned about this sinful relationship would have occasion to say, "If that's what Christianity is about, I don't want any part of it!" Paul said not even the Gentiles or the unbelievers would do such a thing.

There were some in the church who were "puffed up", or who were caught up in the grip of pride as they compared themselves and their spiritual growth to this one who was caught in sin. Their attitude was probably like "Well, at least I am not like old Joe there. I haven't even thought of doing such a thing as he has done." Paul said that they should have been mourning over the situation.

The sin issue in any believer's life is not a light thing that it should be laughed at, or minimalized or encouraged.

Every Born Again believer is a Temple of the Living God *(1 Cor 3:16)*. That isn't just a metaphor. The Holy Spirit has taken residence in us to enable us to live as children of God. It is a serious thing to defile the Temple of God.

If we love God, we will mourn if His Temple is defiled, and we will want to see His Temple restored.

Neh 1:3 And they said unto me, The remnant that are left of the captivity there in the province are

Notes:

in great affliction and reproach: the wall of Jerusalem also is broken down, and the gates thereof are burned with fire.

4 And it came to pass, when I heard these words, that I sat down and wept, and mourned certain days, and fasted, and prayed before the God of heaven

Many Christians are in great affliction and reproach because of their sin against God. In the lives of each of these individuals, the temple of the Lord has been defiled. Should we point our fingers and condemn? That's not God's Way. See what Nehemiah's reaction was concerning the state of the physical temple.

Remember that he fasted, mourned and prayed before the God of Heaven on behalf of His people:

Neh 1:5 And said, I beseech thee, O LORD God of heaven, the great and terrible God, that keepeth covenant and mercy for them that love him and observe his commandments:

6 Let thine ear now be attentive, and thine eyes open, that thou mayest hear the prayer of thy servant, which I pray before thee now, day and night, for the children of Israel thy servants, and confess the sins of the children of Israel, which we have sinned against thee: both I and my father's house have sinned.

7 We have dealt very corruptly against thee, and have not kept the commandments, nor the statutes, nor the judgments, which thou commandedst thy servant Moses.

8 Remember, I beseech thee, the word that thou commandedst thy servant Moses, saying, If ye transgress, I will scatter you abroad among the nations:

9 But if ye turn unto me, and keep my commandments, and do them; though there were of you cast out unto the uttermost part of the heaven, yet will I gather them from thence, and will bring them unto the place that I have chosen to set my name there.

10 Now these are thy servants and thy people,

whom thou hast redeemed by thy great power, and by thy strong hand.

Regardless of our current state of captivity to sin, we are God's servants, and His people, whom He has redeemed by His great Power and His strong Hand. Notice that Nehemiah did not say "*they* have sinned against you" - he got personal and included his own failures before the Holy and Pure God. He said "*We* have sinned against you" (Vs 7). *Nehemiah was a good illustration of what a person who is "poor in spirit" would be like.*

Jeremiah was burdened greatly by the false prophets that flourished in Israel, and mourned that the people of Israel were led into error because of their false teachings. He said his heart was broken, and that he shook because of the fact that the land was full of adulterers, and the Lord's Judgment upon the land was imminent (*Jer. 23:9-40*).

Joel spoke of the Day of the Lord which was to come, and told the people to turn to the Lord with all their heart and with fasting, weeping and mourning over their sin. He said it may be that the Lord will repent of His Anger (*Joel 2:11-14*). The people were called to a solemn assembly, of repentance, and the priests and the ministers of the Lord were called upon to weep and to intercede on behalf of the people, begging Him for His Mercy (*Vss 15-17*).

Our mourning is not only to be for the failure of the Church and our own wickedness...it should also be for the Lord, because we have forsaken Him, the Fountain of Living Waters. In Zechariah 7:3-5, the Lord asks, "In the seventy years that you were in captivity and fasted and mourned, did you fast and mourn to me?" The inference was that the people were fasting and mourning in repentance before the Lord for their own desires, like "Woe is me, because I was bad, this wickedness is being visited upon me! Lord, have mercy on me and forgive me for my sin."

But it appears that they did not pray a prayer like this: "Lord, I have sinned against You, and I have forsaken You. My punishment is Just, because You are Righteous. But I have sinned against You even

Notes:

---

though You have been so Good to me." The people should have mourned that they had done wrong to the God Who had only intended good for them.

Zec 7:4 Then came the word of the LORD of hosts unto me, saying,
5 Speak unto all the people of the land, and to the priests, saying, When ye fasted and mourned in the fifth and seventh month, even those seventy years, did ye at all fast unto me, even to me?
6 And when ye did eat, and when ye did drink, did not ye eat for yourselves, and drink for yourselves?
7 Should ye not hear the words which the LORD hath cried by the former prophets, when Jerusalem was inhabited and in prosperity, and the cities thereof round about her, when men inhabited the south and the plain?

They did not consider the possibility that they had insulted the Lord through their disobedience. When we sin against God, we don't think of it as insulting Him. But we can insult the Almighty God:

Heb 10:28 He that despised Moses' law died without mercy under two or three witnesses:
29 Of how much sorer punishment, suppose ye, shall he be thought worthy, who hath trodden under foot the Son of God, and hath counted the blood of the covenant, wherewith he was sanctified, an unholy thing, and hath done despite unto the Spirit of grace?

The phrase "hath done despite" actually means "insulted". The genuine Christian will be grieved over the fact that he or she has insulted the God who has given them so abundantly of His Mercy. They will mourn over the lack of compassion they have had toward their brothers and sisters.

Zec 7:8 And the word of the LORD came unto Zechariah, saying,
9 Thus speaketh the LORD of hosts, saying, Execute true judgment, and show mercy and compassions every man to his brother:
10 And oppress not the widow, nor the

G1796

ἐνυβρίζω enubrizō en-oo-brid'-zo

From G1722 and G5195; to *insult:* - do despite unto.

Notes

fatherless, the stranger, nor the poor; and let none of you imagine evil against his brother in your heart.

11 But they refused to hearken, and pulled away the shoulder, and stopped their ears, that they should not hear.

12 Yea, they made their hearts as an adamant stone, lest they should hear the law, and the words which the LORD of hosts hath sent in his spirit by the former prophets: therefore came a great wrath from the LORD of hosts.

13 Therefore it is come to pass, that as he cried, and they would not hear; so they cried, and I would not hear, saith the LORD of hosts:

14 But I scattered them with a whirlwind among all the nations whom they knew not. Thus the land was desolate after them, that no man passed through nor returned: for they laid the pleasant land desolate.

Jam 4:8 Draw nigh to God, and he will draw nigh to you. Cleanse your hands, ye sinners; and purify your hearts, ye double minded.
9 Be afflicted, and mourn, and weep: let your laughter be turned to mourning, and your joy to heaviness.

As you examine yourself in the light of this study of the Doctrine of Jesus, do you see that you have not mourned for the state of the Church or the state of our nation, or the state of your own wicked heart, and the ways you have insulted your Redeemer and Your Lord?

You might throw up your hands and say "Well, I am not making the grade, that's for sure. And even as I read this, I don't find myself being grieved over my wretched state or the church's. What am I to do? "

Jam 4:10 Humble yourselves in the sight of the Lord, and he shall lift you up.

Understand the depths of the spiritual poverty that you actually are in, and repent of your indifference. Open your heart to the Lord, and ask Him to change you from the inside out. Ask Him to take your heart of stone and make it flesh once more. Say "Whatever it takes, Lord, change me into who you would have me to be". Once you do that, you will be blessed. You won't be able to look at others in the light of your self righteous opinions of who you are. Then you will mourn for your brothers, and your sisters and yourself.

Don't fall in the trap of pointing your fingers at your brothers and sisters, and laughing at or ridiculing or condemning them for their sin. That is not the Way of Christ. Seek ways to see them restored. Mourn for them. Pray for them. Love covers a multitude of sin.

Jesus said ***"Blessed are they that mourn, for they shall be comforted."*** The word translated as "comforted" is also translated in several places as "beseech" or "besought" (Matt 8:31, 34, 14:36, 18:29, Mk 5:10,12, etc.).

As we mourn for the sins of our brothers and sisters in Christ, and for our own sins, as well as the state our nation and the world is in, we will be comforted as we begin to see the lives of those we have interceded for being transformed.

As we mourn for our sins and the sins of others, we will become more compassionate, and people will recognize that genuine compassion that shines through us, and they will be drawn to that compassion that they see in us.

We will see how others "beseech" us to pray for them, to minister to them, to counsel them. We will see lives being restored, and wounded hearts being healed, because we have the compassion to minister to those who need somebody to care.

And as we are used of God, we will be comforted, because the Lord is permitting us to be used for His Glory to work a change in some people's lives. What a comfort that is to any thirsty soul! There is no higher honor than to be used by the True and Living God.

Isa 58:9 Then shalt thou call, and the LORD shall answer; thou shalt cry, and he shall say, Here I am. If thou take away from the midst of thee the yoke, the putting forth of the finger, and speaking vanity;
10 And if thou draw out thy soul to the hungry, and satisfy the afflicted soul; then shall thy light rise in obscurity, and thy darkness be as the noonday:
11 And the LORD shall guide thee continually, and satisfy thy soul in drought, and make fat thy bones: and thou shalt be like a watered garden, and like a spring of water, whose waters fail not.
12 And they that shall be of thee shall build the old waste places: thou shalt raise up the foundations of many generations; and thou shalt be called, The repairer of the breach, The restorer of paths to dwell in.

The true minister of God is meant to be a repairer of the breach...

2Co 5:18 And all things *are* of God, who hath reconciled us to himself by Jesus Christ, and hath given to us the ministry of reconciliation; 19 To wit, that God was in Christ, reconciling the world unto himself, not imputing their trespasses unto them; and hath committed unto us the word of reconciliation.

Someone who truly mourns over the state of the Kingdom of God will be doing what they can to make it right.

For personal use:

As you examine yourself in the light of this study, in what areas have you not mourned as you ought to have?

_____
_____
_____
_____
_____
_____
_____
_____
_____
_____

Are there individuals you know personally who need to be reconciled to God? What can you do about that? What WILL you do about it?

_____
_____
_____
_____
_____
_____
_____

What revelations, if any, have you had from the study of this chapter about yourself and how your Christian Ministry should be conducted?

_____
_____
_____
_____
_____
_____
_____
_____
_____

> "You can never pray 'the prayer of faith' (*James 5:15*) if you look at the person who is needing it; there is only one place to look, and that is to Jesus."

Smith Wigglesworth

MEEK:

G4239

πραΰς praus *prah-ooce'*

Apparently a primary word; *mild*, that is, (by implication) *humble:* - meek. See also G4235.

Notes:

_____

Chapter 4
BLESSED ARE THE MEEK

A CHARACTERISTIC OF THE TRUE MINISTER OF GOD IS THAT THEY WALK IN MEEKNESS

SO FAR we have seen that

1) The effective servant of God is driven by the Love of Christ Who dwells within him or her to do the work of the ministry.

2) The servant of God is "Poor in Spirit"; he or she truly understands that all they have that is of any worth as far as ministry goes is that which the Lord has given them. They don't lean on their own understanding of "how to make this or that work".

3) The servant of God mourns over the state of the Body of Christ and over individual Christians who are not walking according to the Will of God. They mourn over the fact that they have insulted God through their sin.

Mat 5:5 Blessed are the meek: for they shall inherit the earth.

The characteristics of genuine ministers of God are such that they work in harmony with one another, because they understand that the Work of the Kingdom of God isn't an undertaking that can be accomplished by a single individual. The Body of Christ needs every member functioning together in order to effectively further the Kingdom of God.

The one who is poor in spirit will be so aware of his or her lack before God that they will mourn their own inability to walk in the righteousness of God. This understanding will cause him to be meek or humble before God. What does it mean to be meek?

Jesus, in His doctrine taught that the meek are blessed by God.

Notes:

His statement is a direct quotation from Psalm 37:11, which says:

Psa 37:11 But the meek shall inherit the earth; and shall delight themselves in the abundance of peace.

I believe that the verses prior to verse 11 give a clear definition as to what it is to be meek:

**Psa 37:1 A Psalm of David. Fret not thyself because of evildoers, neither be thou envious against the workers of iniquity.
2 For they shall soon be cut down like the grass, and wither as the green herb.
3 Trust in the LORD, and do good; so shalt thou dwell (ABIDE, PERMANENTLY RESIDE) in the land, and verily thou shalt be fed.**

"Fret not" in the Hebrew means don't be furious or get all riled up over the fact that men can be so evil. Sometimes a Christian will get angry over an individual or a political situation that is absolutely against Christ. When we are furious concerning a thing, it is hard to let Christ's Love show through us, and remember, *Love* is the primary ingredient to effective ministry in Christ.

Jesus assured us that iniquity would increase (Matt 24). There is no need to allow your peace to be taken away from you because of this. Jesus warned us two thousand years ago that it would happen.

On the opposite side of the spectrum, we are not to be envious against those who are wicked. Christians have a tendency to get frustrated over the fact that although they are very careful to keep their minds stayed on the Lord, it seems that the careless sinners prosper and live better lives than they do. Verse 2 says that they will soon be cut down as the grass, and wither as the green herb.

Jesus spoke of the self righteous religious leaders who liked to be seen in their feigned piety. He said they have their reward (*Matt 6:1-8*). Although they may prosper a little here in this life, there will be no reward for them in the Life to come.

Notes:

H982

בָּטַח

bâṭach   *baw-takh'*

A primitive root; properly to *hie* for refuge (but not so *precipitately* as H2620); figuratively to *trust*, be *confident* or *sure:* - be bold (confident, secure, sure), careless (one, woman), put confidence, (make to) hope, (put, make to) trust.

Col 3:1 If ye then be risen with Christ, seek those things which are above, where Christ sitteth on the right hand of God. 2 Set your affection on things above, not on things on the earth. 3 For ye are dead, and your life is hid with Christ in God.

The meek person is not furious over the work of the evildoers in the land. Nor is he envious of them. He just exhibits the Love of Jesus to them, knowing that if the wicked die without Jesus, even though they may have seemed to have prospered abundantly in this life, they will have lost their very soul (*Matt 16:26*). The meek understand that God is not willing that *any* should perish.

THOSE WHO ARE WALKING IN HUMILTIY TRUST IN THE LORD, AND THEY DO GOOD, AND ARE CONTENT WITH THAT WHICH THE LORD PROVIDES.

Act 10:38 How God anointed Jesus of Nazareth with the Holy Ghost and with power: who went about doing good, and healing all that were oppressed of the devil; for God was with him.

Ps 37:3 Trust in the LORD, and do good; so shalt thou dwell in the land, and verily thou shalt be fed.

Those who are meek will understand that their TRUST is in the Lord. He is their Provider, and He will supply all their needs according to His Riches in Glory. The Hebrew word translated as "Trust" is ⬅ indicative of a person relying on something or someone for their refuge and protection.

The meek Christian will have his affections set on those things that are above (Col 3:2) and will be content, regardless of what state he may be in (Phil 4:11-12).

1Ti 6:6 But godliness with contentment is great gain.
7 For we brought nothing into this world, and it is certain we can carry nothing out.
8 And having food and raiment let us be therewith content.

Those who are meek have their priorities set. Their priority is that they seek first the Kingdom of God above all else. They Trust in the Lord for their provision as they make the furtherance of the Kingdom of God their priority.

Notes:

Mat 6:31 Therefore take no thought, saying, What shall we eat? or, What shall we drink? or, Wherewithal shall we be clothed?
32 (For after all these things do the Gentiles seek:) for your heavenly Father knoweth that ye have need of all these things.
33 But seek ye first the kingdom of God, and his righteousness; and all these things shall be added unto you.

The meek Christian is confident that as he walks in obedience to the Lord, he will be fed and taken care of by the God that he trusts. The opposite of "Meek" is to be prideful and self reliant.

THOSE WHO ARE MEEK ARE YIELDED TO THE WILL OF GOD IN THEIR LIVES.

Ps 37:4 Delight (be pliable) thyself also in the LORD; and he shall give thee the desires of thine heart.

The Hebrew word translated as "Delight" means to be pliable, soft, or delicate. Just as clay is in the hands of the Potter, the Christian who is meek will be pliable in the Hands of the Father.

God upbraided His people several times in His Word as being stiffnecked (*Ex 32:9, 33:3, 33:5, 34:9; Deu 9:6,13, 10:16; 2 Chron 30:8*), which would be the opposite of being soft, and delicate and pliable. The meek Christian is yielded to the Work of the Father in his or her life.

Their attitude is that of Jesus' in the garden as He prayed: "**...O my Father, if it be possible, let this cup pass from me: nevertheless not as I will, but as thou wilt.**" (*Mat 26:39*)

Isa 64:8 But now, O LORD, thou art our father; we are the clay, and thou our potter; and we all are the work of thy hand.

Jer 18:1 The word which came to Jeremiah from the LORD, saying,
2 Arise, and go down to the potter's house, and there I will cause thee to hear my words.
3 Then I went down to the potter's house, and,

Notes:

behold, he wrought a work on the wheels.

4 And the vessel that he made of clay was marred in the hand of the potter: so he made it again another vessel, as seemed good to the potter to make it.

5 Then the word of the LORD came to me, saying,

6 O house of Israel, cannot I do with you as this potter? saith the LORD. Behold, as the clay is in the potter's hand, so are ye in mine hand, O house of Israel.

In order for clay to be of any use to the potter, the clay must be pliable. Many people rush to the altar call that invites them to come forth if they wish to be used of God. The minister who makes the invitation will say, "For those of you who have a sincere heart to follow the Lord, and who wish to truly surrender, and want to ask the Lord 'Whatever it takes for me to conform to Your Image, Lord, I invite You to have Your way' come up to the altar now, and surrender to Him."

People will flood the altar because they believe it's a good thing to do (*and it is*). They will pray "Not my Will, but Yours, oh Lord!" But when opportunities to share the gospel with others arise, worldly concerns will come in to hinder them from sharing the Grace of God with others. "I'd go, but I need to talk to my lawyer about this divorce I am going through". "Oh?", the one who invited him may say; "I thought you surrendered your will to God the other night. God hates divorce." "You don't understand. This marriage is irreconcilable. When I went to the altar the other night, I didn't mean I wasn't going to go through with the divorce!" How pliable or meek is that?

Or, the Christian may go through many trials and hardships following that altar call, and it may seem to him that God isn't there, and he may shake his fist at God, yelling "But God, I have lived for You, and served You with all my heart, and now you allow this disaster to come on me?" He eventually turns away from God and goes back into sin. Or he may simply fall into sin of his own accord, saying, "God, I know this is wrong, but I want to do it anyway. You made me like this, and if You won't take it from me, well, it must be Your fault that I am like this!"

Any number of scenarios could be drawn out of how the professing Christian fails and refuses to yield to God because of the fact that he isn't pliable to the Lord. His heart has become hard, and is not delicate before the Lord, fit for His Use.

Stephen addressed those leaders of Israel who were not pliable or meek:

Act 7:51 Ye stiffnecked and uncircumcised in heart and ears, ye do always resist the Holy Ghost: as your fathers did, so do ye.

We have seen that the meek person:

1) Does not get excited, frustrated or angry over the evil in the world
2) He does not envy the apparent successes of the wicked ones
3) He understands that God Alone is his refuge and his salvation
4) He is pliable or tender to the work that the Lord is doing in his life.

ANOTHER ATTRIBUTE OF A PERSON WHO IS MEEK IS THAT THEY WILLINGLY SUBMIT TO THE DIRECTION THE LORD HAS THEM TO GO.

Ps 37:5 Commit thy way unto the LORD; trust also in him; and he shall bring it to pass.
6 And he shall bring forth thy righteousness as the light, and thy judgment as the noonday.

The Hebrew word translated as "Commit" is to roll, or to flow. The word "way" is the Hebrew "Derek" which means road or path. The Christian who is truly meek will not buck at the direction that the Lord would have him to go. A ball does not roll on its own. It goes in the direction that it is sent by a sender. If you put a vessel in a stream, that vessel will follow the flow of the stream with no resistance of its own.

The genuine Christian will be meek, and one of his or her attributes is that they will not resist the direction the Lord would have them to go. It doesn't matter if the direction of the Lord will entail probable persecution, loss of a job, or even a life endangering situation, the one who is meek will say "here am I, Lord, send me". As the Christian willingly yields to the direction of the Lord for his or her life, the Lord says that *His Will* shall be accomplished, and that the believer's righteousness will be apparent to all.

God is looking for a yielded vessel. Twelve spies went forth to spy out the land. Ten said it looked hopeless. They were not yielded to the Will of God. Two said **"With the Lord all things are possible"**. Joshua and Caleb had committed their way to the Lord, knowing that God would cause His Promises to come to pass (*Num 13:1 - 14:38*).

Shadrach, Meshech and Abednego refused to conform to the standards of the society around them, even though everyone else had. They refused to bow to the statue of the king. They humbled themselves, and went with the Will of God, and where the Lord wanted them to go, even when facing death, and the Lord was Faithful to deliver them all (*Dan 1:7- 3:30*).

Pro 3:5 Trust in the LORD with all thine heart; and lean not unto thine own understanding. 6 In all thy ways (Derek = road) acknowledge him, and he shall direct thy paths (Orach = well trodden road).

GENUINE MEEKNESS IN A CHILD OF GOD WILL RESULT IN A CHRISTIAN BEING SILENT BEFORE GOD IN COMPLETE SUBMISSION TO HIS WILL.

Ps 37:7 Rest in the LORD, and wait patiently for him: fret not thyself because of him who prospereth in his way, because of the man who bringeth wicked devices to pass.

The Hebrew word translated as "Rest" here actually means to keep silent, to be dumb, to be still, or to wait. We always hear the testimonies of the professing Christian who says "I was mad at God, and I gave Him a piece of my mind. I stood on His Promises and reminded Him what He had promised." And more often than not they will testify that God eventually blessed them. A lot of well known speakers in the "Christian entertainment industry" have this type of testimony. They will get their audience to agree that they are not content with the place they are in, and encourage them to flood the altar, demanding the Lord to give their petitions. They are the blind leading the blind.

A genuine Christian Minister is humble, and genuine meekness is Biblically defined as silently acquiescing to the Wisdom and Will of God for our lives.

True faith in God manifests itself in the humble and complete surrender of the Christian to the Will of God for his or her life. The countenance of the one who is meek will not reflect hostility or anger toward

H639

אַף

'aph

BDB Definition:

1) nostril, nose, face

2) anger

Part of Speech: noun masculine

Notes:

_____

_____

_____

_____

_____

_____

_____

_____

_____

_____

_____

_____

_____

_____

_____

_____

_____

_____

_____

_____

_____

_____

_____

_____

_____

_____

others, because he refuses to allow anger to have a hold on him.

Ps 37:8 Cease from anger, and forsake wrath: fret not thyself in any wise to do evil.

The word "anger" actually carries with it the idea of the countenance reflecting the anger of an individual. We have all heard the expression "If looks could kill..." Many times this word is translated as "face" or as "nostrils" as when a person huffs in anger. Actually the Hebrew word sounds like "huff". "Wrath" is the fulfillment of that angry countenance - the actions taken to get even with those who have insulted us or have done us wrong.

The meek person turns the other cheek when he is slapped. The meek person doesn't render railing for railing.

The meek person doesn't figure out ways to get even with those who do him wrong.

The meek person understands that "yet a little while", and the wicked will not be.

But as he walks with the Lord, pliable, submissive, and going with the flow of God's Plan for his life without questioning "WHY?", more people will look to him as a true picture of what God's children are like. They will see Jesus in him. People will be drawn to him for counsel and comfort. People will be saved. Lives will be changed, and the land will be taken for the Kingdom of God.

Psalms 149:4 mentions the meek:

149:4 For the LORD taketh pleasure in his people: he will beautify the meek with salvation.

A meek person will rejoice in the things of God, and God *beautifies* the meek with salvation. I remember a time when I was not saved, and I could identify a genuine Christian just by their countenance. Sin takes its toll. I have met 40 year old people who look like they are 70 years old because of the marks of sin

Eph 6:10 Finally, my brethren, be strong in the Lord, and in the power of his might.
11 Put on the whole armour of God, that ye may be able to stand against the wiles of the devil.
12 For we wrestle not against flesh and blood, but against principalities, against powers, against the rulers of the darkness of this world, against spiritual wickedness in high *places*.
Notes:

_____
_____
_____
_____
_____
_____
_____
_____
_____
_____
_____
_____
_____
_____
_____
_____
_____
_____
_____
_____

Rev 11:15 And the seventh angel sounded; and there were great voices in heaven, saying, The kingdoms of this world are become *the kingdoms* of our Lord, and of his Christ; and he shall reign for ever and ever.

on their faces. But the Lord beautifies His people with His salvation.

Those of us who are Born Again have been enlisted in the Army of the Lord. We are engaged in spiritual battle on a daily basis. Ephesians 6 speaks of the warfare the Christian is engaged in.

Ps 149 speaks of the authority the Lord allows His children to walk in.

Ps 149:5 Let the saints be joyful in glory: let them sing aloud upon their beds.
6 Let the high praises of God be in their mouth, and a twoedged sword in their hand;
7 To execute vengeance upon the heathen, and punishments upon the people;
8 To bind their kings with chains, and their nobles with fetters of iron;
9 To execute upon them the judgment written: this honor have all his saints.

Praise the LORD! The saints of the Most High God have the honor of engaging in the battle and seeing victory in those battles.

Jesus was the meekest of men, and yet when He fulfilled His Purpose, He was named the King of Kings and the Lord of Lords.

Genuine Christianity is reflected in the servant of God who walks in humility. Great authority is entrusted to those who are meek. If the church in America would take on the character of Authentic Christianity, we would inherit the earth.

Ps 37:9 For evildoers shall be cut off: but those that wait upon the LORD, they shall inherit the earth.
10 For yet a little while, and the wicked shall not be: yea, thou shalt diligently consider his place, and it shall not be.
11 But the meek shall inherit the earth; and shall delight themselves in the abundance of peace.

Psa 25:9 The meek will he guide in judgment: and the meek will he teach his way.

Mat 11:28 Come unto me, all ye that labour and are heavy laden, and I will give you rest.
29 Take my yoke upon you, and learn of me; for I am meek and lowly in heart: and ye shall find rest unto your souls.
30 For my yoke is easy, and my burden is light.

Notes:

_____
_____
_____
_____
_____
_____
_____
_____
_____
_____
_____
_____
_____
_____
_____
_____
_____
_____
_____
_____
_____
_____
_____
_____
_____
_____
_____

10 All the paths of the LORD *are* mercy and truth unto such as keep his covenant and his testimonies.

Those who walk in true humility before God realize their utter need for His involvement in every aspect of their lives. Jesus said "The Words that I speak are the Father's". He said "The Works that I do are the Father working in me". He didn't lean on His own understanding. In all His Ways, He acknowledged the Father, and was led by His Spirit and accomplished awesome and mighty things.

He said *you* can do the same thing. Whose report will you believe?

SERVANT OF GOD: ARE YOU PLIABLE TO THE WILL OF GOD IN YOUR LIFE?

DO YOU TRUST THE LORD YOUR GOD?

ARE YOU WILLING TO GO WHERE THE LORD WOULD SEND YOU?

ARE YOU WILLING TO DO WHAT THE LORD WOULD REQUIRE OF YOU?

ARE YOU SILENT BEFORE GOD?

HAVE YOU FORSAKEN AN ANGRY COUNTENANCE AND WRATH?

THE MEEK SHALL BE BEAUTIFIED WITH SALVATION!

Psa 25:9 The meek will he guide in judgment: and the meek will he teach his way.
10 All the paths of the LORD *are* mercy and truth unto such as keep his covenant and his testimonies.

Mat 7:21 Not every one that saith unto me, Lord, Lord, shall enter into the kingdom of heaven; but he that doeth the will of my Father which is in heaven.

Mat 12:50 For whosoever shall do the will of my

1Jn 2:6 He that saith he abideth in him ought himself also so to walk, even as he walked.

Notes:

_____
_____
_____
_____
_____
_____
_____
_____
_____
_____
_____
_____
_____
_____
_____
_____
_____
_____
_____
_____
_____
_____
_____
_____
_____
_____
_____
_____
_____
_____
_____
_____
_____

Father which is in heaven, the same is my brother, and sister, and mother. (Mar 3:35)

Joh 4:34 Jesus saith unto them, My meat is to do the will of him that sent me, and to finish his work.

Joh 6:38 For I came down from heaven, not to do mine own will, but the will of him that sent me.

Joh 7:16 Jesus answered them, and said, My doctrine is not mine, but his that sent me.
17 If any man will do his will, he shall know of the doctrine, whether it be of God, or whether I speak of myself.
18 *He that speaketh of himself seeketh his own glory: but he that seeketh his glory that sent him, the same is true, and no unrighteousness is in him.*

Joh 9:31 Now we know that God heareth not sinners: but if any man be a worshiper of God, and doeth his will, him he heareth.

1Jo 5:14 And this is the confidence that we have in him, that, if we ask any thing according to his will, he heareth us:
15 And if we know that he hear us, whatsoever we ask, we know that we have the petitions that we desired of him.
16 If any man see his brother sin a sin which is not unto death, he shall ask, and he shall give him life for them that sin not unto death. There is a sin unto death: I do not say that he shall pray for it.
17 All unrighteousness is sin: and there is a sin not unto death.

Joh 15:6 If a man abide not in me, he is cast forth as a branch, and is withered; and men gather them, and cast them into the fire, and they are burned.
7 If ye abide in me, and my words abide in you, ye shall ask what ye will, and it shall be done unto you.
8 Herein is my Father glorified, that ye bear

much fruit; so shall ye be my disciples.
9 As the Father hath loved me, so have I loved you: continue ye in my love.
10 If ye keep my commandments, ye shall abide in my love; even as I have kept my Father's commandments, and abide in his love.
11 These things have I spoken unto you, that my joy might remain in you, and that your joy might be full.
12 This is my commandment, That ye love one another, as I have loved you.
13 Greater love hath no man than this, that a man lay down his life for his friends.
14 Ye are my friends, if ye do whatsoever I command you.
15 Henceforth I call you not servants; for the servant knoweth not what his lord doeth: but I have called you friends; for all things that I have heard of my Father I have made known unto you.
16 Ye have not chosen me, but I have chosen you, and ordained you, that ye should go and bring forth fruit, and that your fruit should remain: that whatsoever ye shall ask of the Father in my name, he may give it you.

Some teachers say "Just because you are meek doesn't mean you have to be a door mat", and teach Christians in the way of pride.

This is the example of true humility for a minister of God:

Php 2:5 Let this mind be in you, which was also in Christ Jesus:
6 Who, being in the form of God, thought it not robbery to be equal with God:
7 But made himself of no reputation, and took upon him the form of a servant, and was made in the likeness of men:
8 And being found in fashion as a man, he humbled himself, and became obedient unto death, even the death of the cross.

1Pe 2:21 For even hereunto were ye called: because Christ also suffered for us, leaving us an example, that ye should follow his steps:
22 Who did no sin, neither was guile found in his mouth:
23 Who, when he was reviled, reviled not again; when he suffered, he threatened not; but committed *himself* to him that judgeth righteously:
24 Who his own self bare our sins in his own body on the tree, that we, being dead to sins, should live unto righteousness: by whose stripes ye were healed.
25 For ye were as sheep going astray; but are now returned unto the Shepherd and Bishop of your souls.

1) Take some quality time here (at least a half-hour or more) to pray and seek God's Face as to what areas you need to work on humility. In what areas of your life do you see that you need to become more like Jesus?

_____
_____
_____
_____
_____
_____
_____
_____
_____
_____

2) In what areas do you see in your life that you are walking like Jesus?

_____
_____
_____
_____
_____
_____
_____
_____
_____
_____
_____
_____
_____
_____
_____

3) Ask someone you know to honestly evaluate your walk with Jesus, and the areas you need improvement. Either have them fill out their answers here or you record their response and resolve to work on those areas:_____

_____
_____
_____
_____
_____
_____
_____
_____
_____
_____

CHAPTER 5
HUNGRY FOR MORE

Mat 5:6 Blessed Are They Which Do Hunger And Thirst After Righteousness: For They Shall Be Filled.

IN MATT 4:2, we see a good definition of what the "hunger" for righteousness that Jesus was referring to is. After Jesus had fasted for forty days and forty nights, the Word of God tells us that "He was afterward hungry".

My experience with fasting has been that after about three days, the hunger leaves you, and you are pretty much free to choose to eat or not to eat. You can do with or without it. After about five days, my sense of smell becomes very acute, although hunger pains don't accompany that heightened sense of smell. But the food that I smell smells ***GOOD!***

After about 7 or 8 days it seems like I can actually taste the food that I smell. The longest period of time I have personally fasted as of this writing was for 21 days, and the only reason I quit was not because of hunger, but because I felt the fast was over. But I understand that somewhere between twenty-five and forty days of not eating, maybe even sooner, depending on your body's constitution, a person's body begins to kick into the survival mode, since it is on the verge of starvation. At that point, *Hunger* begins to make itself known.

Jesus experienced that kind of hunger, and it appears that it wasn't too long after He had gone through His temptation to turn the stones into bread to satisfy His hunger that He taught His doctrine about the Characteristics of the Genuine child of God (the *Be-Attitudes*), and mentioned how blessed those who hunger and thirst for Righteousness are.

On a personal level, we have seen

1) That the one who understands his or her utter spiritual dependency on God for an effective

Notes:

ministry (*Blessed are the poor in spirit*), will **2)** sincerely grieve (*Blessed are they that mourn*) over his or her propensity toward sin and the state of the Church and our nation, and **3)** being aware of his absolute dependence on God's intervention in his life on a daily basis, he will have no place for boasting (*Blessed are the meek*), and will be yielded to God's Will for his or her life. **4)** Knowing his lack, and loving his Father, the child of God will strongly desire to be conformed to His Image (*Blessed are they that hunger and thirst for righteousness*).

Fully aware of his utter spiritual poverty, the humble servant of God understands that he cannot live up to God's Standard of Righteousness by his own merit, but there is an insatiable desire to attain to that place, because he or she is a child of God, and they want to reflect their Father.

Isa 64:5 Thou meetest him that rejoiceth and worketh righteousness, those that remember thee in thy ways: behold, thou art wroth; for we have sinned: in those is continuance, and we shall be saved.
6 But we are all as an unclean thing, and all our righteousnesses are as filthy rags; and we all do fade as a leaf; and our iniquities, like the wind, have taken us away.

In Isaiah 64:6 the confession is made that we are ALL as an unclean thing. All our righteousness is as filthy rags. *Nothing* that I can do will ever measure up to the Righteousness that is of God. Many who profess Christ are content with simply quoting that verse, and resting in the "I'll never be perfect" mindset. But as a child of God, my desire should be to be like my Father. I want to reflect His Righteousness to the world, but I understand my utter incapability to do so because of the struggle between the flesh and the Spirit of God. As such I am dependant on Him to finish the Work He has begun in me.

Jesus gave a provocative challenge to His hearers when He told them that they had to outshine the religious leaders in their righteousness.

Joh 3:3 Jesus answered and said unto him, Verily, verily, I say unto thee, Except a man be born again, he cannot see the kingdom of God.

Notes:

_____
_____
_____
_____
_____
_____
_____
_____
_____
_____
_____
_____
_____
_____
_____
_____
_____
_____
_____
_____
_____
_____
_____
_____
_____
_____
_____
_____
_____
_____
_____
_____

Mat 5:20 For I say unto you, that except your righteousness shall exceed the righteousness of the scribes and Pharisees, ye shall in no case enter into the kingdom of heaven.

The religious leaders had a form of righteousness. Every jot and tittle according to the laws and traditions of the Jewish religion were to be carefully observed. They *looked* righteous. But they could not fulfill the Law. The endless sacrifices they had to make on their own behalf testified to that. But Jesus insisted that a child of God's righteousness had to exceed that of a Pharisee's.

The Righteousness of God is a righteousness that is (super)naturally born from a heartfelt love for the things of God, not a self-styled righteousness which is attained through complying to regulations, laws and rules. The first and greatest commandment is that we should love the Lord our God with all our heart, with all our soul and all our mind. This means that God and the things of God should have the priority in our lives over the things of the world.

Our tendency is to view this saying as a future event - entering the kingdom of heaven after I die - but remember what Jesus said about the kingdom of God? He said:

Luk 17:20 And when he was demanded of the Pharisees, when the kingdom of God should come, he answered them and said, The kingdom of God cometh not with observation: 21 Neither shall they say, Lo here! or, lo there! for, behold, the kingdom of God is within you.

We can see that the phrase "the Kingdom of Heaven" and "the Kingdom of God" can be synonymous with one another:

Mat 13:10 And the disciples came, and said unto him, Why speakest thou unto them in parables? 11 He answered and said unto them, Because it is given unto you to know the mysteries of the kingdom of heaven, but to them it is not given.

Notes:

Luk 8:10 And he said, Unto you it is given to know the mysteries of the kingdom of God: but to others in parables; that seeing they might not see, and hearing they might not understand.

Understanding that the Kingdom of God isn't necessarily a future event can help us see more clearly what Jesus was saying in the following verse:

Mar 10:14 But when Jesus saw *it,* he was much displeased, and said unto them, Suffer the little children to come unto me, and forbid them not: for of such is the kingdom of God.
15 Verily I say unto you, Whosoever shall not receive the kingdom of God as a little child, he shall not enter therein.

The "Kingdom of God" and the "Kingdom of Heaven" are used interchangeably, but they are both present and future events:

Luk 18:24 And when Jesus saw that he was very sorrowful, he said, How hardly shall they that have riches enter into the kingdom of God!
25 For it is easier for a camel to go through a needle's eye, than for a rich man to enter into the kingdom of God.
26 And they that heard *it* said, Who then can be saved?
27 And he said, The things which are impossible with men are possible with God.
28 Then Peter said, Lo, we have left all, and followed thee.
29 And he said unto them, Verily I say unto you, There is no man that hath left house, or parents, or brethren, or wife, or children, for the kingdom of God's sake,
30 Who shall not receive manifold more in this *present* time, and *in the world to come* life everlasting.

Jesus' doctrine instructs us to seek FIRST the Kingdom of God *and* His Righteousness.

Mat 6:31 Therefore take no thought, saying, What shall we eat? or, What shall we drink? or, Wherewithal shall we be clothed?

2Co 5:21 For he hath made him to be sin for us, who knew no sin; that we might be made the righteousness of God in him.

2Co 5:17 Therefore if any man be in Christ, he is a new creature: old things are passed away; behold, all things are become new.

Notes:

_____
_____
_____
_____
_____
_____
_____
_____
_____
_____
_____
_____
_____
_____

G1492

εἴδω eidō *i'-do*

A primary verb; used only in certain past tenses, the others being borrowed from the equivalent, G3700 and G3708; properly to see (literally or figuratively); by implication (in the perfect only) to know: - be aware, behold, X can (+ not tell), consider, (have) known (-ledge), look (on), perceive, see, be sure, tell, understand, wist, wot. Compare G3700.

32 (For after all these things do the Gentiles seek:) for your heavenly Father knoweth that ye have need of all these things.
33 But seek ye first the kingdom of God, and his righteousness; and all these things shall be added unto you.
34 Take therefore no thought for the morrow: for the morrow shall take thought for the things of itself. Sufficient unto the day is the evil thereof.

There is an ongoing creative process that God is doing in the lives of His children. Christ became sin for us, so that we would be made the Righteousness of God in Him (*2 Cor 5:21*). Despite what some teachers would have you believe, that *doesn't* mean that even though we spend our lives in sin, God only sees us as righteous.

What it does mean is that Christ died for us so that we could have victory over sin and that we could walk in *His* Righteousness. Just a few verses before that, we see that if any man is in Christ, he is a new creature. *Old things have passed away; behold, All things become new (2nd Cor 5:17)*.

There is a supernatural transformation that takes place when a person surrenders their will to the Will of God, and asks Jesus to be the Lord of his or her life. The first time we are born into the world, we are born in the flesh, and we are subject to the demands of the flesh. Self gratification is the primary goal of such a person. But Jesus spoke about a new birth.

Joh 3:3 Jesus answered and said unto him, Verily, verily, I say unto thee, Except a man be born again, he cannot see the kingdom of God.

The phrase "*born again*" is better translated as "*born from above*". The first birth is the birth of the fleshly or carnal man. From the moment of birth, our flesh demands our attention, as the infant seeks his or her mother's breast to satisfy their hunger.

The word translated as "see" in John 3:3 actually means to perceive, or to experience; to understand a thing. Until one is born of the spirit, he or she can only engage in philosophical ideas concerning

Rom 8:5 For they that are after the flesh do mind the things of the flesh; but they that are after the Spirit the things of the Spirit.
6 For to be carnally minded is death; but to be spiritually minded is life and peace.
7 Because the carnal mind is enmity against God: for it is not subject to the law of God, neither indeed can be.
8 So then they that are in the flesh cannot please God.

Rom 6:12 Let not sin therefore reign in your mortal body, that ye should obey it in the lusts thereof.
13 Neither yield ye your members *as* instruments of unrighteousness unto sin: but yield yourselves unto God, as those that are alive from the dead, and your members *as* instruments of righteousness unto God.
14 For sin shall not have dominion over you: for ye are not under the law, but under grace.

Tit 2:11 For the grace of God that bringeth salvation hath appeared to all men,
12 Teaching us that, denying ungodliness and worldly lusts, we should live soberly, righteously, and godly, in this present world;
13 Looking for that blessed hope, and the glorious appearing of the great God and our Saviour Jesus Christ;
14 Who gave himself for us, that he might redeem us from all iniquity, and purify unto himself a peculiar people, zealous of good works.

the Kingdom of God. But once a person is born from above, a supernatural transformation begins to take place, and their understanding is enlightened to the Ways of God.

Once they have been born of the Spirit, they need to mature in the things of God, which they do as they forsake their carnal inclinations and pursue the Will of God for their lives.

IN CHRIST, we are a new Creation.

As we mature and learn to walk according to the Spirit, we demonstrate the transformation from the domination of sin in our lives to the prevalence of Christ's Righteousness in our lives to the world.

To walk in anything less than the Righteousness that Christ has imputed to us is to declare that the Word of God is not true, and that the Work that Jesus Christ did on the cross was of no effect.

To say that we are incapable of manifesting His Righteousness in our lives is to negate the Word of God, which teaches us to yield our bodies as instruments (weapons) of righteousness unto God (Rom 6:13).

If we *are* incapable of yielding our bodies as instruments of righteousness to God, we are accusing God of being a hard Taskmaster Who expects more of us than we are able to do. It would be unfair of God to demand something of us that we were incapable of doing. Christ's Work on the cross has enabled us to walk in His Righteousness.

It is a matter of *yielding* to His Will for our lives. If we say we are unable to obey His Word and to yield our bodies as instruments of righteousness to God, we insult the Spirit of Grace, which teaches us that denying ungodliness and worldly lusts, we should live soberly, righteously, and godly in this present world (Tit 2:11, 12).

THOUGH THE NEW BIRTH, CHRIST HAS ENABLED THE CHILD OF GOD TO WALK IN OBEDIENCE TO HIS WORD.

Knowing that this is the case, a Born Again child of God will be grieved for his or her failure to walk in Christ's Righteousness, and will have an overwhelming desire to manifest His Righteousness to the world. It is at this time that he or she will encounter those in the church who will tell them not to worry about it, "because God understands that we are not perfect". If they aren't careful, they will allow others to extinguish their desire to be conformed to the image of Jesus.

A minister of the Gospel will hunger and thirst on a daily basis to be able to walk in the Righteousness of Christ because they understand that they are a representative of God.

2Co 5:17 Therefore if any man be in Christ, he is a new creature: old things are passed away; behold, all things are become new.
18 And all things are of God, who hath reconciled us to himself by Jesus Christ, and hath given to us the ministry of reconciliation;
19 To wit, that God was in Christ, reconciling the world unto himself, not imputing their trespasses unto them; and hath committed unto us the word of reconciliation.
20 Now then we are ambassadors for Christ, as though God did beseech you by us; we pray you in Christ's stead, be ye reconciled to God.
21 For he hath made him to be sin for us, who knew no sin; that we might be made the righteousness of God in him.

Jesus Christ bore our sins so that while we *were* dead in our sins, now we are dead to sin, and are free to live a life of righteousness.

1Pe 2:24 Who his own self bare our sins in his own body on the tree, that we, being dead to sins, should live unto righteousness: by whose stripes ye were healed.
25 For ye were as sheep going astray; but are now returned unto the Shepherd and Bishop of your souls.

Rom 6:11 Likewise reckon ye also yourselves to be dead indeed unto sin, but alive unto God through Jesus Christ our Lord.
12 Let not sin therefore reign in your mortal body, that ye should obey it in the lusts thereof.
13 Neither yield ye your members *as* instruments of unrighteousness unto sin: but yield yourselves unto God, as those that are alive from the dead, and your members *as* instruments of righteousness unto God.
14 For sin shall not have dominion over you: for ye are not under the law, but under grace.

Notes:

_____
_____
_____
_____
_____
_____
_____
_____
_____
_____
_____
_____
_____
_____
_____
_____
_____
_____
_____
_____
_____
_____

The phrase "Being dead to sins" literally means "to be absent from sins".

We have been redeemed and are new creatures through the Blood of the Lamb. Sin can no longer dominate our lives (**Rom 6:14**), because we have been made free from the power of sin by the sacrifice of our Lord Jesus Christ and the supernatural transformation that takes place at the event of our new birth.

Having been purchased through His Precious Blood, we are enabled (and as such are obligated) to live unto righteousness.

**2Pe 2:20 For if after they have escaped the pollutions of the world through the knowledge of the Lord and Savior Jesus Christ, they are again entangled therein, and overcome, the latter end is worse with them than the beginning.
21 For it had been better for them not to have known the way of righteousness, than, after they have known it, to turn from the holy commandment delivered unto them.
22 But it is happened unto them according to the true proverb, The dog is turned to his own vomit again; and the sow that was washed to her wallowing in the mire.**

Choices are put before the child of God. Each day there is a choice to serve God in righteousness or to wallow in the mire of unrighteousness. The fact that there is a choice shows us that we are able to resist sin. We have not been saved to wallow in the mire.

1Jo 2:29 If ye know that he is righteous, ye know that every one that doeth righteousness is born of him.

The genuine Minister of God does not *practice* sin. He *practices* walking in righteousness.

He may have some sins that continually beset him and ensnare him or her, but the child of God takes no pleasure in the fact that these sins have such a foothold in his life. I have met many miserable backsliders. The true Christian will loathe his sin, and will desire to walk in righteousness before God.

Every Christian goes through the experience Paul spoke of in Romans 7:15-23, and they will also feel the frustration that Paul felt as well:

Rom 7:15 For that which I do I allow not: for what I would, that do I not; but what I hate, that do I.
16 If then I do that which I would not, I consent unto the law that it is good.
17 Now then it is no more I that do it, but sin that dwelleth in me.
18 For I know that in me (that is, in my flesh,) dwelleth no good thing: for to will is present with me; but how to perform that which is good I find not.
19 For the good that I would I do not: but the evil which I would not, that I do.
20 Now if I do that I would not, it is no more I that do it, but sin that dwelleth in me.
21 I find then a law, that, when I would do good, evil is present with me.
22 For I delight in the law of God after the inward man:
23 But I see another law in my members, warring against the law of my mind, and bringing me into captivity to the law of sin which is in my members.
24 O wretched man that I am! who shall deliver me from the body of this death?
25 I thank God through Jesus Christ our Lord. So then with the mind I myself serve the law of God; but with the flesh the law of sin.

Paul declared that there is conflict that takes place in a person's life as they walk the Christian walk.

He doesn't do what he knows is right, but does the things that he hates. Even when he wants to do right, he finds he can't do it. Instead of doing what he knows to be right, he does wrong. He understands his wretched state before God and man.

Because of this struggle, and because of his hunger and thirst to do that which is right, he cries out in frustration: "O wretched man that I am! who shall deliver me from the body of this death?" (Rom 7:24) His answer is immediate. The *only* One Who can deliver him from his dilemma is Jesus Christ through the Work of the Holy Spirit in his life (Rom. 7:25, 8:1).

Today, because of wrong theology ("We're just sinners saved by Grace"), many professing Christians do not have a hunger and a thirst to do what is right. They do not understand their own wretchedness, because they have been lulled to complacency by the false doctrines that divest them of their responsibility before God.

THE GENUINE MINISTER OF GOD RESPONDS TO BIBLICAL TRUTH IN OBEDIENCE TO THE WORD, AND ENCOURAGES OTHERS TO DO THE SAME.

For the genuine Christian, sin is the exception to the rule, instead of the rule. The Christian *strives* against sin (Heb 12:4). His life is to be one of resistance against temptation (Jas 4:7). We have a mandate to remain in Christ and to resist the devil.

Jas 4:7 Submit yourselves therefore to God. Resist the devil, and he will flee from you.
8 Draw nigh to God, and he will draw nigh to you. Cleanse *your* hands, *ye* sinners; and purify *your* hearts, *ye* double minded.

The Genuine Christian, despite his faults and tendencies toward sin, will have a strong desire to manifest the Righteousness of Christ in his life. As a minister of the Gospel, Christ's righteousness in you should be obvious to all.

1Jo 3:5 And ye know that he was manifested to take away our sins; and in him is no sin.
6 Whosoever abideth in him sinneth not: whosoever sinneth hath not seen him, neither known him.
7 Little children, let no man deceive you: he that doeth righteousness is righteous, even as he is righteous.
8 He that committeth sin is of the devil; for the devil sinneth from the beginning. For this purpose the Son of God was manifested, that he might destroy the works of the devil.
9 Whosoever is born of God doth not commit sin; for his seed remaineth in him: and he cannot sin, because he is born of God.
10 In this the children of God are manifest, and the children of the devil: whosoever doeth not righteousness is not of God, neither he that loveth not his brother.

"He that committeth sin" speaks of the person who continues in sin with no regard to his lifestyle or responsibility as a Christian.

Rom 10:9 That if thou shalt confess with thy mouth the Lord Jesus, and shalt believe in thine heart that God hath raised him from the dead, thou shalt be saved.
10 For with the heart man believeth unto righteousness; and with the mouth confession is made unto salvation.
11 For the Scripture saith, Whosoever believeth on him shall not be ashamed.

Christianity is a heart issue. If a person continues in sin with little or no regard to his sin after he has prayed to ask Jesus into his heart, there is a question as to whether or not he has believed with his heart. If we believe with our heart, we will strive to live in accordance to the Will of God. Sometimes our fleshly desires or lusts may get the better of us, but we will understand that is exactly why we are in need of a Savior, to save us from our sins. We will earnestly desire to be conformed to His Image.

Rom 14:17 For the kingdom of God is not meat and drink; but righteousness, and peace, and joy in the Holy Ghost.
18 For he that in these things serveth Christ is acceptable to God, and approved of men.
19 Let us therefore follow after the things which make for peace, and things wherewith one may edify another.

As we hunger and thirst for His Righteousness, Jesus promised that we would be filled, or satisfied with that desire. We will reflect His Righteousness in our lives.

But there are many who profess to be Christians who do not even attempt to walk in His Righteousness. In the Book of Romans, it speaks of those who *hold the truth* (they possess the Truth) in unrighteousness. These are those who profess to be Christians, yet who justify their sin by saying "I am just a sinner saved by Grace" and who do little or nothing to resist their sin. They have a promise from God that they can rely on:

"The Wrath of God is revealed from heaven against all ungodliness and unrighteousness of men who hold the truth in unrighteousness" (*Rom 1:18*).

These reprobate Christians who walk in self-justification and who have changed the Truth of God into a lie, worship and serve the created thing (their own lusts and their own will) more than the Creator.

One day they will have to give account to God for their hypocrisy. But in the meantime, those who are not yet Christians see their example and use it as an excuse not to come to Christ.

1Jn 3:5 And ye know that he was manifested to take away our sins; and in him is no sin.

Rom 6:13 Neither yield ye your members *as* instruments of unrighteousness unto sin: but yield yourselves unto God, as those that are alive from the dead, and your members *as* instruments of righteousness unto God.
14 For sin shall not have dominion over you: for ye are not under the law, but under grace.

Joh 15:1 I am the true vine, and my Father is the husbandman.
2 Every branch in me that beareth not fruit he taketh away: and every *branch* that beareth fruit, he purgeth it, that it may bring forth more fruit.
3 Now ye are clean through the word which I have spoken unto you.
4 Abide in me, and I in you. As the branch cannot bear fruit of itself, except it abide in the vine; no more can ye, except ye abide in me.
5 I am the vine, ye *are* the branches: He that abideth in me, and I in him, the same bringeth forth much fruit: for without me ye can do nothing
6 If a man abide not in me, he is cast forth as a branch, and is withered; and men gather them, and cast *them* into the fire, and they are burned.

Many Professing Christians have asked Jesus into their hearts because they are looking for fire insurance. They don't want to go to hell, but they don't want to give up their sin, either. They search for teachers who will scratch their ears and teach those things that justify their sinfulness (*2 Tim 4:3*). They don't hunger and thirst for righteousness. They have a form of godliness (they go to church and speak fluent Christianese), but they deny the transforming power of it (*2 Tim 3:5*).

Rom 6:16 Know ye not, that to whom ye yield yourselves servants to obey, his servants ye are to whom ye obey; whether of sin unto death, or of obedience unto righteousness?
17 But God be thanked, that ye were the servants of sin, but ye have obeyed from the heart that form of doctrine which was delivered you.
18 Being then made free from sin, ye became the servants of righteousness.

The Gospel teaches us that Jesus Christ has freed us from our sins (*1 Jn 3:5*). It teaches that sin no longer has any dominion over us (*Rom 6:14*). It teaches us that we have a responsibility to remain IN Him (*John 15:1-6*). We have a responsibility to turn away from a lifestyle of ungodliness and worldliness, and that we should live soberly, righteously and godly in this present world, because Jesus gave Himself for us, that we should be redeemed from ALL iniquity (*Titus 2:11-14*).

This is true for every Christian, but particularly for those who have responded to the call of ministry, and who are ambassadors of Christ. We are to be examples to those on the outside of what Freedom in Christ is.

The preacher who goes out of the church building after the service and smokes with the rest of the congregation cannot effectively minister freedom to someone who is in bondage to drugs.

Tit 2:7 In all things shewing thyself a pattern of good works: in doctrine *shewing* uncorruptness,
 gravity, sincerity,
8 Sound speech, that cannot be condemned; that he that is of the contrary part may be ashamed, having no evil thing to say of you.

1Pe 5:1 The elders which are among you I exhort, who am also an elder, and a witness of the sufferings of Christ, and also a partaker of the glory that shall be revealed:
2 Feed the flock of God which is among you, taking the oversight *thereof,* not by constraint, but willingly; not for filthy lucre, but of a ready mind;
3 Neither as being lords over *God's* heritage, but being ensamples to the flock.

Notes:
_____
_____
_____
_____
_____
_____
_____
_____
_____
_____
_____
_____
_____
_____
_____
_____
_____
_____
_____
_____
_____

You can't preach about the Covenant between God and men if you yourself have grown distant from your spouse and have divorced and remarried.

You cannot teach humility if you are caught up in pride.

You cannot teach self control if you don't have control of your own lusts and emotions, and if you are given to a gluttonous appetite.

You can't cast out devils if he's alive in you.

A minister of the Gospel is to be an example to others. We are representing the Kingdom of God.

Christian: do you feel inadequate before God? You truly ought to. That will cause you to be in the right position before him, where you hunger and thirst for His Righteousness.

Resolve today that you will fight the good fight of faith (*1 Tim 6:12*). That you will strive against sin (*Heb 12:4*). That you will resist the devil (*James 4:7*). That you will bring your body in subjection to the will of God (*1 Cor 9:27*). The more you realize your utter helplessness to accomplish these things by your own strength, the more you will hunger and thirst for the righteousness that only God can clothe you with.

When you finally want that righteousness to be manifested in your life above all things, the Lord will do such a work in you that you *will* be filled.

**Pro 10:11 The mouth of a righteous man is a well of life: but violence covereth the mouth of the wicked.
12 Hatred stirreth up strifes: but love covereth all sins.**

**1Pe 4:7 But the end of all things is at hand: be ye therefore sober, and watch unto prayer.
8 And above all things have fervent charity among yourselves: for charity shall cover the multitude of sins.
9 Use hospitality one to another without grudging.**

10 As every man hath received the gift, *even so* minister the same one to another, as good stewards of the manifold grace of God.

11 If any man speak, *let him speak* as the oracles of God; if any man minister, *let him do it* as of the ability which God giveth: that God in all things may be glorified through Jesus Christ, to whom be praise and dominion for ever and ever. Amen.

1) What, in your opinion, is the difference between self righteousness and righteousness? _____

_____
_____
_____
_____
_____
_____

2) List 3 passages from the Bible that encourages believers to be examples to others. _____

_____
_____
_____
_____

3) Write down and memorize 1 Jn 3:7 _____

_____
_____
_____

4) Fill in the blanks:

1Jn 3:6 Whosoever abideth in him sinneth not: whosoever _____ hath not seen him, neither _____ him.

7 Little children, let no man deceive you: he that doeth _____ is _____, even as he is _____.

8 He that _____ sin is of the _____; for the _____ sinneth from the beginning. For this purpose the Son of God was _____, that he might _____ the works of the _____.

9 Whosoever is _____ of God doth not _____ sin; for his seed remaineth in him: and he _____ sin, because he is _____ of God.

10 In this the _____ are manifest, and the _____

_____: whosoever doeth not _____ is not of God, neither he that _____ his brother.

5) What areas in your life have you compromised concerning living your life in righteousness?

_____

_____

_____

_____

_____

_____

_____

_____

_____

_____

Chapter 6

Merciful Mendicants

Mat 5:7 Blessed *are* the merciful: for they shall obtain mercy.

IN THE BEGINNING of His discourse to His ministers in training, Jesus said "Blessed are the poor in spirit", and we have seen that this was referring to the one who understands his or her total dependence on God. As we grow in our knowledge of God's work of Grace in every aspect of our lives, we will manifest His Grace to others. But one cannot effectively manifest Grace to others unless he or she is fully aware of the depths of God's Grace that has been demonstrated toward them. All that we are, all that we will ever be is because of the Grace of God.

So far we have seen that Jesus is telling His disciples that as ministers of God, *1)* we must understand our utter spiritual dependency on God in order to be effective in ministry (Blessed are the poor in spirit); and as a result, we will *2)* sincerely grieve (Blessed are they that mourn) over our propensity toward sin. *3)* Being aware of our absolute dependence on God's intervention in our life on a daily basis, we will have no place for boasting (Blessed are the meek), and will be yielded to God's Will for our life. *4)* Knowing our lack, and loving our Father, the child of God will strongly desire to be conformed to His Image (Blessed are they that hunger and thirst for righteousness). *5)* As we walk in His Righteousness and not in our own, His Mercy will manifest itself in our lives toward others, because God's Righteousness demands mercy on a people who are incapable in themselves of living free from sin.

The only other place where this word *Merciful* is used is in Hebrews 2:17, where we can get an idea how the Ultimate Minister conducts His Ministry.

Mercy imitates God, and disappoints Satan.

John Chrysostom

Mendicant

MEND'ICANT, a. [L. mendicans, from mendico, to beg; allied to L.mando, to command, demand.]

1. Begging; poor to a state of beggary; as reduced to a mendicant state.

2. Practicing beggary; as a mendicant friar.

MEND'ICANT, n. A beggar; one that makes it his business to beg alms; one of the begging fraternity of the Romish church.

Notes:

_____
_____
_____
_____
_____
_____
_____
_____
_____
_____
_____
_____
_____
_____
_____
_____
_____
_____
_____
_____

Merciful

G1655

ἐλεήμων eleēmōn

el-eh-ay'-mone

From G1653; compassionate (actively): - merciful.

1Jn 2:6 He that saith he abideth in him ought himself also so to walk, even as he walked.

Notes:

_____
_____
_____
_____
_____
_____
_____
_____
_____
_____
_____
_____
_____
_____
_____
_____
_____
_____
_____
_____
_____
_____
_____
_____
_____
_____
_____

Heb 2:11 For both he that sanctifieth and they who are sanctified *are* all of one: for which cause he is not ashamed to call them brethren,
12 Saying, I will declare thy name unto my brethren, in the midst of the church will I sing praise unto thee.
13 And again, I will put my trust in him. And again, Behold I and the children which God hath given me.
14 Forasmuch then as the children are partakers of flesh and blood, he also himself likewise took part of the same; that through death he might destroy him that had the power of death, that is, the devil;
15 And deliver them who through fear of death were all their lifetime subject to bondage.
16 For verily he took not on *him the nature of* angels; but he took on *him* the seed of Abraham.
17 Wherefore in all things it behoved him to be made like unto his brethren, that he might be a merciful and faithful high priest in things pertaining to God, to make reconciliation for the sins of the people.
18 For in that he himself hath suffered being tempted, he is able to succour them that are tempted.

Christ was our example in all aspects of life. He came in the form of a servant in order to teach us how to live our lives as servants to each other. As He was merciful, so we also should be merciful to others.

Just as no one would hold a mentally disabled person accountable for his or her deficiencies, God understands our spiritual deficiencies as well, and has given us Grace. As such we also should be consciously demonstrating Grace to those we are called to minister to.

Temptations come in all forms. What is a temptation for one person may not be an issue with another. I suppose when I was younger in Christ, and had gotten deliverance from nicotine, being around someone who smoked would be a temptation to me.

Rom 8:26 Likewise the Spirit also helpeth our infirmities: for we know not what we should pray for as we ought: but the Spirit itself maketh intercession for us with groanings which cannot be uttered.
27 And he that searcheth the hearts knoweth what *is* the mind of the Spirit, because he maketh intercession for the saints according to *the will of* God.
28 And we know that all things work together for good to them that love God, to them who are the called according to *his* purpose.

Notes:

But after I walked free from its hold on me for five years or so, I could be in a room filled with smokers, and the temptation wouldn't be there any longer. But does that mean that I am free from all temptations? No. I have overcome that one and many others, but there are still enticements to incline toward the lust of the flesh rather than the Will of God. Knowing that I myself at one time struggled with the addiction to nicotine, how could I ever stand in condemnation of those who are still struggling?

Unfortunately there are those who forget where they have come from, and who do walk in condemnation of those who are not where they are in their walk with Jesus. But that should never be the case with the Christian minister.

As I have grown in maturity in my walk with the Lord, I now understand that I have the ability to resist the devil in ANY area of temptation with Jesus' help, and as such, I am able to help others who are struggling with temptations.

Those who are merciful will have compassion instead of condemnation for those who are struggling. As we have seen, *Hebrews 2:17* declares that Christ endured those things that He went through so He could be a merciful high priest on our behalf. He understands what we are going through in our life, and He is there to comfort us during those times, so we can comfort others who are in turn going through the same struggles that we have gone through ourselves.

2Co 1:3 Blessed *be* God, even the Father of our Lord Jesus Christ, the Father of mercies, and the God of all comfort;
4 Who comforteth us in all our tribulation, that we may be able to comfort them which are in any trouble, by the comfort wherewith we ourselves are comforted of God.
5 For as the sufferings of Christ abound in us, so our consolation also aboundeth by Christ.
6 And whether we be afflicted, *it is* for your consolation and salvation, which is effectual in the enduring of the same sufferings which we also

2Co 5:18 And all things are of God, who hath reconciled us to himself by Jesus Christ, and hath given to us the ministry of reconciliation;
19 To wit, that God was in Christ, reconciling the world unto himself, not imputing their trespasses unto them; and hath committed unto us the word of reconciliation.

Gal 6:1 Brethren, if a man be overtaken in a fault, ye which are spiritual, restore such an one in the spirit of meekness; considering thyself, lest thou also be tempted.
2 Bear ye one another's burdens, and so fulfil the law of Christ.
3 For if a man think himself to be something, when he is nothing, he deceiveth himself.

Jas 5:19 Brethren, if any of you do err from the truth, and one convert him;
20 Let him know, that he which converteth the sinner from the error of his way shall save a soul from death, and shall hide a multitude of sins.

1Jn 5:16 If any man see his brother sin a sin *which is* not unto death, he shall ask, and he shall give him life for them that sin not unto death. There is a sin unto death: I do not say that he shall pray for it.

suffer: or whether we be comforted, *it is* for your consolation and salvation.

The effective minister of God will not judge another person according to how he or she thinks that person should be ("If I was them, I wouldn't do what they are doing"); they will treat them with the Compassion that Jesus had.

I have met many who have compared their victories over sin with other's failures. They will say something like "When I got saved, I lost all desire for alcohol," and they will insist that the Christian who still struggles with alcohol didn't really get saved. There is no mercy in that attitude.

The minister needs to understand that there are variables in every person's life. No one is the same as the other person. Their situations are not the same. Instead of looking at people from our skewed carnal perspective, we should look at them through Jesus' Eyes, always aware that even while *we* were yet sinners, Christ died for us. That means He never pronounced us as hopeless, regardless of the depths of our degradation. Christ knew the woman at the well was an adulteress, and He never spoke condemnation to her, but ministered Words of Life to her.

There is a lot of false doctrine that has crept into the Church. Jesus warned His disciples that it would be so. Paul said there would be false teachers and false apostles who would creep into the Church. John spoke about the spirit of antichrist that would prevail in the last days. Peter warned about false prophets. James and Jude also wrote about error that would creep in to the Church through false teachers.

Where does mercy fit into all of this? Sometimes you can confuse that which is real with that which is false. We all have an inclination to error. And it is usually easier to see the faults of others than it is our own. We are co-laborers with Jesus and with each other in the Kingdom of God. And as such, Jesus should be our model for ministry.

Jud 1:22 And of some have compassion, making a difference:
23 And others save with fear, pulling them out of the fire; hating even the garment spotted by the flesh.

Notes:

_____
_____
_____
_____
_____
_____
_____
_____
_____
_____
_____
_____
_____
_____
_____
_____
_____
_____
_____
_____
_____
_____
_____
_____
_____
_____
_____
_____

We should be ready to expose false doctrine, but not so quick to name names. Through our example some who were caught in error may see their fault, and repent.

Sometimes a tare can look like wheat, and sometimes a stalk of wheat can be mistaken for a tare. It's not for the minister of the Gospel to uproot the tares; it is our job to warn against false doctrine that some may teach, but we are always to understand that *ours is a ministry of reconciliation, not a ministry of condemnation.* Even those who teach error could be doing so out of wrong understanding.

Mat 13:24 Another parable put he forth unto them, saying, The kingdom of heaven is likened unto a man which sowed good seed in his field:
25 But while men slept, his enemy came and sowed tares among the wheat, and went his way.
26 But when the blade was sprung up, and brought forth fruit, then appeared the tares also.
27 So the servants of the householder came and said unto him, Sir, didst not thou sow good seed in thy field? from whence then hath it tares?
28 He said unto them, An enemy hath done this. The servants said unto him, Wilt thou then that we go and gather them up?
29 But he said, Nay; lest while ye gather up the tares, ye root up also the wheat with them.
30 Let both grow together until the harvest: and in the time of harvest I will say to the reapers, Gather ye together first the tares, and bind them in bundles to burn them: but gather the wheat into my barn.

Sowing Mercy will result in having mercy bestowed on you when you stand before the King.

Mat 18:23 Therefore is the kingdom of heaven likened unto a certain king, which would take account of his servants.
24 And when he had begun to reckon, one was brought unto him, which owed him ten thousand talents.

Gal 6:7 Be not deceived; God is not mocked: for whatsoever a man soweth, that shall he also reap.
8 For he that soweth to his flesh shall of the flesh reap corruption; but he that soweth to the Spirit shall of the Spirit reap life everlasting.
9 And let us not be weary in well doing: for in due season we shall reap, if we faint not.
10 As we have therefore opportunity, let us do good unto all *men,* especially unto them who are of the household of faith.

Heb 12:14 Follow peace with all *men,* and holiness, without which no man shall see the Lord:
15 Looking diligently lest any man fail of the grace of God; lest any root of bitterness springing up trouble *you,* and thereby many be defiled;

1Jn 2:6 He that saith he abideth in him ought himself also so to walk, even as he walked.

Notes:

_____
_____
_____
_____
_____
_____
_____
_____
_____
_____
_____
_____
_____
_____

25 But forasmuch as he had not to pay, his lord commanded him to be sold, and his wife, and children, and all that he had, and payment to be made.
26 The servant therefore fell down, and worshipped him, saying, Lord, have patience with me, and I will pay thee all.
27 Then the lord of that servant was moved with compassion, and loosed him, and forgave him the debt.
28 But the same servant went out, and found one of his fellowservants, which owed him an hundred pence: and he laid hands on him, and took *him* by the throat, saying, Pay me that thou owest.
29 And his fellowservant fell down at his feet, and besought him, saying, Have patience with me, and I will pay thee all.
30 And he would not: but went and cast him into prison, till he should pay the debt.
31 So when his fellowservants saw what was done, they were very sorry, and came and told unto their lord all that was done.
32 Then his lord, after that he had called him, said unto him, O thou wicked servant, I forgave thee all that debt, because thou desiredst me:
33 Shouldest not thou also have had compassion (mercy) on thy fellowservant, even as I had pity on thee?
34 And his lord was wroth, and delivered him to the tormentors, till he should pay all that was due unto him.
35 So likewise shall my heavenly Father do also unto you, if ye from your hearts forgive not every one his brother their trespasses.

The law of sowing and reaping is obvious here. Those who walk in unforgiveness and who do not have compassion toward their brothers and sisters in Christ will live a life of inner conflict or torment. Bitterness and anger are the opposite of Mercy, and they afford a heavy burden for those who carry them.

The minister who has issues of unforgiveness will

carry those issues into his or her ministry, and their relationship with others.

A person who has issues of unresolved unforgiveness or bitterness is generally critical in their dealings with others. You will find little in the way of a disposition of mercy in the life of one who is walking in bitterness. Distrust and a judgmental attitude toward others are generally indicative of a root of bitterness.

In *Hebrews 12:15*, we see that Christians are to avoid any root of bitterness. The disciple is admonished to be careful that he or she does not "fail of the Grace of God". The word "fail" can mean to "lack". Our walk should reflect God's abounding Grace toward others.

If a person fails to learn to reflect God's Grace in their ministry to others, they will often do more damage to people who have already been damaged and are demonstrating that damage in their sinful behavior.

It is important that the reader pause here for a moment, and take an accurate assessment of your life, and those who have hurt, betrayed, or disappointed you.

Make a list of those people and write down the way they have caused you hurt. Then write how you think the issue could be resolved, or if you think it could ever be resolved. Don't allow your heart to deceive you. As a child of God, these issues *must* be resolved, if you hope to live an overcoming Christian life and to be an effective minister in the Kingdom of God.

_____

_____

_____

_____

_____

_____

_____

_____

_____

_____

_____

_____

_____

_____

_____

_____

_____

_____

_____

_____

_____
_____
_____
_____
_____
_____
_____
_____
_____
_____
_____
_____
_____
_____
_____
_____
_____
_____
_____
_____
_____
_____
_____
_____
_____
_____
_____
_____
_____
_____

If you are going through this book in a class room setting, pray about sharing what you wrote with the others, and minister healing and deliverance to one another.

Maybe you aren't ready yet to deal with these things publicly, because the pain is too great. That's O.K.. But be assured that the longer you keep these things bottled up inside you, the greater a hindrance they will be in your Christian walk. Sooner or later, you will have to let someone get close enough to help you

Gal 6:7 Be not deceived; God is not mocked: for whatsoever a man soweth, that shall he also reap.
8 For he that soweth to his flesh shall of the flesh reap corruption; but he that soweth to the Spirit shall of the Spirit reap life everlasting.
9 And let us not be weary in well doing: for in due season we shall reap, if we faint not.
10 As we have therefore opportunity, let us do good unto all *men,* especially unto them who are of the household of faith.

Notes:

carry your burdens, so you will be better qualified to help others carry *their* burdens.

GENUINE CHRISTIANS WALK IN COMPASSION TOWARD OTHERS JUST AS CHRIST WALKED IN COMPASSION TOWARD THOSE HE ENCOUNTERED.

Since He is the Source of our salvation, we can safely assume that the words that Jesus spoke concerning His Doctrine were of the utmost importance, and since chapter seven concludes his dialogue of chapters 5, 6, and 7 with "*And it came to pass, when Jesus had ended these sayings, the people were astonished at his doctrine:" (Matt 7:28*), then we can conclude that everything Jesus spoke from Matthew 5:3 – Matt 7:28 was doctrinal as well.

In John 7:16, Jesus said that the Doctrine He taught was not His Own, but that of His Father's.

When we search the Old Testament, we can see a parallel to these Words which Jesus spoke in Matthew 5:7 with 2 Sa 22:26, and Psalms 18:25.

2Sa 22:22 For I have kept the ways of the LORD, and have not wickedly departed from my God.
23 For all his judgments were before me: and as for his statutes, I did not depart from them.
24 I was also upright before him and have kept myself from mine iniquity.
25 Therefore the LORD hath recompensed me according to my righteousness; according to my cleanness in his eye sight.
26 With the merciful thou wilt show thyself merciful, and with the upright man thou wilt show thyself upright.
27 With the pure thou wilt show thyself pure; and with the froward thou wilt show thyself unsavory.
28 And the afflicted people thou wilt save: but thine eyes are upon the haughty, that thou mayest bring them down.

Notes:

And again, in Psalm 18:23-26, we read the same words:

**Psa 18:23 I was also upright before him, and I kept myself from mine iniquity.
24 Therefore hath the LORD recompensed me according to my righteousness, according to the cleanness of my hands in his eyesight.
25 With the merciful thou wilt show thyself merciful; with an upright man thou wilt show thyself upright;
26 With the pure thou wilt show thyself pure; and with the froward thou wilt show thyself froward.
27 For thou wilt save the afflicted people; but wilt bring down high looks.
28 For thou wilt light my candle: the LORD my God will enlighten my darkness.**

***Blessed Are The Merciful, For They Shall Obtain Mercy*...**

Luk 6:36 Be ye therefore merciful, as your Father also is merciful.

It was God's Mercy that came wrapped in a cloak of flesh and shrouded in the weakness of mortality, Who beheld our rebellion and wept over it.

It was God's Mercy that willingly went to the cross and bore the sins of humanity, a Perfect Sacrifice for all who had no perfection to offer.

It was God's Mercy revealed in a vessel of Compassion that fed the multitude, that healed the sick, that freed the captive, that saved the lost.

It was God's Mercy that beheld the multitude mocking Him as He suffered on the cross for them, and said "Father, forgive them, for they know not what they do". He practiced what He preached.

Mat 5:7 Blessed are the merciful: for they shall obtain mercy.

Mat 18:21 Then came Peter to him, and said, Lord, how oft shall my brother sin against me, and I forgive him? till seven times?

22 Jesus saith unto him, I say not unto thee, Until seven times: but, Until seventy times seven.

23 Therefore is the kingdom of heaven likened unto a certain king, which would take account of his servants.

24 And when he had begun to reckon, one was brought unto him, which owed him ten thousand talents.

25 But forasmuch as he had not to pay, his lord commanded him to be sold, and his wife, and children, and all that he had, and payment to be made.

26 The servant therefore fell down, and worshiped him, saying, Lord, have patience with me, and I will pay thee all.

27 Then the lord of that servant was moved with compassion and loosed him, and forgave him the debt.

28 But the same servant went out, and found one of his fellow servants, which owed him a hundred pence: and he laid hands on him, and took *him* by the throat, saying, Pay me that thou owest.

29 And his fellowservant fell down at his feet, and besought him, saying, Have patience with me, and I will pay thee all.

30 And he would not: but went and cast him into prison, till he should pay the debt.

31 So when his fellowservants saw what was done, they were very sorry, and came and told unto their lord all that was done.

The verse so often used before the offering plate is passed is really talking about mercy, not a means to financial blessings:

Luk 6:31 And as ye would that men should do to you, do ye also to them likewise.
32 For if ye love them which love you, what thank have ye? for sinners also love those that love them.
33 And if ye do good to them which do good to you, what thank have ye? for sinners also do even the same.
34 And if ye lend to them of whom ye hope to receive, what thank have ye? for sinners also lend to sinners, to receive as much again.
35 But love ye your enemies, and do good, and lend, hoping for nothing again; and your reward shall be great, and ye shall be the children of the Highest: for he is kind unto the unthankful and to the evil.
36 Be ye therefore merciful, as your Father also is merciful.
37 Judge not, and ye shall not be judged: condemn not, and ye shall not be condemned: forgive, and ye shall be forgiven:
38 Give, and it shall be given unto you; good measure, pressed down, and shaken together, and running over, shall men give into your bosom. For with the same measure that ye mete withal it shall be measured to you again.

We are taught by those who are intent on building their kingdom that Luke 6:38 is speaking of giving a generous offering into the plate, and if we do, we will get more in our wallet. But Jesus was teaching His disciples the Way of Mercy.

If you give mercy you'll get mercy when you need it.

A minister of God is to sow Mercy to those who least deserve it. Isn't that what God did for you?

Eph 4:1 I therefore, the prisoner of the Lord, beseech you that ye walk worthy of the vocation wherewith ye are called,
2 With all lowliness and meekness, with longsuffering, forbearing one another in love;

32 Then his lord, after that he had called him, said unto him, O thou wicked servant, I forgave thee all that debt, because thou desiredst me:
33 Shouldest not thou also have had compassion on thy fellow servant, even as I had pity on thee?
34 And his lord was wroth, and delivered him to the tormentors, till he should pay all that was due unto him.
35 So likewise shall my heavenly Father do also unto you, if ye from your hearts forgive not every one his brother their trespasses.

Mic 6:8 He hath showed thee, O man, what *is* good; and what doth the LORD require of thee, but to do justly, and to love mercy, and to walk humbly with thy God?

Jam 3:17 But the wisdom that is from above is first pure, then peaceable, gentle, *and* easy to be entreated, full of mercy and good fruits, without partiality, and without hypocrisy.

Mat 9:11 And when the Pharisees saw *it,* they said unto his disciples, Why eateth your Master with publicans and sinners?
12 But when Jesus heard *that,* he said unto them, They that be whole need not a physician, but they that are sick.
13 But go ye and learn what *that* meaneth, I will have mercy, and not sacrifice: for I am not come to call the righteous, but sinners to repentance.

3 Endeavoring to keep the unity of the Spirit in the bond of peace.

Pro 21:13 Whoso stoppeth his ears at the cry of the poor, he also shall cry himself, but shall not be heard.

In Isaiah 58, we see that God isn't interested in His people fasting to afflict their souls like some kind of self sacrifice for Him; walking in mercy toward others is the fast that pleases Him.

In fact, in Matthew 9:13 we read that God desires Mercy over sacrifice.

Again, as you read these passages you can see the Law of sowing and reaping at work:

Isa 58:6 *Is* not this the fast that I have chosen? to loose the bands of wickedness, to undo the heavy burdens, and to let the oppressed go free, and that ye break every yoke?
7 *Is it* not to deal thy bread to the hungry, and that thou bring the poor that are cast out to thy house? when thou seest the naked, that thou cover him; and that thou hide not thyself from thine own flesh?
8 Then shall thy light break forth as the morning, and thine health shall spring forth speedily: and thy righteousness shall go before thee; the glory of the LORD shall be thy rearward.
9 Then shalt thou call, and the LORD shall answer; thou shalt cry, and he shall say, Here I *am.* If thou take away from the midst of thee the yoke, the putting forth of the finger, and speaking vanity;
10 And *if* thou draw out thy soul to the hungry, and satisfy the afflicted soul; then shall thy light rise in obscurity, and thy darkness *be* as the noonday:
11 And the LORD shall guide thee continually, and satisfy thy soul in drought, and make fat thy bones: and thou shalt be like a watered garden, and like a spring of water, whose waters fail not.
12 And *they that shall be* of thee shall build the old waste places: thou shalt raise up the

foundations of many generations; and thou shalt be called, The repairer of the breach, The restorer of paths to dwell in.

In our previous study we looked at those who hunger and thirst for Righteousness. A definitive quality of a person who walks in righteousness is found in the following verses, and that is that he is ever merciful toward those he deals with.

Psa 37:25 I have been young, and *now* am old; yet have I not seen the righteous forsaken, nor his seed begging bread.
26 *He is* ever merciful, and lendeth; and his seed *is* blessed.
27 Depart from evil, and do good; and dwell forevermore.
28 For the LORD loveth judgment, and forsaketh not his saints; they are preserved forever: but the seed of the wicked shall be cut off.
29 The righteous shall inherit the land, and dwell therein forever.
30 The mouth of the righteous speaketh wisdom, and his tongue talketh of judgment.
31 The law of his God *is* in his heart; none of his steps shall slide.

1) Explain Isaiah 58 in your own words:

_____
_____
_____
_____
_____
_____
_____
_____

2) How does bitterness and unforgiveness stand in the way of a person who would walk in mercy? _____

_____
_____
_____
_____
_____
_____

3) Read 1 Cor 13:3. These are obvious acts of mercy, but without love as a motivating factor, they are of no profit to the one who does them. Give examples of the difference between religious works, and true works of mercy

_____

_____
_____
_____
_____
_____
_____
_____

4) Personal inventory: Where have you failed in demonstrating mercy to others?

_____
_____
_____
_____
_____
_____
_____
_____
_____
_____
_____

5) Take some time to seek God in prayer and ask Him to give you the Compassion of Christ.

"It is safe to tell the pure in heart that they shall see God, for only the pure in heart want to."

— C.S. Lewis, The Problem of Pain

Chapter 7
The Pure in Heart.

Mat 5:8 Blessed *Are* The Pure In Heart: For They Shall See God.

WHAT DOES IT MEAN to be pure in heart for one who is a minister of the gospel? Psalm 24 can give us an idea:

Pure:

G2513

καθαρός   katharos
Thayer Definition:

1) clean, pure
1a) physically
1a1) purified by fire
1a2) in a similitude, like a vine cleansed by pruning and so fitted to bear fruit
1b) in a levitical sense
1b1) clean, the use of which is not forbidden, imparts no uncleanness
1c) ethically
1c1) free from corrupt desire, from sin and guilt
1c2) free from every admixture of what is false, sincere genuine
1c3) blameless, innocent
1c4) unstained with the guilt of anything

Part of Speech: adjective

Notes:

**Psa 24:3 Who shall ascend into the hill of the LORD? or who shall stand in his holy place?
4 He that hath clean hands, and a pure heart; who hath not lifted up his soul unto vanity, nor sworn deceitfully.
5 He shall receive the blessing from the LORD, and righteousness from the God of his salvation.
6 This *is* the generation of them that seek him, that seek thy face, O Jacob. Selah**

A similar Psalm is Psalm 15, which I believe defines a little clearer what it is to have a pure heart:

**Psa 15:1 A Psalm of David. LORD, who shall abide in thy tabernacle? who shall dwell in thy holy hill?
2 He that walketh uprightly, and worketh righteousness, and speaketh the truth in his heart.
3 *He that* backbiteth not with his tongue, nor doeth evil to his neighbour, nor taketh up a reproach against his neighbour.
4 In whose eyes a vile person is contemned; but he honoureth them that fear the LORD. *He that* sweareth to *his own* hurt, and changeth not.
5 *He that* putteth not out his money to usury, nor taketh reward against the innocent. He that doeth these *things* shall never be moved.**

Those who have a pure heart walk uprightly.

Mat 5:33 Again, ye have heard that it hath been said by them of old time, Thou shalt not forswear thyself, but shalt perform unto the Lord thine oaths:
34 But I say unto you, Swear not at all; neither by heaven; for it is God's throne:
35 Nor by the earth; for it is his footstool: neither by Jerusalem; for it is the city of the great King.
36 Neither shalt thou swear by thy head, because thou canst not make one hair white or black.
37 But let your communication be, Yea, yea; Nay, nay: for whatsoever is more than these cometh of evil.

Notes:

_____
_____
_____
_____
_____
_____
_____
_____
_____
_____
_____
_____
_____
_____
_____
_____
_____
_____
_____
_____
_____
_____
_____
_____
_____

This speaks of integrity. A minister of the Gospel must be a person of integrity.

Those who have a pure heart work righteousness. It's what they do. A minister of the gospel must be able to see the opportunities that are before him to do good to all men.

1Jn 3:7 Little children, let no man deceive you: he that doeth righteousness is righteous, even as he is righteous.

The pure in heart speaks truth, and never seeks to deceive. They must be a man or a woman of their word. A minister must always speak the truth, seasoned with love. They are not to be respecters of persons.

Those who are pure in heart won't gossip or speak about others behind their back. A minister must practice confidentiality in all areas. Trust is a crucial factor in any relationship, but especially between a representative of God and those he or she ministers to.

The pure in heart will not do evil to his neighbor. A minister of the gospel can't carry an attitude of "getting even". Jesus told His ministers in training:

**Mat 5:38 Ye have heard that it hath been said, An eye for an eye, and a tooth for a tooth:
39 But I say unto you, That ye resist not evil: but whosoever shall smite thee on thy right cheek, turn to him the other also.
40 And if any man will sue thee at the law, and take away thy coat, let him have *thy* cloke also.
41 And whosoever shall compel thee to go a mile, go with him twain.
42 Give to him that asketh thee, and from him that would borrow of thee turn not thou away.**

"...Nor taketh up a reproach against his neighbor". Not only will the pure in heart not back bite or gossip about others, they won't allow themselves to believe an unsubstantiated report

Jas 4:13 Go to now, ye that say, To day or to morrow we will go into such a city, and continue there a year, and buy and sell, and get gain:
14 Whereas ye know not what shall be on the morrow. For what is your life? It is even a vapour, that appeareth for a little time, and then vanisheth away.
15 For that ye ought to say, If the Lord will, we shall live, and do this, or that.
16 But now ye rejoice in your boastings: all such rejoicing is evil.
17 Therefore to him that knoweth to do good, and doeth it not, to him it is sin.

From Webster's 1828 Dictionary

Integrity

INTEG'RITY, n. [L. integritas, from integer.]

2. The entire, unimpaired state of any thing, particularly of the mind; moral soundness or purity; incorruptness; uprightness; honesty. Integrity comprehends the whole moral character, but has a special reference to uprightness in mutual dealings, transfers of property, and agencies for others.

about someone else. In counseling others, a minister of the gospel always has to remain neutral, understanding that there are three sides to a story, and God's side is the one that matters.

The pure in heart won't associate with evil people. They will minister to them, but they won't put themselves in a place where they are associated with their evil doings. It's one thing to minister to a drunk. It's another thing to befriend him in such a way that it appears as if you approve of what he is doing. The pure in heart won't approve of the ungodliness of the wicked, or condone it, knowing that it will only reinforce their path to destruction. The pure in heart will distinguish between what is acceptable before God and what is not.

The one who is pure in heart will honor those who fear the Lord. They will live in unity with and walk in love toward other Christians. The minister of the Gospel will strive for unity with other ministers to further the Kingdom of God. This word "Honor" is the Hebrew Word "Kabad", and it has a variety of meanings.

It carries with it the idea of something that is weighty, or of Great substance. In the positive sense, when used of God, it means to glorify Him.

This word is what the word which speaks of God's Glory comes from, "Kabod". If you want to look it up in Strong's Concordance, you can find it under the reference number 3519, and you will find that it comes from 3513, which is our word "kabad". In the context of Psalm 15:4, to honor those who fear the Lord would be to hold them in high esteem, and to value them greatly.

1Ti 5:17 Let the elders that rule well be counted worthy of double honour, especially they who labour in the word and doctrine.

When the early Church was established, we see that the people of God gave of their substance to ensure that those who were in the Church who lacked didn't

_____
_____
_____
_____
_____
_____
_____
_____
_____
_____
_____
_____
_____
_____
_____
_____
_____
_____
_____
_____
_____
_____
_____
_____
_____
_____
_____
_____
_____
_____
_____
_____
_____
_____
_____
_____
_____
_____
_____
_____

lack. They honored their brothers and sisters who feared the Lord with their substance.

Act 2:43 And fear came upon every soul: and many wonders and signs were done by the apostles.
44 And all that believed were together, and had all things common;
45 And sold their possessions and goods, and parted them to all *men*, as every man had need.
46 And they, continuing daily with one accord in the temple, and breaking bread from house to house, did eat their meat with gladness and singleness of heart,
47 Praising God, and having favour with all the people. And the Lord added to the church daily such as should be saved.

In Proverbs, we can see that we are to honor the Lord with our *substance, our income.*

Pro 3:5 Trust in the LORD with all thine heart; and lean not unto thine own understanding.
6 In all thy ways acknowledge him, and he shall direct thy paths.
7 Be not wise in thine own eyes: fear the LORD, and depart from evil.
8 It shall be health to thy navel, and marrow to thy bones.
9 Honour the LORD with thy substance, and with the firstfruits of all thine increase:
10 So shall thy barns be filled with plenty, and thy presses shall burst out with new wine.

Not only are we to honor our brothers and sisters in Christ, and not only are we to honor God, but God honors those who are in that place of walking with a pure heart.

He that sweareth to his own hurt, and changeth not. Sometimes we say we will do something and end up realizing that it may conflict with our own personal well being. An ambassador for the Kingdom of God must keep his or her word regardless of the cost.

Jas 4:13 Go to now, ye that say, To day or to morrow we will go into such a city, and continue there a year, and buy and sell, and get gain:
14 Whereas ye know not what *shall be* on the morrow. For what *is* your life? It is even a vapour, that appeareth for a little time, and then vanisheth away.
15 For that ye *ought* to say, If the Lord will, we shall live, and do this, or that.

_____

Notes:

_____
_____
_____
_____
_____
_____
_____
_____
_____
_____
_____
_____
_____
_____
_____
_____
_____
_____
_____
_____
_____
_____
_____
_____
_____

Those who are pure in heart will keep their word, even if it means that they may suffer loss from it. Wisdom dictates that before you promise or commit to anything, you need to carefully factor in the unknown; a family emergency, an unexpected expense can throw off the most carefully laid plans. It is better to say "If the Lord Wills, I will do such and such a thing."

The one who is pure in heart will give to those who are in need without an ulterior motive of personal gain when they help someone.

Again the operative word here is *integrity*.

"He that doeth these *things* shall never be moved."

Pro 22:11 He who loves purity of heart, and whose speech is gracious, will have the king as his friend. (English Standard Version)

Paul was able to in good conscience declare himself as "pure from the blood of all men" because he ministered in integrity:

**Act 20:17 And from Miletus he sent to Ephesus, and called the elders of the church.
18 And when they were come to him, he said unto them, Ye know, from the first day that I came into Asia, after what manner I have been with you at all seasons,
19 Serving the Lord with all humility of mind, and with many tears, and temptations, which befell me by the lying in wait of the Jews:
20 And how I kept back nothing that was profitable unto you, but have shewed you, and have taught you publickly, and from house to house,
21 Testifying both to the Jews, and also to the Greeks, repentance toward God, and faith toward our Lord Jesus Christ.
22 And now, behold, I go bound in the spirit unto Jerusalem, not knowing the things that shall befall me there:
23 Save that the Holy Ghost witnesseth in every city, saying that bonds and afflictions abide me.
24 But none of these things move me, neither**

count I my life dear unto myself, so that I might finish my course with joy, and the ministry, which I have received of the Lord Jesus, to testify the gospel of the grace of God.

25 And now, behold, I know that ye all, among whom I have gone preaching the kingdom of God, shall see my face no more.

26 Wherefore I take you to record this day, that I am pure from the blood of all men.

27 For I have not shunned to declare unto you all the counsel of God.

28 Take heed therefore unto yourselves, and to all the flock, over the which the Holy Ghost hath made you overseers, to feed the church of God, which he hath purchased with his own blood.

29 For I know this, that after my departing shall grievous wolves enter in among you, not sparing the flock.

30 Also of your own selves shall men arise, speaking perverse things, to draw away disciples after them.

31 Therefore watch, and remember, that by the space of three years I ceased not to warn every one night and day with tears.

32 And now, brethren, I commend you to God, and to the word of his grace, which is able to build you up, and to give you an inheritance among all them which are sanctified.

33 I have coveted no man's silver, or gold, or apparel.

34 Yea, ye yourselves know, that these hands have ministered unto my necessities, and to them that were with me.

35 I have shewed you all things, how that so labouring ye ought to support the weak, and to remember the words of the Lord Jesus, how he said, It is more blessed to give than to receive.

Those ministers who are pure in heart will walk in genuine love toward others.

1Ti 1:5 Now the end of the commandment is charity out of a pure heart, and *of* a good conscience, and *of* faith unfeigned:

6 From which some having swerved have turned aside unto vain jangling;

7 Desiring to be teachers of the law; understanding neither what they say, nor whereof they affirm.

Having a pure heart is our responsibility before God Who has enabled us to do so:

1Pe 1:22 Seeing ye have purified your souls in obeying the truth through the Spirit unto unfeigned love of the brethren, *see that ye* love one another with a pure heart fervently:

23 Being born again, not of corruptible seed, but of incorruptible, by the word of God, which liveth and abideth for ever.

24 For all flesh *is* as grass, and all the glory of man as the flower of grass. The grass withereth, and the flower thereof falleth away:

25 But the word of the Lord endureth for ever. And this is the word which by the gospel is preached unto you.

Those who are in ministry will walk in continual integrity, not just before men, but also God, whereby we can serve Him in pure conscience.

1Ti 3:8 Likewise *must* the deacons (ministers) *be* grave, not doubletongued, not given to much wine, not greedy of filthy lucre; 9 Holding the mystery of the faith in a _pure conscience_.

2Ti 1:3 I thank God, whom I serve from *my* forefathers with _pure conscience_, that without ceasing I have remembrance of thee in my prayers night and day;

2Ti 2:22 Flee also youthful lusts: but follow righteousness, faith, charity, peace, with them that call on the Lord out of a _pure heart_.

Tit 1:15 Unto the pure all things *are* pure: but unto them that are defiled and unbelieving *is* nothing pure; but even their mind and conscience is defiled. 16 They profess that they know God; but in works they deny *him*, being abominable, and disobedient, and unto every good work reprobate.

2Ti 2:22 Flee also youthful lusts: but follow righteousness, faith, charity, peace, with them that call on the Lord out of a _pure heart_.

1) In your own words, define what it is to be Pure in Heart: _____

_____
_____
_____
_____
_____

2) As a Minister of the Gospel, what areas do you see in your life that would indicate you are not as pure in heart as you should be? (if you are in a group setting, only share those things you feel comfortable sharing with the group, but be honest in your personal assessment here so you can refer to it periodically and see where you have grown, and where you are still in need of growth)_____

_____
_____
_____

_____
_____
_____

3) Fill in the blank:

Mat 5:8 Blessed *are* the pure in heart: for _____

4) What does that mean to you? _____

_____
_____
_____
_____
_____

It is so hard to see when my eyes are on me.
 (Keith Green, song "I Pledge My Head to Heaven)

"We say, "Just confess the Lord and you are in!"
He says, "Not everyone who says to me Lord, Lord will enter the kingdom."
We say, "Just pray this prayer and it's done."
He says, "If anyone would come after me he must deny himself, take up his cross and follow me."
We say, "Just come to the alter it will only take a minute!"
He says "make every effort to enter through the narrow door."
Who do you think is right?"
(Doctor Michael Brown, "How Saved Are We?")

Pro 10:10 He that winks with his eyes deceitfully, procures griefs for men; but he that reproves boldly is a peacemaker. (Septuagint)

Boldly - παρρησία

parrhēsia par-rhay-see'-ah

From G3956 and a derivative of G4483; *all* out *spokenness*, that is, *frankness, bluntness, publicity*; by implication *assurance:* - bold (-ly, -ness, -ness of speech), confidence, freely, openly, plainly (-ness).

Notes:
_____
_____
_____
_____
_____
_____

Chapter 8
Peaceably Persistent

Mat 5:9 Blessed *Are* The Peacemakers: For They Shall Be Called The Children Of God.

JESUS WAS THE Ultimate Peacemaker:

**Col 1:20 And, having made peace through the blood of his cross, by him to reconcile all things unto himself; by him, *I say,* whether *they be* things in earth, or things in heaven.
21 And you, that were sometime alienated and enemies in *your* mind by wicked works, yet now hath he reconciled
22 In the body of his flesh through death, to present you holy and unblameable and unreproveable in his sight:
23 If ye continue in the faith grounded and settled, and *be* not moved away from the hope of the gospel, which ye have heard, *and* which was preached to every creature which is under heaven; whereof I Paul am made a minister;**

How about you?

Are you a child of God? If you are a Peacemaker, you are.

What exactly is a Peacemaker? The Biblical definition might surprise you:

Pro 10:10 He that winks with his eyes deceitfully, procures griefs for men; but he that reproves boldly is a peacemaker. (Septuagint)

"He that reproves boldly" is a peacemaker.

To hear church folk talk today, you would think that he who reproves boldly is a trouble maker. But consider once again that Jesus was the Ultimate Peacemaker, and see how He reproved those who needed reproof:

Mat 23:13 But woe unto you, scribes and Pharisees, hypocrites! for ye shut up the kingdom

of heaven against men: for ye neither go in yourselves, neither suffer ye them that are entering to go in.

14 Woe unto you, scribes and Pharisees, hypocrites! for ye devour widows' houses, and for a pretence make long prayer: therefore ye shall receive the greater damnation.

15 Woe unto you, scribes and Pharisees, hypocrites! for ye compass sea and land to make one proselyte, and when he is made, ye make him twofold more the child of hell than yourselves.

16 Woe unto you, ye blind guides, which say, Whosoever shall swear by the temple, it is nothing; but whosoever shall swear by the gold of the temple, he is a debtor!

17 Ye fools and blind: for whether is greater, the gold, or the temple that sanctifieth the gold?

Mat 23:33 Ye serpents, ye generation of vipers, how can ye escape the damnation of hell?

Mat 12:33 Either make the tree good, and his fruit good; or else make the tree corrupt, and his fruit corrupt: for the tree is known by his fruit.

34 O generation of vipers, how can ye, being evil, speak good things? for out of the abundance of the heart the mouth speaketh. "

Mar 8:33 But when he had turned about and looked on his disciples, he rebuked Peter, saying, Get thee behind me, Satan: for thou savourest not the things that be of God, but the things that be of men.

Though they may be stinging words, bold reproof may result in causing men and women who are in error to see their error and repent.

Those who are in ministry and who are abusing their position of leadership need to be reproved stronger than others.

If you notice, Jesus only had harsh words (strong reproof) for His disciples who were ministers in training and for those who were in ministry. He called His disciples "Ye of little Faith", and part of a "perverse generation", and at one time called Peter

Rom 2:21 Thou therefore which teachest another, teachest thou not thyself? thou that preachest a man should not steal, dost thou steal? **22** Thou that sayest a man should not commit adultery, dost thou commit adultery? thou that abhorrest idols, dost thou commit sacrilege? **23** Thou that makest thy boast of the law, through breaking the law dishonourest thou God?

Notes:

_____
_____
_____
_____
_____
_____
_____
_____
_____
_____
_____
_____
_____
_____
_____
_____
_____
_____
_____
_____
_____
_____
_____

"Satan". He called the Religious leaders "Hypocrites" and "Blind leaders of the blind", "serpents" and "vipers", as well as "white washed tombs". One day He will reprove some who thought they were doing the Work of God and tell them "I never knew you. Depart from me, you workers of iniquity" (*Matthew 7:23*). That will be a terrible place to find oneself in.

One who enters into ministry is a "watchman'; a person who stands watch over the Kingdom of God. Error needs to be addressed. But first it needs to be dealt with in our personal life before we deal with it in other's lives.

A lot of people who are in sin, whether they are Christians or not, are quick to quote Matthew 7:1:

Mat 7:1 Judge not, that ye be not judged.

As a minister of the Gospel who isn't afraid to speak the Truth in love, you will hear that verse quoted to you numerous times.

The majority who quote that verse are actually walking in sin themselves, and they don't want to be confronted with it. There is a difference between *discerning* whether a person is walking in sin, and *condemning* the person who is walking in sin.

The Word of God says that if we see a brother who has been "overtaken in a fault", we who are spiritual are supposed to restore him in a spirit of meekness. A judgment call has to be made as to whether the brother is overtaken in a fault or not. We who are Christians should always be about restoration and reconciliation. Judgment calls have to be made before we can undertake the work of restoration.

Jesus said you would know false prophets by their fruit. That requires a judgment call on your part.

Jesus called the religious leaders vipers, serpents and hypocrites, as well as white washed tombs. Sounds like some pretty strong judgment calls doesn't it? But Jesus was just calling "a spade a spade" as the saying goes.

He Himself said that God didn't send Him into the world to condemn the world.

Joh 3:17 For God sent not his Son into the world to condemn the world; but that the world through him might be saved.

He made judgment calls and used those judgment calls to warn the transgressors of their danger of imminent hell fire.

It is God's Love that compels a man or a woman of God to warn others from imminent danger. It is God's love that calls sin "sin", and reminds those who are caught up in it of the consequences of that sin. That is called righteous judgment, which we are commanded to do. It is not our place to condemn others to hell. But it *is* our place to warn them and to bring them to place of reconciliation with God. You should be ready to answer the one who quotes Matthew 7:1 with John 7:24:

Joh 7:24 Judge not according to the appearance, but judge righteous judgment.

Even the vipers and serpents and hypocrites can be saved, if they repent. Some people aren't even aware of their hypocrisy until it is pointed out to them. A judgment call must be made, but it must be made righteously.

If a person confronts someone for fornicating, they should make sure they aren't caught up in porn or fornication themselves. A glutton who has no control over his eating addiction shouldn't be quick to confront a drunk or a drug addict. An adulterer shouldn't point fingers at the homosexual. A person who always thinks they need more money, or more things shouldn't preach against the idolatry of a Catholic or a Hindu.

The sin isn't in calling a sinner a sinner. You are *called* to do that. The sin is in condemning them for the very thing you yourself are guilty of.

Rom 2:1 Therefore thou art inexcusable, O man, whosoever thou art that judgest: for wherein thou

judgest another, thou condemnest thyself; for thou that judgest doest the same things.

Paul addressed this very issue in his epistle to the Saints who were in Rome:

**Rom 2:17 Behold, thou art called a Jew, and restest in the law, and makest thy boast of God,
18 And knowest his will, and approvest the things that are more excellent, being instructed out of the law;
19 And art confident that thou thyself art a guide of the blind, a light of them which are in darkness,
20 An instructor of the foolish, a teacher of babes, which hast the form of knowledge and of the truth in the law.
21 Thou therefore which teachest another, teachest thou not thyself? thou that preachest a man should not steal, dost thou steal?
22 Thou that sayest a man should not commit adultery, dost thou commit adultery? thou that abhorrest idols, dost thou commit sacrilege?
23 Thou that makest thy boast of the law, through breaking the law dishonourest thou God?
24 For the name of God is blasphemed among the Gentiles through you, as it is written.**

Jesus said before you make a judgment call, make sure you are in right standing before God, so you can see clearly to help others with their issue.

**Mat 7:3 And why beholdest thou the mote that is in thy brother's eye, but considerest not the beam that is in thine own eye?
4 Or how wilt thou say to thy brother, Let me pull out the mote out of thine eye; and, behold, a beam is in thine own eye?
5 Thou hypocrite, first cast out the beam out of thine own eye; and then shalt thou see clearly to cast out the mote out of thy brother's eye.**

A mote is a mote. It is an affliction that needs to be removed. If you see a mote, you will make a judgment call that it is what it is. Jesus is saying get the beam out of your eye so you can really help your brother with his mote.

Rom 2:21 Thou therefore which teachest another, teachest thou not thyself? thou that preachest a man should not steal, dost thou steal?
22 Thou that sayest a man should not commit adultery, dost thou commit adultery? thou that abhorrest idols, dost thou commit sacrilege?
23 Thou that makest thy boast of the law, through breaking the law dishonourest thou God?

A peacemaker will want to help others with their motes and beams. The goal is always to help each other to successfully complete this walk as a Bride who has made herself ready for the Coming of the Groom.

Those who are in ministry have been entrusted with the responsibility of leading the people of God in being a kingdom of priests, a royal priesthood. But those that Jesus rebuked were men who were interested in their own personal kingdoms. And so it is today. Many who are in leadership are in need of strong rebuke because they've neglected their responsibility to equip the saints of God to be effective ambassadors and soldiers for Christ.

It is important that an individual doesn't become a self styled heretic hunter, carefully looking for errors in others so they can let them know about it.

But if they are wrong, they are wrong, and are in need of bold reproof:

1Ti 5:19 Against an elder receive not an accusation, but before two or three witnesses.
20 Them that sin rebuke before all, that others also may fear.
21 I charge thee before God, and the Lord Jesus Christ, and the elect angels, that thou observe these things without preferring one before another, doing nothing by partiality.

Bold reproof, if done in genuine love for the soul that is being reproved, and if it is then received, will result in sincere repentance. If it is rejected, then pride is usually the culprit.

A peacemaker strives to make peace between God and men.

Sometimes your brothers and sisters in Christ and even those who are in leadership won't know they are in error concerning a thing, and sometimes that will require some bold rebuke.

Tit 2:11 For the grace of God that bringeth salvation hath appeared to all men,
12 Teaching us that, denying ungodliness and worldly lusts, we should live soberly, righteously, and godly, in this present world;
13 Looking for that blessed hope, and the glorious appearing of the great God and our Saviour Jesus Christ;
14 Who gave himself for us, that he might redeem us from all iniquity, and purify unto himself a peculiar people, zealous of good works.
15 These things speak, and exhort, and rebuke with all authority. Let no man despise thee.

Honor those who have been commissioned to a place of leadership to equip you.

But don't be afraid to bring correction where correction is needed. One day they will have to stand before God and give an account for their abuses. Be a peacemaker.

Act 4:31 And when they had prayed, the place was shaken where they were assembled together; and they were all filled with the Holy Ghost, and they spake the word of God with boldness.

Php 1:20 According to my earnest expectation and _my_ hope, that in nothing I shall be ashamed, but _that_ with all boldness, as always, _so_ now also Christ shall be magnified in my body, whether _it be_ by life, or by death.

A peacemaker strives to live peaceably with all men....

Rom 12:17 Recompense to no man evil for evil. Provide things honest in the sight of all men.
18 If it be possible, as much as lieth in you, live peaceably with all men.
19 Dearly beloved, avenge not yourselves, but _rather_ give place unto wrath: for it is written, Vengeance _is_ mine; I will repay, saith the Lord.
20 Therefore if thine enemy hunger, feed him; if he thirst, give him drink: for in so doing thou shalt heap coals of fire on his head.
21 Be not overcome of evil, but overcome evil with good.

**Rom 14:17 For the kingdom of God is not meat and drink; but righteousness, and peace, and joy in the Holy Ghost.
18 For he that in these things serveth Christ *is* acceptable to God, and approved of men.
19 Let us therefore follow after the things which make for peace, and things wherewith one may edify another.**

Notes:

_____
_____
_____
_____
_____
_____
_____
_____
_____
_____
_____
_____
_____
_____
_____
_____
_____
_____
_____
_____
_____
_____
_____
_____
_____
_____

A peacemaker is interested in seeing people achieve their potential in Christ. They edify or build others up in the faith.

Rom 14:19 Let us therefore follow after the things which make for peace, and things wherewith one may edify another.

Peace is an outgrowth of the fruit of the Spirit. Those who mature in Christ will naturally be about bringing peace into whatever situations they find themselves in.

Gal 5:22 But the fruit of the Spirit is love, joy, peace, longsuffering, gentleness, goodness, faith, 23 Meekness, temperance: against such there is no law.

A child of God is to pursue peace.

2Ti 2:22 Flee also youthful lusts: but follow righteousness, faith, charity, peace, with them that call on the Lord out of a pure heart.

Pursuing peace with the Body of Christ is an attribute of the child of God.

Rom 16:17 Now I beseech you, brethren, mark them which cause divisions and offences contrary to the doctrine which ye have learned; and avoid them.

There is a great spirit of division in the Church today that hinders the Kingdom of God from going forward.

Just for the record, there is a difference between the Church that Christ founded and the church that men oversee. For the sake of this writing, the Church that Christ founded will be designated with capital "C". The buildings that many congregate in and the institutions that men have called "Church" will be designated with a lowercase "c". You can read about the difference between the two on page 287 in the Appendix of this book.

Heresies:

G139

αἵρεσις hairesis

Thayer Definition:

1) act of taking, capture: e.g. storming a city
2) choosing, choice
3) that which is chosen 4) a body of men following their own tenets (sect or party)
 4a) of the Sadducees 4b) of the Pharisees
4c) of the Christians
5) dissensions arising from diversity of opinions and aims

Rom 16:17 Now I beseech you, brethren, mark them which cause divisions and offences contrary to the doctrine which ye have learned; and avoid them.

Notes:

_____
_____
_____
_____
_____
_____
_____
_____
_____
_____
_____
_____
_____
_____
_____
_____
_____
_____

Pastors of different denominations or even different fellowships refuse to come together with other pastors because they hold different doctrinal positions than others.

They encourage this division in their churches and in the mindset of their congregations through their refusal to participate with other leaders in the Body of Christ for the furtherance of the Kingdom of God.

Such isolation is a cultic characteristic that encourages a worship or adoration of a personality and faithfulness to that person and his church in place of God.

The refusal of a church to come together with the rest of the Body of Christ is actually defined as a heresy:

1Co 11:19 For there must be also heresies among you, that they which are approved may be made manifest among you.

One major instance of this heretical behavior (but not the only one) is demonstrated by the fact that those who are of the opinion that the Gifts of the Holy Spirit are not active today have been taught to isolate themselves from those who do.

Likewise, those who operate in the Gifts of the Holy Spirit ridicule those who don't, and avoid fellowship with them. According to the definition, that is heretical behavior.

Generally it has been my personal observation that it is the "Cessationists" who are more inclined to avoid fellowshipping with the Pentecostals or the Charismatics than it is the other way around. But either way, it should not be so.

In *Romans 16:17,* we see that Paul said to the Church that they should mark them which cause divisions and offenses contrary to the doctrine which they have learned, and avoid them.

Many in the church will say that since others don't agree with their church doctrine, then they have an obligation to be separate from them, but that is not

Notes:

what Paul is referring to here. The doctrine he is referring to is NOT a local church's doctrine, nor a denominational doctrine. He is talking about the apostle's doctrine, which was taught to them by Christ.

Is a church teaching contrary to Christ's teachings? Then by all means, you should avoid them.

How do we know Christ's doctrine?

Read the red.

We are told what the First Principles of the Doctrine of Christ are in Hebrews Chapter 6:1-2. My first book in this series deals with the First Principles of the Fundamentals of Christianity. I would recommend the reader familiarize himself with the First Principles if he or she is going to minister to others.

**Heb 6:1 Therefore leaving the principles of the doctrine of Christ, let us go on unto perfection; not laying again the foundation of repentance from dead works, and of faith toward God,
2 Of the doctrine of baptisms, and of laying on of hands, and of resurrection of the dead, and of eternal judgment.**

Christ taught His followers to further the Kingdom of God, not to advance the kingdom of men. Christ taught the importance of the Unity of the Church, not the division of the churches:

**Joh 17:11 And now I am no more in the world, but these are in the world, and I come to thee. Holy Father, keep through thine own name those whom thou hast given me, that they may be one, as we are.
12 While I was with them in the world, I kept them in thy name: those that thou gavest me I have kept, and none of them is lost, but the son of perdition; that the scripture might be fulfilled.
13 And now come I to thee; and these things I speak in the world, that they might have my joy fulfilled in themselves.
14 I have given them thy word; and the world**

hath hated them, because they are not of the world, even as I am not of the world.

15 I pray not that thou shouldest take them out of the world, but that thou shouldest keep them from the evil.

16 They are not of the world, even as I am not of the world.

17 Sanctify them through thy truth: thy word is truth.

18 As thou hast sent me into the world, even so have I also sent them into the world.

19 And for their sakes I sanctify myself, that they also might be sanctified through the truth.

20 Neither pray I for these alone, but for them also which shall believe on me through their word;

21 That they all may be one; as thou, Father, art in me, and I in thee, that they also may be one in us: that the world may believe that thou hast sent me.

22 And the glory which thou gavest me I have given them; that they may be one, even as we are one:

23 I in them, and thou in me, that they may be made perfect in one; and that the world may know that thou hast sent me, and hast loved them, as thou hast loved me.

It's real simple to tell if you are in a church or if you are part of the Church:

Is your pastor actively working toward bringing the Church into a place of Unity with other ministries in his area? Or is he always talking about how to get the membership up in "his" church?

Does he talk about getting together with other ministries to impact the area for the Kingdom of God, or does he tell you to invite people to come to his church?

According to Paul, one is approved of God, and the other is a heretic.

Is Christ divided? Did He only die for one and not the other? Can the hand say to the foot "I have no need of thee, because you are not the hand?" Yet carnal minded leaders of the churches that they "shepherd" pick and choose who in the Body of Christ is worth spending time with, instead of trying to come together and to learn from one another, or at the least, to agree to disagree in matters which are not essential to salvation.

Pastors and ministers who pick and choose who they will fellowship with in the Body of Christ are by the Biblical definition, *heretics*, concerned with the growth of their own church more than they are the Church of Christ (and no, I am not referring to the denominational church of Christ).

According to the Word of God, those who strive to bring Unity to the Body of Christ are approved of God. These are peacemakers. As a minister of the

Kingdom of God, one of your primary pursuits should be to bring Unity to the Body of Christ.

There must be a reformation in the mindset of those who are in leadership of the churches if the Church is to advance. Those who have been heretical and isolationists in their position need to repent, and if they won't repent, then those who have a heart for God need to come out from among them, no matter how great of a speaker they may be, or regardless of their charismatic personality.

We (the Church) can't afford anymore of the "us four and no more" mentality that has prevailed in the church.

Our Nation is falling into moral and social decay because the Church is divided. Jesus said a house divided cannot stand.

I believe that there is no other way to the Father Who is the ONE True God, but through Jesus Christ, and Jesus Christ alone. There is no other Name by which men can be saved, except the Name Of Christ. I believe that it was through the Blood which He spilled on the cross, and through His Death, Burial and Resurrection that mankind has the hope of reconciliation between God and man. Christ paid for my sins, which I was unable to do. I believe that just as He was the minister of reconciliation between God and man, Jesus Christ has called us to be ministers of reconciliation as well. I believe that when I called upon the Name of Jesus Christ to be my Lord and my Savior, I became a child of God, and I became a part of one big Family of God, the Church, and I am to walk in love toward my brothers and sisters in Christ, and work with them to further the Kingdom of God.

I believe those are the primary things Christ taught. If you believe that as well, then we can fellowship together. It's imperative that we do so.

Rom 14:15 But if thy brother be grieved with *thy* meat, now walkest thou not charitably. Destroy not him with thy meat, for whom Christ died.
16 Let not then your good be evil spoken of:
17 For the kingdom of God is not meat and drink; but righteousness, and peace, and joy in the Holy Ghost.
18 For he that in these things serveth Christ *is* acceptable to God, and approved of men.
19 Let us therefore follow after the things which make for peace, and things wherewith one may edify another.

There is no peace in contention. A minister of God needs to be careful not to engage in arguments that will foster division.

2Ti 2:22 Flee also youthful lusts: but follow righteousness, faith, charity, peace, with them that call on the Lord out of a pure heart.

23 But foolish and unlearned questions avoid, knowing that they do gender strifes.

The next verses are verses that should become a guiding principle for all who are in ministry:

2Ti 2:24 And the servant of the Lord must not strive; but be gentle unto all *men*, apt to teach, patient,
25 In meekness instructing those that oppose themselves; if God peradventure will give them repentance to the acknowledging of the truth;
26 And *that* they may recover themselves out of the snare of the devil, who are taken captive by him at his will.

Holiness and Peacemaking walk closely with one another:

Heb 12:14 Follow peace with all *men*, and holiness, without which no man shall see the Lord:

Christ was our example. He came to make peace between mankind and God. As His servants, our focus should be to make peace with each other and between men and God.

Eph 2:14 For he is our peace, who hath made both one, and hath broken down the middle wall of partition *between us;*
15 Having abolished in his flesh the enmity, *even* the law of commandments *contained* in ordinances; for to make in himself of twain one new man, *so* making peace;
16 And that he might reconcile both unto God in one body by the cross, having slain the enmity thereby:
17 And came and preached peace to you which were afar off, and to them that were nigh.

Col 1:19 For it pleased *the Father* that in him should all fulness dwell;
20 And, having made peace through the blood of his cross, by him to reconcile all things unto

Notes:

himself; by him, *I say,* whether *they be* things in earth, or things in heaven.

21 And you, that were sometime alienated and enemies in *your* mind by wicked works, yet now hath he reconciled

22 In the body of his flesh through death, to present you holy and unblameable and unreproveable in his sight:

23 If ye continue in the faith grounded and settled, and *be* not moved away from the hope of the gospel, which ye have heard, *and* which was preached to every creature which is under heaven; whereof I Paul am made a minister;

The Gospel is the Gospel of Peace. Ministers of God are peacemakers.

Rom 10:13 For whosoever shall call upon the name of the Lord shall be saved.

14 How then shall they call on him in whom they have not believed? and how shall they believe in him of whom they have not heard? and how shall they hear without a preacher?

15 And how shall they preach, except they be sent? as it is written, How beautiful are the feet of them that preach the gospel of peace, and bring glad tidings of good things!

Eph 6:14 Stand therefore, having your loins girt about with truth, and having on the breastplate of righteousness;

15 And your feet shod with the preparation of the gospel of peace-

Always be prepared to be a Peacemaker.

1) Jesus said the Peacemakers are blessed because they shall be called

_____

2) Proverbs 10 defines who a peacemaker is:

Pro 10:10 He that winks with his eyes deceitfully, procures griefs for men; but he that reproves boldly is a peacemaker. (Septuagint)

Give an example how someone who reproves boldly could be a peacemaker

_____
_____
_____
_____
_____
_____
_____
_____

_____

3) In Proverbs 10:10 it mentions "He that winks with his eyes deceitfully". In your own words, what does that look like? _____

_____
_____
_____
_____
_____
_____
_____
_____

4) 2Ti 4:3 For the _____ will _____ when they will not endure _____ _____; but after their own _____ shall they _____ to themselves _____, having _____ _____;

5) Jesus was a peacemaker between _____ and _____. As such, those who are in ministry should be peacemakers between _____ and _____.

6) Heb 12:14 Follow _____ with _____, and _____, without which _____:

7) What is the Biblical definition of a heretic? _____

_____
_____

8) Rom 16:17 says: Now I beseech you, brethren, mark them which cause divisions and offences contrary to the doctrine which ye have learned; and avoid them. Which doctrine is Paul referring to?_____

_____
_____

9) In what areas do you think that you could be a peacemaker as a minister of God in your sphere of influence (workplace, fellowship, family, etc) ? _____

_____
_____
_____
_____
_____
_____

10) Take some time to formulate ideas on how this could be accomplished. _____

_____
_____
_____
_____
_____
_____
_____
_____
_____
_____
_____

"While women weep, as they do now, I'll fight; while children go hungry, as they do now I'll fight; while men go to prison, in and out, in and out, as they do now, I'll fight; while there is a drunkard left, while there is a poor lost girl upon the streets, while there remains one dark soul without the light of God, I'll fight, I'll fight to the very end!" —

William Booth

Notes:

_____
_____
_____
_____
_____
_____
_____
_____
_____
_____
_____
_____
_____
_____
_____
_____
_____
_____
_____
_____
_____
_____
_____
_____
_____
_____
_____
_____

Chapter 9
What Price For Ministry

Mat 5:10 Blessed *are* they which are persecuted for righteousness' sake: for theirs is the kingdom of heaven.
11 Blessed are ye, when *men* shall revile you, and persecute *you*, and shall say all manner of evil against you falsely, for my sake.
12 Rejoice, and be exceeding glad: for great *is* your reward in heaven: for so persecuted they the prophets which were before you.

AFTER JESUS LISTED the characteristics of a minister of God, He concluded with these words that promise persecution to those who serve Him in ministry.

The one who studies to show himself approved of God will suffer persecution.

2Ti 3:12 Yea, and all that will live godly in Christ Jesus shall suffer persecution.

It is generally the *religious* people of the man-centered church who are the primary source of persecution against the Church. The leaders of the Jewish people were the ones who came out against Jesus and His disciples.

The great persecution of the early Church came as a result of Christians refusing to engage in the emperor worship that the Roman Caesars demanded.

As of this writing, the world in which we live is full of religious persecution against Christians. Islamists are beheading and torturing Christians in the middle East, in Africa, India and Asia. Adherents of the Hindu religion are persecuting and killing Christians in India.

In China and other communist countries, where man's abilities are exalted above the belief in God, the Church has been forced to go underground, meeting secretly in home fellowships.

Even those who profess themselves to be Christians will persecute and shun the Christian who strives to be all that Christ has called him or her to be.

As we should have been able to see by now, there is a difference between the showmanship of professional clergy and the one whose heart is reserved only for God.

The servant of God has no agenda but to please God. The only popularity he seeks is that which can be found at the throne of Grace.

Just as Noah found Grace in the eyes of God, and Job was known in the assembly of the heavenly host to be more righteous than all of humanity, a true servant of God lives his or her life in such a way that they hope to hear the Lord Himself say "Well done, thou good and faithful servant".

He gives himself to serve those who are least likely to benefit him, just as Jesus did.

The only recognition the servant of God seeks is the recognition given by the Lord Jesus Christ as He says "Well done, thou good and faithful servant, enter into the Joy of the Lord".

The accolades and acceptance of men have no great attraction for a servant of God whose heart is only to please the Father. Pride seeks recognition from the masses, but a soul that's been converted desires recognition only from His Lord. Religious people distance themselves from such a one, because he or she doesn't fit into the "clique".

The servant of God realizes how utterly spiritually impoverished he is, entirely dependent on God's daily Intervention to keep him on the right path.

But those who strive for "professionalism" and recognition in Christian religious circles are in danger of becoming self sufficient rather than being dependent on God as their Source in all things. They are not poor in sprit, and cannot be, as long as "success" is their aim.

This is the plight of the messenger of the Church of Laodicea.

Laodicean ministers are content with maintaining the status quo. They ride the waves of popularity and self fulfillment. They fail to understand the importance of equipping the saints entrusted to their care for the work of the ministry, preferring to keep them content with faithfully occupying the pews every Sunday.

They think they are sufficient in themselves, and shun the fellowship of the greater Body of Christ.

Rev 3:17 Because thou sayest, I am rich, and increased with goods, and have need of nothing; and knowest not that thou art wretched, and miserable, and poor, and blind, and naked:
18 I counsel thee to buy of me gold tried in the fire, that thou mayest be rich; and white raiment, that thou mayest be clothed, and that the shame of thy nakedness do not appear; and anoint thine eyes with eyesalve, that thou mayest see.

In the religious circles of Christianity, success is measured by recognition in a type of celebrity status. Jets, fine cars, and personal wealth are the standard by which "godly faith" is measured in some ministerial circles. But the Word of God says we should avoid these types of ministries.

1Ti 6:5 Perverse disputings of men of corrupt minds, and destitute of the truth, *supposing that gain is godliness*: from such withdraw thyself.

The heart is deceitful above all things.

It is best for the minister of God to pursue after those Character traits that Jesus mentioned in Matthew 5:3-9, and not to succumb to the temptation to think that ministry is a means to personal gain and recognition by men.

1Ti 6:6 But godliness with contentment is great gain.
7 For we brought nothing into this world, and it is certain we can carry nothing out.

As a minister of Christ, we don't need "*armor bearers*," as some religious leaders have. The truth is, the one who feels the need to have "armor bearers" needs to learn to be *burden bearers* for others.

Gal 6:2 Bear ye one another's burdens, and so fulfil the law of Christ.

Notes:

As a minister of Christ, we don't need to receive honor from men. We need to esteem others better than ourselves.

Php 2:3 Let nothing be done through strife or vainglory; but in lowliness of mind let each esteem other better than themselves.

As a minister of Christ, we are not to seek our own success or comfort, but we are to do what we can to help others succeed.

Php 2:4 Look not every man on his own things, but every man also on the things of others.

As a minister of Christ, we are to be *like Christ*, not like what men say we ought to be like.

**Php 2:5 Let this mind be in you, which was also in Christ Jesus:
6 Who, being in the form of God, thought it not robbery to be equal with God:
7 But made himself of no reputation, and took upon him the form of a servant, and was made in the likeness of men:
8 And being found in fashion as a man, he humbled himself, and became obedient unto death, even the death of the cross.**

There are many who are in ministry who clothe themselves with a kind of spiritual diplomatic immunity. They are quick to quote the words "Touch not mine anointed," leading some to think that grave harm will befall them if they speak against them or expose their error.

There are many who insist on being honored or highly esteemed by their followers to the point that it becomes almost cultish. If someone leaves the fellowship of some churches they are seen as "backslid" or not wanting to hear "the truth", or unwilling to submit to authority. In some cases that may be true, but in other cases, those phrases are just a form of control that many "shepherds" employ. These men are almost revered by their congregation like the pope is by his religious Catholic groupies.

Eze 28:12 Son of man, take up a lamentation upon the king of Tyrus, and say unto him, Thus saith the Lord GOD; Thou sealest up the sum, full of wisdom, and perfect in beauty. **13** Thou hast been in Eden the garden of God; every precious stone *was* thy covering, the sardius, topaz, and the diamond, the beryl, the onyx, and the jasper, the sapphire, the emerald, and the carbuncle, and gold: the workmanship of thy tabrets and of thy pipes was prepared in thee in the day that thou wast created. **14** Thou *art* the anointed cherub that covereth; and I have set thee *so:* thou wast upon the holy mountain of God; thou hast walked up and down in the midst of the stones of fire. **15** Thou *wast* perfect in thy ways from the day that thou wast created, till iniquity was found in thee. **16** By the multitude of thy merchandise they have filled the midst of thee with violence, and thou hast sinned: therefore I will cast thee as profane out of the mountain of God: and I will destroy thee, O covering cherub, from the midst of the stones of fire.

G5092
τιμή timē
Thayer Definition:
1) a valuing by which the price is fixed
1a) of the price itself
1b) of the price paid or received for a person or thing bought or sold
2) honour which belongs or is shown to one
2a) of the honour which one has by reason of rank and state of office which he holds
2b) deference, reverence

Others shame their congregation for not being faithful to attend the special services they may be having, or try to present their ministry as *THE* Ministry where God is going to move in a mighty way. Leaders like these are deceived by their own conceit, and are actually treading on the same ground as Lucifer, who exalted himself to a place which was not his to have. We need to understand that we plant, we water, but it is God Who gives the increase.

The danger of being in a place of authority or leadership over others is the tendency to misuse or abuse that position. There is no shame, guilt trips or manipulation in Christ. Better to have a few under your charge who are hungry to fulfill the Will of God than many who must be coerced or bribed to walk in obedience.

Leadership in the world system demands respect and submissive servitude from those who are being led.

But leadership in the Kingdom of God demands that those who are in a position of authority submit to a life of servitude to those they lead, not demanding servitude from those they lead.

One must learn to submit to authority before they can effectively exercise authority.

Giving Honor Where Honor Is Due

Those who are in leadership positions are deserving of being shown honor from those who they serve, but that honor should never be demanded or even expected.

1Ti 5:17 Let the elders that rule well be counted worthy of double honour, especially they who labour in the word and doctrine.

It is interesting to note that the word "honour" here doesn't only mean to revere and respect a person, but it also refers to a *monetary value* placed on something, or money paid.

1Pe 5:1 The elders which are among you I exhort, who am also an elder, and a witness of the sufferings of Christ, and also a partaker of the glory that shall be revealed:
2 Feed the flock of God which is among you, taking the oversight *thereof,* not by constraint, but willingly; not for filthy lucre, but of a ready mind;
3 Neither as being lords over *God's* heritage, but being ensamples to the flock.
4 And when the chief Shepherd shall appear, ye shall receive a crown of glory that fadeth not away.

Notes:

_____
_____
_____
_____
_____
_____
_____
_____
_____
_____
_____
_____
_____
_____
_____
_____
_____
_____
_____
_____
_____
_____

In context, *1 Ti 5:17* appears to be saying that those who rule well should be counted worthy of a "double payment", since the very next verse speaks about not muzzling the ox and that the laborer is worthy of his hire:

1Ti 5:18 For the scripture saith, Thou shalt not muzzle the ox that treadeth out the corn. And, The labourer is worthy of his reward.

1 Co 9:9-14 mentions this truth again, that those who preach the gospel should live of the gospel.

1Co 9:6 Or I only and Barnabas, have not we power to forbear working?
7 Who goeth a warfare any time at his own charges? who planteth a vineyard, and eateth not of the fruit thereof? or who feedeth a flock, and eateth not of the milk of the flock?

8 Say I these things as a man? or saith not the law the same also?
9 For it is written in the law of Moses, Thou shalt not muzzle the mouth of the ox that treadeth out the corn. Doth God take care for oxen?
10 Or saith he it altogether for our sakes? For our sakes, no doubt, this is written: that he that ploweth should plow in hope; and that he that thresheth in hope should be partaker of his hope.
11 If we have sown unto you spiritual things, is it a great thing if we shall reap your carnal things?
12 If others be partakers of this power over you, are not we rather? Nevertheless we have not used this power; but suffer all things, lest we should hinder the gospel of Christ.
13 Do ye not know that they which minister about holy things live of the things of the temple? and they which wait at the altar are partakers with the altar?
14 Even so hath the Lord ordained that they which preach the gospel should live of the gospel.

The Bible is clear that those who are in active ministry are worthy of support from those they minister to, but *if they expect to be supported by others, they are defined as "hirelings".*

We are not to be in ministry for personal gain, or treat it as a "job" or a vocation by which we make a living. The provision is incidental to the ministry.

Personally, I don't condemn those who make appeals for support for "their ministry"; that is between them and God.

But I do think it demonstrates a lack of Faith on their part. In my personal walk I have found that if God gives me a vision, He will supply the Provision. That's not just a "cute cliché". He has always been Faithful in that regard.

I am very grateful to those who do support the ministry the Lord has called us to, but the Lord has made it plain from our first step into ministry that HE was to be our Source and our Hope, and not man. I believe those who come alongside us in support are partakers of the fruit of the ministry. But they do so at the Lord's Bidding and not as a result of our appeals for "help".

I find that in that way I don't look at people as "potential contributors", so I don't have to "watch what I say" for fear of losing support, or becoming a "respecter of persons".

Heb 13:5 Let your conversation be without covetousness; and be content with such things as ye have: for he hath said, I will never leave thee, nor forsake thee.
6 So that we may boldly say, The Lord is my helper, and I will not fear what man shall do unto me.

The Kingdom of God is absolutely contrary to the Kingdoms of this world.

The world system teaches us that we are to climb the ladder to success.

The Kingdom of God teaches us that to be a success, we have to descend the ladder of worldly success, to help others find their way down to the position of servitude where the true Blessings are.

Mat 20:25 But Jesus called them unto him, and said, Ye know that the princes of the Gentiles exercise dominion over them, and they that are great exercise authority upon them.
26 But it shall not be so among you: but whosoever will be great among you, let him be your minister;
27 And whosoever will be chief among you, let him be your servant:
28 Even as the Son of man came not to be ministered unto, but to minister, and to give his life a ransom for many.

A minister of the Gospel is to live his or her life as an example to others. Faith is just a word and a concept to those who really have not learned to trust in the Lord with all their heart. Someone preaching about faith while asking their audience for donations to help support their ministry actually sends a mixed signal.

Do you have faith in your ability to drum up support from others, or is your faith solely in God, who has promised that He will supply all our needs according to His Riches in Glory?

Some of the things that are done today in the name of ministry are done because of tradition or manmade doctrine. We need to be careful to try to determine what is of God and what is of man. *Good* ideas are not necessarily *God* ideas.

The price that must be paid for successful ministry is everything. Jesus said:

Luk 14:26 If any *man* come to me, and hate not his father, and mother, and wife, and children, and brethren, and sisters, yea, and his own life also, he cannot be my disciple.
27 And whosoever doth not bear his cross, and come after me, cannot be my disciple.

28 For which of you, intending to build a tower, sitteth not down first, and counteth the cost, whether he have *sufficient* to finish *it?*
29 Lest haply, after he hath laid the foundation, and is not able to finish *it,* all that behold *it* begin to mock him,
30 Saying, This man began to build, and was not able to finish.
31 Or what king, going to make war against another king, sitteth not down first, and consulteth whether he be able with ten thousand to meet him that cometh against him with twenty thousand?
32 Or else, while the other is yet a great way off, he sendeth an ambassage, and desireth conditions of peace.
33 So likewise, whosoever he be of you that forsaketh not all that he hath, he cannot be my disciple.
34 Salt *is* good: but if the salt have lost his savour, wherewith shall it be seasoned?
35 It is neither fit for the land, nor yet for the dunghill; *but* men cast it out. He that hath ears to hear, let him hear.

It is important to note that Jesus uses the same phrase here as He does in His letters to the messengers of the churches in Revelation 2 and 3: "*He that hath ears to hear, let him hear*". As a minister of the Gospel of the Kingdom of God, you are on the same footing as those messengers of Revelation are. The minister of the Gospel carries a serious responsibility wherever he goes. Others who are in the Valley of Decision are watching you, and your conduct may be factor that influences their decision.

In the above passage of scripture, Jesus was teaching that those who "put their hand to the plow" have no retirement plans. Ministry is not a job. It is a *privilege* that God has entrusted you with. He said you should really count the cost and understand what it means to be His disciple. A person who has been pastoring for fifty years may get to a place where he cannot operate in that capacity any longer, but just because he steps down from that position does not mean that he has retired from ministry. Ministry is a Christian's lifestyle.

The demands that the flesh makes on us are decidedly anti Christian and are opposed to the Will of God. That is why Paul speaks of "beating his body into submission" as a minister of the Gospel.

1Co 9:22 To the weak became I as weak, that I might gain the weak: I am made all things to all *men,* that I might by all means save some.
23 And this I do for the gospel's sake, that I might be partaker thereof with *you.*
24 Know ye not that they which run in a race run all, but one receiveth the prize? So run, that ye may obtain.
25 And every man that striveth for the mastery is temperate in all things. Now they *do it* to obtain a corruptible crown; but we an incorruptible.

26 I therefore so run, not as uncertainly; so fight I, not as one that beateth the air:

27 But I keep under my body, and bring *it* into subjection: lest that by any means, when I have preached to others, I myself should be a castaway.

Gal 5:24 And they that are Christ's have crucified the flesh with the affections and lusts.

The sermon on the mount is a message principally meant for _____

All Christians are called to _____

The definition of a disciple is: _____

_____

A minister of the Gospel is to live his or her life as an _____ to others.

1Ti 5:17 Let the elders that rule well be counted worthy of _____, especially they who labour in the word and doctrine.

What does the above verse actually mean?

_____

_____

_____

Describe the difference between leadership in the world and leadership in the Kingdom of God.

_____

_____

_____

_____

One must learn to _____ to _____ before they can effectively exercise authority.

SECTION TWO

WALKING IN THE GIFTS AND THE AUTHORITY OF GOD

"When God has specially promised the thing, we are bound to believe we shall receive it when we pray for it. You have no right to put in an 'if', and say, 'Lord, if it be thy will...'' This is to insult God. To put an 'if' in God's promise when God has put none there, is tantamount to charging God with being insincere."

— **Charles Grandison Finney**

Chapter 10
Temptation In Ministry

"In answer to your inquiry, I consider that the chief dangers which confront the coming century will be religion without the Holy Ghost, Christianity without Christ, forgiveness without repentance, salvation without regeneration, politics without God, and heaven without hell."

— *William Booth*

"You can go to hell with the "gifts of the Spirit" but not the fruit of the Spirit."
- David Popovici,

Notes:

_____
_____
_____
_____
_____
_____
_____
_____
_____
_____
_____
_____
_____
_____
_____
_____
_____
_____
_____
_____
_____
_____
_____
_____
_____
_____
_____

THE FIRST SECTION of this book has been about the *character* or the *attributes* that are necessary for a disciple to become a successful minister of the Gospel. Once we learn to conduct ourselves as Ambassadors of Christ should conduct themselves, then we will be able to operate effectively in the authority that Christ has given us.

The first thing we need to grasp is that we *do* have authority in Christ, *but not everyone who operates in the Power and Authority of Christ are Christ's.* Every minister of Christ will be tempted to abuse that authority in one way or another.

Mat 7:21 Not every one that saith unto me, Lord, Lord, shall enter into the kingdom of heaven; but he that doeth the will of my Father which is in heaven.
22 Many will say to me in that day, Lord, Lord, have we not prophesied in thy name? and in thy name have cast out devils? and in thy name done many wonderful works?
23 And then will I profess unto them, I never knew you: depart from me, ye that work iniquity.

The Word of God says that those who are Christ's should conduct themselves as Christ conducted Himself.

1Jn 2:6 He that saith he abideth in him ought himself also so to walk, even as he walked.

What does that look like in a practical sense?

Php 2:5 Let this mind be in you, which was also in Christ Jesus:
6 Who, being in the form of God, thought it not robbery to be equal with God:

Notes:

_____
_____
_____
_____
_____
_____
_____
_____
_____
_____
_____
_____
_____
_____

**Mat 4:1 Then was Jesus led up of the Spirit into the wilderness to be tempted of the devil.
2 And when he had fasted forty days and forty nights, he was afterward an hungred.
3 And when the tempter came to him, he said, If thou be the Son of God, command that these stones be made bread.**

Notes:

_____
_____
_____
_____
_____
_____
_____
_____
_____
_____
_____
_____
_____
_____
_____

**7 But made himself of no reputation, and took upon him the form of a servant, and was made in the likeness of men:
8 And being found in fashion as a man, he humbled himself, and became obedient unto death, even the death of the cross.**

It is when we walk in the *Character* of Christ, that we are able to avoid misusing the God-given Authority He intends for us to walk in. Notice the first thing He did was to make Himself of no reputation. What's your purpose for ministry? If you are seeking recognition, acceptance and fame, you *might* achieve it. But that isn't what Christ was about. You might just discover that you already received your reward here on earth when you stand before Him.

In Matthew 4, we can see that there are four areas in which a minister of the Gospel will be tempted. If the devil had enough audacity to tempt Christ, you can be sure he will tempt you as well.

THE FIRST AREA of temptation is to question whether you are called to ministry or not.

Jesus was the Son of God. God Himself had declared that in Matthew 3:17.

Mat 3:17 And lo a voice from heaven, saying, This is my beloved Son, in whom I am well pleased.

Yet the tempter whispered "if thou be the Son of God"- or "Prove it". Some tempters will come to you and ask you who you are licensed under, or under whose authority (covering) do you minister, or what school you went to, or who sent you out, or how do you know that you are supposed to be doing what you are doing?

You are called to be a saint (*1 Cor 1:2*), yet the devil continually tries to whisper that you are a sinner saved by Grace, and not a saint. Religion has taught you to believe that a saint is some individual who has been specially elevated by God above other

Rev 1:6   And hath made us kings and priests unto God and his Father; to him *be* glory and dominion for ever and ever. Amen.

1Pe 2:9   But ye *are* a chosen generation, a royal priesthood, an holy nation, a peculiar people; that ye should shew forth the praises of him who hath called you out of darkness into his marvellous light:

Eph 4:11   And he gave some, apostles; and some, prophets; and some, evangelists; and some, pastors and teachers; 12   For the perfecting of the saints, for the work of the ministry, for the edifying of the body of Christ:

Notes:

_____

_____

_____

_____

_____

_____

_____

_____

_____

_____

_____

_____

_____

_____

_____

_____

_____

_____

_____

_____

_____

individuals, like Saint Christopher, Saint Francis, Saint Paul, or Saint Peter, yet that is not what the Word of God teaches. Answer the devil's temptation to believe otherwise with the Word of God that declares you to be a saint of the Most High God.

Not only are you a *saint,* you are *called* to be a minister of God (*Eph 4:1-12, 1 Pet 2:9*). Don't let anyone prevent you from fulfilling your Purpose in Christ.

***THE SECOND AREA* of temptation is to be overly concerned with one's personal livelihood.**

Pro 3:5   Trust in the LORD with all thine heart; and lean not unto thine own understanding. 6   In all thy ways acknowledge him, and he shall direct thy paths.

Satan's whisper to you will be to convince you to try to figure out what you need to do to make *your* ministry a success.

The mantra of self is to look out for number one. The command of Jesus is to seek FIRST the Kingdom of God.

Jesus had gone for forty days with nothing to eat. The Word of God says after that, He was hungry, and when He was in a weakened state, the tempter came to him.

Mat 4:3   And when the tempter came to him, he said, If thou be the Son of God, command that these stones be made bread.

Sounds like *"You're a King's kid. You deserve the best. Exercise your faith to get that new _____. You have not because you ask not."*

You won't be tempted to compromise your integrity as a minister of the gospel when you are strong and on top of the game. Jesus couldn't have been tempted to make stones into bread when He had just eaten. But now, after forty days of fasting, there was a serious need to consider nourishing His Body.

2Co 9:6 But this *I say,* He which soweth sparingly shall reap also sparingly; and he which soweth bountifully shall reap also bountifully.
7 Every man according as he purposeth in his heart, *so let him give;* not grudgingly, or of necessity: for God loveth a cheerful giver.

Notes:

_____
_____
_____
_____
_____
_____
_____
_____
_____
_____
_____
_____
_____
_____
_____
_____
_____
_____
_____
_____
_____
_____
_____
_____
_____
_____
_____
_____

In moments of weakness or personal challenges, the enemy will whisper to the children of God in an attempt to get them to question their relationship with the Father. *"If you are a child of God, why are you going through this?"*

It is important to comprehend this Truth: Christ didn't exercise His Faith to turn the stones into bread so He could meet His own *personal* needs. He understood that His Father would take care of Him, and He rested in that knowledge.

But later on in His Ministry, he exercised His Faith to feed a multitude with five loaves of bread and two fish.

He understood that His ministry was about others, and not about Himself. His Father was more than able to supply His needs; He in turn was called to help others in their needs.

Christ's First Purpose was to seek and to save that which was lost; to reconcile fallen humanity to God.

As you show mercy to others, you yourself will receive mercy in your time of need. As you give unselfishly of your substance to others, others will give unto you. As you invest your life in the furtherance of the Kingdom, those things you have need of will be given unto you.

There are many teachers who teach their followers to "sow their seed according to their need," to give sacrificially in the offering so you can reap an abundance.

But as good as that may sound, that isn't what Christ taught. He taught His followers to *live a lifestyle* of giving, to live a lifestyle of Love, to live a *lifestyle* of selflessness toward others. *Your lifestyle* should be one of sowing liberally, not just when you find yourself in a tight spot.

Luk 6:35 But love ye your enemies, and do good, and lend, hoping for nothing again; and your reward shall be great, and ye shall be the children of the Highest: for he is kind unto the unthankful and to the evil.

Notes:

36 Be ye therefore merciful, as your Father also is merciful.
37 Judge not, and ye shall not be judged: condemn not, and ye shall not be condemned: forgive, and ye shall be forgiven:

Jesus is talking about a lifestyle here, not some occasional *"I'll do that when it seems convenient to me"* time. *As you live the lifestyle of Christ, God will take care of your needs in life.*

Luk 6:38 Give, and it shall be given unto you; good measure, pressed down, and shaken together, and running over, shall men give into your bosom. For with the same measure that ye mete withal it shall be measured to you again.

The one who professes a belief in the Power of God to heal may be tested by the enemy with a life threatening illness. Will you trust God, or the physicians?

The one who professes a belief in God for provision may be tested by the enemy in the area of finances. Will you believe God, or will you send out urgent appeals for donations? Or will you max out your credit card to get you out of trouble?

These two scenarios mentioned above will require serious consideration on the part of a believer. Am I implying you should never go to a doctor, or that you should never make an appeal for financial help? That is entirely between you and God.

Faith is not something we manufacture through making confessions until we believe them.

Faith is a place of rest in the Christian's walk, not just understanding what the Word of God says about it, but being absolutely convinced that the Promises of God are all "Yea" and "Amen".

There will always be questions whispered by the enemy *"Yea, hath God truly said..."*

Faith toward God takes us beyond the hypothetical myriads of "what ifs" of a situation, and into a place

Notes:

of knowing that "*All things work together for good for those who love God and are the called according to His Purpose.*"

As ministers of the Gospel, if we say we have faith, our lives must reflect our confession.

Heb 11:6 But without faith it is impossible to please him: for he that cometh to God must believe that he is, and that he is a rewarder of them that diligently seek him.

Whatever the situation looks like; in order to be successful in ministry (in the Eyes of God), we need to be resolved to stand firm in the Faith, and not to compromise the Integrity of the Word of God.

Jesus rebuked His ministers in training on a few occasions for having "little faith".

They couldn't rest in the midst of the storm, and Jesus accused them of having "*little faith*". A lot of ministers have a good appearance of having faith until a real crisis confronts them. They preach about faith, they teach about faith, but it is how they react in the midst of personal crisis that will determine whether they rest in God or not. In fact, many turn from God "because He wasn't there in the storm".

Peter allowed the visible circumstances to cause him to lose faith in his ability to do what Jesus was doing (walk on the water), although he'd begun to do it. But when he began to be challenged by things he saw happening (leaning on his own understanding), he began to sink. And Jesus rebuked him for having little faith. Notice He didn't say, "Well, you began good. Keep on trying and you will get it". No, instead He said "*O thou of little faith, wherefore didst thou doubt?*" (*Mat 14:31*).

Peter was like many Christians today. They read about the things that the Lord did, and the fact that He said that those who believe in Him will be able to do the things that He did, and even greater things, because He went to the Father; and they seek the Lord to call them into ministry:

Mat 14:28 And Peter answered him and said, Lord, if it be thou, bid me come unto thee on the water.

And the Lord grants them their wish.

Mat 14:29 And he said, Come. And when Peter was come down out of the ship, he walked on the water, to go to Jesus.

A Christian who steps into ministry by faith will often times be initially encouraged by situations in which the Lord's intervention is obvious. Most of the time (I'm inclined to believe *all the time*) the Lord will give confirmation of a person's Calling to a particular ministry through seemingly coincidental situations that occur that could only have taken place by God's Hand in the matter. Peter began to walk on the water. It must have been a totally exhilarating moment, until life happened, and the storm became real in his mind.

Mat 14:30 But when he saw the wind boisterous, he was afraid; and beginning to sink, he cried, saying, Lord, save me.

A minister of God has success when he or she understands it is Christ's Ability in them that does the Work, and not their own. Life happens. And Christ *never* fails. *If He calls you to it, He will see you through it.*

2 Cor 5:7 says that we walk by faith, not by sight. Peter's crises of faith began when he started to be moved by what he saw happening around him.

There has to come a time in our lives when we truly understand that God is in charge, and circumstances will never thwart God's Plan for us. There is a difference between trusting in

God in every circumstance, and trusting in God when things are going good. Things will not always go the way we think they should. The Truth is, they rarely will, if we are walking in faith.

Mat 14:31 And immediately Jesus stretched forth *his* hand, and caught him, and said unto him, O thou of little faith, wherefore didst thou doubt?

Like Peter who asked Jesus to call him out of the boat, many Christians ask God to call them into ministry, and they fall away when things begin to get rough. It *will* get rough. Life will happen. Going forth in Faith is not without its' challenges. Jesus was hungry after 40 days of fasting. Sometimes the storms will seem constant. But God wants us to be able to trust Him more than we trust the storm's ability to destroy us or to keep us from God's Purpose.

The Great missionary to Africa, David Livingstone said this:

"I am immortal till my work is accomplished, and although I see few results, future missionaries will see conversions following every sermon. May they not forget the pioneers who worked in the thick gloom with few rays to cheer, except such as flow from faith in the precious promises of God's Word."

Concerning God's Ability to provide food and clothing, Jesus accused them of having "little faith".

As a minister of the Gospel, our dependence shouldn't be on others to enable us to do the Work He has called us to. God will raise up those who understand that the laborer is worthy of his hire. These are people who have been vested with the Gift of helps. You shouldn't need to convince people that they have a gift of helps to help you. But that will come as we make His Kingdom our first priority. And if there are those who refuse God's prompting to

Mat 6:30 Wherefore, if God so clothe the grass of the field, which to day is, and to morrow is cast into the oven, *shall he* not much more *clothe* you, O ye of little faith?
31 Therefore take no thought, saying, What shall we eat? or, What shall we drink? or, Wherewithal shall we be clothed?
32 (For after all these things do the Gentiles seek:) for your heavenly Father knoweth that ye have need of all these things.

support His laborers, God can even put a coin in a fish's mouth to provide the need.

Many who are in ministry today have more faith in their ability to drum up provision for their "cause" than they have faith in God who gave them the vision in the first place. The endless appeals for donations are a great point of stumbling for many both in the Church and outside it. I am convinced that many today who say they are "faith based" would fold up quickly if they stopped making appeals for finances.

On the other hand Jesus commended others of having "Great faith": the centurion who understood Jesus' Authority over sickness and disease; and the woman who understood His Power to deliver those who are held captive by the devil, even though they were not yet in Covenant with God.

A minister of the Gospel must be absolutely settled in his or her heart that God is All Powerful, and the devil and his demons are not.

Matt 4:4 But he answered and said, It is written, Man shall not live by bread alone, but by every word that proceedeth out of the mouth of God.

Because Jesus passed this test, He was able to say with absolute conviction to His disciples (ministers in training):

Mat 6:30 Wherefore, if God so clothe the grass of the field, which today is, and tomorrow is cast into the oven, shall he not much more clothe you, O ye of little faith?
31 Therefore take no thought, saying, What shall we eat? or, What shall we drink? or, Wherewithal shall we be clothed?
32 (For after all these things do the Gentiles seek:) for your heavenly Father knoweth that ye have need of all these things.
33 But seek ye first the kingdom of God, and his righteousness; and all these things shall be added unto you.
34 Take therefore no thought for the morrow: for the morrow shall take thought for the things of itself. Sufficient unto the day is the evil thereof.

Jesus practiced what He preached. Through demonstration of a life yielded to God, he could encourage those who had little or nothing in the way of finances or material possessions or natural talent to go forward into ministry.

Lack or abundance should never determine a willingness or an ability to minister in the capacity that Jesus called you to.

It costs NOTHING except your time to minister healing to a sick person, to lend a hearing ear to the lonely, to lift up your voice in the marketplace and proclaim the Gospel, to hand someone a tract as you walk by them, to cast out a devil from an afflicted soul, or to comfort someone who is mourning.

Programs and men's devices and ambitions cost money. The ministry of the Holy Spirit working in you and through you costs nothing.

As it has been stated elsewhere, "Where the Lord Guides, He Provides". Whatever your circumstance may be, it should not limit your ability to minister.

As we walk in the authority of the Gospel, we are not to use that authority for a means of personal gain.

Jesus sent out the disciples to minister the Gospel:

Mat 10:5 These twelve Jesus sent forth, and commanded them, saying, Go not into the way of the Gentiles, and into *any* **city of the Samaritans enter ye not:**
6 But go rather to the lost sheep of the house of Israel.
7 And as ye go, preach, saying, The kingdom of heaven is at hand.
8 Heal the sick, cleanse the lepers, raise the dead, cast out devils: freely ye have received, freely give.
9 Provide neither gold, nor silver, nor brass in your purses,
10 Nor scrip for *your* **journey, neither two coats, neither shoes, nor yet staves: for the workman is worthy of his meat.**

Notice also that Jesus did not say "send out letters soliciting support for the ministry". He said be about the Kingdom's business first.

Preach and set the captive free. Don't worry about provision, because the Lord, your Employer will see to it that you are taken care of. Notice that the order of Jesus' Commission to the twelve is the same as that which He told them after the resurrection: 1) go and preach, 2) and as you preach, manifest the authority that God has given you.

Mar 16:15 And he said unto them, Go ye into all the world, and preach the gospel to every creature.
16 He that believeth and is baptized shall be saved; but he that believeth not shall be damned.

17 And these signs shall follow them that believe; In my name shall they cast out devils; they shall speak with new tongues;
18 They shall take up serpents; and if they drink any deadly thing, it shall not hurt them; they shall lay hands on the sick, and they shall recover.

The Gospel minister's priority must be the furtherance of the Kingdom of God. First, proclamation must be made that the Kingdom of God is at hand. How is that?

Because the Kingdom of God is within *you*, where you go, the Kingdom is. You are taking the Kingdom of God with you. You are an ambassador to the nations of a Kingdom that is not of this world.

Luk 17:20 And when he was demanded of the Pharisees, when the kingdom of God should come, he answered them and said, The kingdom of God cometh not with observation:
21 Neither shall they say, Lo here! or, lo there! for, behold, the kingdom of God is within you.

As an ambassador of God, you represent the Kingdom to those who you encounter on a daily basis.

2Co 5:19 To wit, that God was in Christ, reconciling the world unto himself, not imputing their trespasses unto them; and hath committed unto us the word of reconciliation.
20 Now then we are ambassadors for Christ, as though God did beseech *you* by us: we pray *you* in Christ's stead, be ye reconciled to God.
21 For he hath made him *to be* sin for us, who knew no sin; that we might be made the righteousness of God in him.

What are you representing to those you encounter?

Are you representing a god who is a theory or an idea, a philosophical concept, or are you representing the Living God, the All Sufficient One, the One Who is known in the Old Testament as Jehovah (Yahweh) Jireh, our Provider?

If He is in the latter group, why do you have to lean on your own understanding to try to make things happen? Jesus turned down the challenge to make the stones into bread, because He knew that His Father would sustain Him, and true ministers of God should turn down the challenge to drum up finances to make the ministry that God has entrusted to them to work.

Jesus was hungry. He was starving. The devil tried to get Him to focus on His need. The devil renders many people powerless and ineffective by causing them to focus on their need, and ultimately that results in a lust for greed.

Notes:

The Word of God says:

Php 4:19 But my God shall supply all your need according to his riches in glory by Christ Jesus.

Remember: All His Promises are Yea and Amen.

As Jesus told His disciples, the Laborer is worthy of his hire. Who is it that has hired us? Won't He be more faithful than any worldly employer? What does that look like in the natural?

The Kingdom minded minister of the Gospel will see the income that he or she accrues either through secular employment or through gifts from others as being a means to provide daily needs and for the work of the ministry that God has called them to.

We are instructed as Christians not to set our affections on things below:

Col 3:1 If ye then be risen with Christ, seek those things which are above, where Christ sitteth on the right hand of God.
2 Set your affection on things above, not on things on the earth.

The less attached we are to the things of the world, the more effective we will be to minister as the Lord has commissioned us to.

The more we set our affections on the things of this world, the more we may accumulate debt. The more debt we have, the more time we will have to spend taking care of that debt, and the less time we will have to fulfill our commission to go and preach the gospel. We become slaves to the lender instead of slaves to the Sender.

I don't know how many times I have heard Christians say "Once we get out of debt, then we will be able to serve the Lord."

Rom 13:8 Owe no man any thing, but to love one another: for he that loveth another hath fulfilled the law.

Pro 19:17 He that hath pity upon the poor lendeth unto the LORD; and that which he hath given will he pay him again.

THE SECOND AREA OF TEMPTATION FOR A MINISTER IS TO TREAT THE GIFTS OF GOD AS AN ENDORSEMENT OF OR VALIDATION OF WHETHER WE ARE APPROVED OF GOD.

Mat 4:6 And saith unto him, If thou be the Son of God, cast thyself down: for it is written, He shall give his angels charge concerning thee: and in *their* hands they shall bear thee up, lest at any time thou dash thy foot against a stone.
7 Jesus said unto him, It is written again, Thou shalt not tempt the Lord thy God.

One of the biggest stumbling blocks for those who are in ministry is the inclination to use our spiritual authority as some kind of proof that we are special in the eyes of God. Christ, on the other hand, made Himself of *no reputation* and lived solely to glorify His Father. He lived a life of obedience to the Father, and as a result, the Father "highly exalted Him".

The supernatural is an area of fascination to the carnal mind, and there will always be a tendency to misuse it or abuse it.

In Matthew 10:8, we read that the second thing that Jesus commissioned the disciples to do after preaching the gospel of the Kingdom of God was to heal the sick, raise the dead, and cast out devils.

As we have seen, He reemphasized that commission after His resurrection:

Mar 16:17 And these signs shall follow them that believe; In my name shall they cast out devils; they shall speak with new tongues;
18 They shall take up serpents; and if they drink any deadly thing, it shall not hurt them; they shall lay hands on the sick, and they shall recover.

There is such a tendency to misuse the Power that is at our disposal because of our fascination with the supernatural, that Paul addressed it in chapters 12, 13, and 14 of his first epistle to the Corinthians.

1Co 12:1 Now concerning spiritual *gifts*, brethren, I would not have you ignorant.

God gives us Gifts to further His Kingdom and to Glorify His Name, not our own.

In 1 Corinthians 12 we are told that God distributes the Gifts of the Holy Spirit as He deems fit to those who are of His Body.

Eph 2:8 For by grace are ye saved through faith; and that not of yourselves: *it is* the gift of God:

9 Not of works, lest any man should boast.

10 For we are his workmanship, created in Christ Jesus unto good works, which God hath before ordained that we should walk in them.

Notes:

_____
_____
_____
_____
_____
_____
_____
_____
_____
_____
_____
_____
_____
_____
_____
_____
_____
_____
_____
_____
_____
_____
_____
_____
_____
_____
_____

1Co 12:6 And there are diversities of operations, but it is the same God which worketh all in all.

7 But the manifestation of the Spirit is given to every man to profit withal.

8 For to one is given by the Spirit the word of wisdom; to another the word of knowledge by the same Spirit;

9 To another faith by the same Spirit; to another the gifts of healing by the same Spirit;

10 To another the working of miracles; to another prophecy; to another discerning of spirits; to another *divers* kinds of tongues; to another the interpretation of tongues:

11 But all these worketh that one and the selfsame Spirit, dividing to every man severally as he will.

We see a similar phrase as that in verse 11, "dividing to every man severally" in the parable of the talents, when the man had called his servants and gave to every man sums of money according to his "several ability":

Mat 25:14 For *the kingdom of heaven is* as a man travelling into a far country, *who* called his own servants, and delivered unto them his goods.

15 And unto one he gave five talents, to another two, and to another one; to every man according to his several ability; and straightway took his journey.

The Lord doesn't expect us to do more than we are able to do, but He does expect us to be faithful with that which He has entrusted to us. If that sounds like a "saved by works" statement, it isn't. There *is* a difference between a wicked and slothful servant, and one who is good and faithful.

While we are *NOT* saved by our works; when we are saved, we are called to do good works.

Tit 2:14 Who gave himself for us, that he might redeem us from all iniquity, and purify unto himself a peculiar people, zealous of good works.

1Ti 6:6 But godliness with contentment is great gain.
7 For we brought nothing into *this* world, *and it is* certain we can carry nothing out.
8 And having food and raiment let us be therewith content.

Notes:

_____
_____
_____
_____
_____
_____
_____
_____
_____
_____
_____
_____
_____
_____
_____
_____
_____
_____
_____
_____
_____
_____
_____
_____
_____
_____
_____
_____
_____
_____

Those who have been redeemed by the Blood of the Lamb naturally become a peculiar people who are zealous of good works. They want to make a difference in the world. They are about furthering the Kingdom of God wherever they go, and understand that the Gifts are given by God to assist them in accomplishing that task.

When Jesus commissioned His disciples, He assured them that *all* authority had been given to Him, and in turn, He delegates His Authority to His disciples:

Mat 28:18 And Jesus came and spake unto them, saying, All power is given unto me in heaven and in earth.
19 Go ye therefore, and teach all nations, baptizing them in the name of the Father, and of the Son, and of the Holy Ghost:
20 Teaching them to observe all things whatsoever I have commanded you: and, lo, I am with you alway, *even* unto the end of the world. Amen.

In Mark 16, we read this:

Mar 16:15 And he said unto them, Go ye into all the world, and preach the gospel to every creature.
16 He that believeth and is baptized shall be saved; but he that believeth not shall be damned.
17 And these signs shall follow them that believe; In my name shall they cast out devils; they shall speak with new tongues;
18 They shall take up serpents; and if they drink any deadly thing, it shall not hurt them; they shall lay hands on the sick, and they shall recover.
19 So then after the Lord had spoken unto them, he was received up into heaven, and sat on the right hand of God.
20 And they went forth, and preached every where, the Lord working with *them,* and confirming the word with signs following. Amen.

Whatever He calls us to, He enables us to do it, and

145

Gal 5:22 But the fruit of the Spirit is love, joy, peace, longsuffering, gentleness, goodness, faith,
23 Meekness, temperance: against such there is no law.
24 And they that are Christ's have crucified the flesh with the affections and lusts.

Notes:

_____
_____
_____
_____
_____
_____
_____
_____
_____
_____
_____
_____
_____
_____
_____
_____
_____
_____
_____

Mat 7:22 Many will say to me in that day, Lord, Lord, have we not prophesied in thy name? and in thy name have cast out devils? and in thy name done many wonderful works?
23 And then will I profess unto them, I never knew you: depart from me, ye that work iniquity.

we are able to do it through the Holy Spirit Who dwells in us. But even though we may understand in principle that it is the Holy Spirit Who does the Work, pride can quickly infiltrate the ministry if we are not careful.

The Word of God says that we are engaged in a spiritual warfare, and the enemy will do all he can to prevent us from accomplishing the Will of God in our lives.

There was a time when the disciples came rejoicing and were in awe of the fact that even the devils were subject to Him. And they were, because Jesus gave them that authority.

Mat 10:1 And when he had called unto him his twelve disciples, he gave them power against unclean spirits, to cast them out, and to heal all manner of sickness and all manner of disease.

Walking in the realm of the supernatural is not a definitive proof that God has placed His stamp of approval on an individual.

Call to mind Jesus' words, when He mentioned that there would be a time when there will be *many* who will remind the Lord that they had cast out demons, prophesied and done many wonderful works in His Name, and He will tell them He never knew them.

Tarot card readers and fortune tellers walk in a type of prophetic gifting; but that gifting isn't from the Lord. Satanic Worshippers and witches have a type of tongues, but those tongues are not from the Lord. Psychologists and psychiatrists give their patients psychotropic drugs to help relieve them from their troubling thoughts, but they can't deliver them from the demonic influence that is behind the thoughts.

As of this writing, I am located in Northeast Alabama, on a 75 mile long by 35 mile wide plateau which is part of the Appalachian mountain chain. Snake handling is still a very real part of some congregations in Appalachia. Their doctrine is based on Mark 16:18, where Jesus mentioned two of the signs that would follow those who believe was that they would take up serpents and if they drink any deadly thing, it will not hurt them.

I've actually visited one of these churches, and have witnessed them passing around a copperhead and a rattlesnake. One member of the congregation held a fire under his chin close enough so the flames were parted and licked at both sides of his face. After the service, there was no evidence of any burn marks on the man's face. They do such things in their service to prove whether they "believe" or not. This is another example akin to the second temptation of Christ. The devil whispers: "If you really believe, you will handle snakes and drink strychnine, so prove that you are really a believer."

But in India snake charmers handle snakes even deadlier than copperheads and rattlesnakes, and they are far from Christ.

There are several accounts of missionaries who in the course of their ministry were unaware that they were given poison by witch doctors as a test to see if they were really representatives of God or not, and were unaffected by the sorcerer's devices, which have led to whole villages coming to Christ, including the witch doctors.

In the 28th chapter of Acts, we read where Paul inadvertently got bit by a viper. When no harm came to him, the people in the region were receptive to the Gospel.

**Act 28:3 And when Paul had gathered a bundle of sticks, and laid *them* on the fire, there came a viper out of the heat, and fastened on his hand.
4 And when the barbarians saw the *venomous* beast hang on his hand, they said among themselves, No doubt this man is a murderer, whom, though he hath escaped the sea, yet vengeance suffereth not to live.
5 And he shook off the beast into the fire, and felt no harm.
6 Howbeit they looked when he should have swollen, or fallen down dead suddenly: but after they had looked a great while, and saw no harm come to him, they changed their minds, and said that he was a god.**

The gifts of God are not meant to be cheapened by some kind of parlor trick mentality, or to be used like a mentalist who can give a "Word of Knowledge", or as a practitioner of divination who can tell someone their future. For every Gift of the Holy Spirit, there is an occultic counterfeit, and the minister of God must be careful not to misuse the Gifts. Pride or a push for personal recognition is a good indicator as to whether the minister of the Gospel is using the Gifts for his personal gain, or for the Glory of God.

The words Jesus spoke to His disciples when He commissioned them applies to each one of us who step into ministry:

Luk 10:17 And the seventy returned again with joy, saying, Lord, even the devils are subject unto us through thy name.
18 And he said unto them, I beheld Satan as lightning fall from heaven.
19 Behold, I give unto you power to tread on serpents and scorpions, and over all the power of the enemy: and nothing shall by any means hurt you.
20 Notwithstanding in this rejoice not, that the spirits are subject unto you; but rather rejoice, because your names are written in heaven.

In 1st Corinthians 12, Paul equates the wrong use of the Spiritual gifts with idolatry.

1Co 12:1 Now concerning spiritual *gifts*, brethren, I would not have you ignorant.
2 Ye know that ye were Gentiles, carried away unto these dumb idols, even as ye were led.

Those of us who have been baptized with the Baptism of the Holy Spirit have supernatural gifts imparted to us through that same Holy Spirit.

Those gifts are given to us for the furtherance of the ministry that God has committed to us, to bring GLORY exclusively to Him. Focusing on the Gifts more than the One Who has bestowed them upon us will lead us into error.

A man receives a brand new high caliber rifle as a gift. He loves to hunt. Initially, he will admire the weight, the action, and the fine qualities of this rifle. He will be anxious to use that rifle, and he may even go out to the range immediately to try it out. What a beautiful weapon! It isn't wrong to admire it and to appreciate it, and to be grateful to the one who gave it to him. But eventually it will become a tool to use to stock his freezer with food.

Being a good hunter, he will use it responsibly and appropriately. He will take care of the rifle, and maintain it, and spend time becoming proficient at using it, but it won't become an idol to him, if he understands it is a tool intended to achieve a goal.

As an effective minister of God whose focus is the furtherance of the Kingdom of God, you will be a good steward of the Gifts God He has bestowed upon you, but you won't allow yourself to be tempted to misuse the Gifts that you have been freely given as a means of proving that you are something special.

Jesus made sure His seventy disciples understood that the most important Gift we have is the Gift of Salvation. And in our walk as ministers of the WORD of God, we need to be mindful that there is the potential to misuse the Gifts that are given to us through the Holy Spirit.

148

1Th 1:5 For our gospel came not unto you in word only, but also in power, and in the Holy Ghost, and in much assurance; as ye know what manner of men we were among you for your sake.
6 And ye became followers of us, and of the Lord, having received the word in much affliction, with joy of the Holy Ghost:
7 So that ye were ensamples to all that believe in Macedonia and Achaia.
8 For from you sounded out the word of the Lord not only in Macedonia and Achaia, but also in every place your faith to God-ward is spread abroad; so that we need not to speak any thing.

Tit 2:7 In all things shewing thyself a pattern (example) of good works: in doctrine *shewing* uncorruptness, gravity, sincerity,
8 Sound speech, that cannot be condemned; that he that is of the contrary part may be ashamed, having no evil thing to say of you.

Notes:
_____
_____
_____
_____
_____
_____
_____
_____
_____
_____
_____
_____

Paul was an instructor of the Word of God, and the letter to the Corinthians was written to a body of believers whose focus was just wrong, because they were carnal in their thinking.

Paul's' Words to Timothy are applicable to all who are aspiring to be ministers of the Gospel:

1Ti 4:12 Let no man despise thy youth; but be thou an example of the believers, in word, in conversation, in charity, in spirit, in faith, in purity.
13 Till I come, give attendance to reading, to exhortation, to doctrine.
14 Neglect not the gift that is in thee, which was given thee by prophecy, with the laying on of the hands of the presbytery.
15 Meditate upon these things; give thyself wholly to them; that thy profiting may appear to all.
16 Take heed unto thyself, and unto the doctrine; continue in them: for in doing this thou shalt both save thyself, and them that hear thee.

In verse 12, we are instructed to be examples of what ministry is to all who we encounter.

Php 3:13 Brethren, I count not myself to have apprehended: but *this* one thing *I do*, forgetting those things which are behind, and reaching forth unto those things which are before,
14 I press toward the mark for the prize of the high calling of God in Christ Jesus.
15 Let us therefore, as many as be perfect, be thus minded: and if in any thing ye be otherwise minded, God shall reveal even this unto you.
16 Nevertheless, whereto we have already attained, let us walk by the same rule, let us mind the same thing.
17 Brethren, be followers (Greek = *Summimates* - Co-imitator) together of me, and mark them which walk so as ye have us for an ensample.

Just as a recap, we have seen that:

Notes:

The first area in which ministers of the Gospel will be tempted is to question whether or not they are really called to the Work.

The second area of temptation is to use the ministry in the area of personal gain.

The third area ministers of the Gospel are tempted in is to misuse the Gifts as an endorsement of who they are, and the ministry becomes more of a show that church people flock to see, rather than a means of furthering the Kingdom of God.

Not only can the minister of the Gospel become more focused on the demonstration of the Power of God which works in him or her than they are on the One Who has given them the Power, but they can also be tempted to abuse the Authority they have been given. It is always important to remember that *it is the meek who are Blessed.*

Jesus taught by example when He resisted the devil's temptation to abuse His Authority.

The fourth area in which a minister of the Gospel will be tempted is to use the Power of God in order to gain personal recognition and status.

Luk 4:5 And the devil, taking him up into an high mountain, shewed unto him all the kingdoms of the world in a moment of time.
6 And the devil said unto him, All this power will I give thee, and the glory of them: for that is delivered unto me; and to whomsoever I will I give it.
7 If thou therefore wilt worship me, all shall be thine.
8 And Jesus answered and said unto him, Get thee behind me, Satan: for it is written, Thou shalt worship the Lord thy God, and him only shalt thou serve.

Php 2:9 Wherefore God also hath highly exalted him, and given him a name which is above every name:

Php 2:5 Let this mind be in you, which was also in Christ Jesus:
6 Who, being in the form of God, thought it not robbery to be equal with God:
7 But made himself of no reputation, and took upon him the form of a servant, and was made in the likeness of men:

Notes:

_____
_____
_____
_____
_____
_____
_____
_____
_____
_____
_____
_____
_____
_____
_____
_____
_____
_____
_____
_____
_____
_____
_____
_____
_____
_____
_____
_____
_____
_____

10 That at the name of Jesus every knee should bow, of *things* in heaven, and *things* in earth, and *things* under the earth;
11 And *that* every tongue should confess that Jesus Christ *is* Lord, to the glory of God the Father.

Many in ministry love the fame and recognition that can follow a person who is truly being used by God. With fame and recognition comes the potential for personal gain of wealth and power. Remember, Jesus made Himself of *no reputation*.

Worldly possessions bring a kind of status quo among certain ministries today as a measure of how much "Faith" they have. Some "Faith" preachers have expensive car collections, or golden toilets - one prominent prosperity teacher has a different car for every day of the week. And we aren't talking about Ford Focus' or Chevy Impalas. Rolls Royce's, Mercedes Benz and the like are in his garage.

And then there are the elite few who have their own personal jet.

They tell their followers that if they could attain the faith that they have, they too could have the finer things in life. But they explain that such things come through "sacrificial giving". And so the congregation gives sacrificially from their bank accounts into the bank account of the preacher, and the preacher gets richer while the congregant works harder at trying to "walk in faith".

God has given us Authority as ministers of the Gospel, and because we are flesh, our inclination is to flaunt that authority, and to lord it over those who have been entrusted to our care.

Jesus was our example of how we are not to abuse that authority. He never "lorded it over" those who were in His care. Just as Jesus was our example, we also must be an example to those who have been entrusted to our care.

2Th 3:7 For yourselves know how ye ought to follow us: for we behaved not ourselves disorderly among you;
8 Neither did we eat any man's bread for nought; but wrought with labour and travail night and day, that we might not be chargeable to any of you:
9 Not because we have not power, but to make ourselves an ensample unto you to follow us.

1Pe 5:1 The elders which are among you I exhort, who am also an elder, and a witness of the sufferings of Christ, and also a partaker of the glory that shall be revealed:
2 Feed the flock of God which is among you, taking the oversight *thereof,* not by constraint, but willingly; not for filthy lucre, but of a ready mind;
3 Neither as being lords over *God's* heritage, but being ensamples to the flock.
4 And when the chief Shepherd shall appear, ye shall receive a crown of glory that fadeth not away.

Ministry should never become viewed as a job or a means of personal gain. "Filthy Lucre" in verse two above means "eagerness for base gain", or financial and material prosperity.

Tit 2:1 But speak thou the things which become sound doctrine:
2 That the aged men be sober, grave, temperate, sound in faith, in charity, in patience.
3 The aged women likewise, that *they be* in behaviour as becometh holiness, not false accusers, not given to much wine, teachers of good things;
4 That they may teach the young women to be sober, to love their husbands, to love their children,
5 *To be* discreet, chaste, keepers at home, good, obedient to their own husbands, that the word of God be not blasphemed.
6 Young men likewise exhort to be sober minded.
7 In all things shewing thyself a pattern of good works: in doctrine *shewing* uncorruptness, gravity, sincerity,
8 Sound speech, that cannot be condemned; that he that is of the contrary part may be ashamed, having no evil thing to say of you.

Some teach that Jesus and His disciples were rich. They point out that Judas was the treasurer of the group, because he "had the bag", or took care of the finances of the group *(John 12:4-6)*. They say that when Jesus was a child, the wise men lavished gifts of gold upon Him, and so He grew up privileged and able to finance his own ministry. He wore the finest clothes, so valuable that the soldiers cast lots for His clothing.

There were people who no doubt gave money to Jesus' ministry. This money was used by Jesus and His disciples to take care of their needs as they travelled. In fact it would become a pattern later of how the early Church conducted its' business, when everyone laid what they had at the apostles' feet, and it was distributed to the saints according to everyone's need. They certainly did not have enough in the way of finances to feed the multitude. And one day, in a time of apparent lack, Jesus had a disciple to catch a fish with a coin in its' mouth in order to pay their taxes. As we pointed out at the beginning of this chapter, Jesus taught that our personal provision was to be of no concern as we work to further the Kingdom of God.

Judas was the one who Christ entrusted to take care of those finances that came to them in the course of the ministry, and a lot of ministries today who call themselves "Faith based" are really of a Judas mentality. They are thieves who care more about what they can get from their audience than they do about the "audience" themselves.

Joseph continued in his vocation as a carpenter after the birth of Jesus, and obviously they lived a simple life as he was growing up, since the people knew Jesus as "the carpenter's" son. Despite what some slick preacher may say, it seems apparent that he did not grow up rich because of the wise men's gold.

What about His expensive garment? By the time he was crucified, Jesus was a famous man. The scripture tells us that the soldiers parted His clothing into four parts, implying that they ripped his clothing so each would have a piece as a bit of memorabilia. But Jesus' coat was such that it had no seams, so they gambled among each other for the whole coat, rather than rip it into four pieces as well.

The Bible doesn't say that it was an expensive piece of clothing. The prosperity teachers who want your money say that. The simple truth is that it just didn't make sense to rip up a perfectly good coat.

Joh 19:23 Then the soldiers, when they had

Col 3:5 Mortify therefore your members which are upon the earth; fornication, uncleanness, inordinate affection, evil concupiscence, and covetousness, which is idolatry:
6 For which things' sake the wrath of God cometh on the children of disobedience:

Notes:

_____
_____
_____
_____
_____
_____
_____
_____
_____
_____
_____
_____
_____
_____
_____
_____
_____
_____
_____
_____
_____
_____
_____
_____
_____
_____

crucified Jesus, took his garments, and made four parts, to every soldier a part; and also *his* coat: now the coat was without seam, woven from the top throughout.
24 They said therefore among themselves, Let us not rend it, but cast lots for it, whose it shall be: that the scripture might be fulfilled, which saith, They parted my raiment among them, and for my vesture they did cast lots. These things therefore the soldiers did.

Covetousness is defined as idolatry in Col 3:5. Jesus understood that fact when He refused the devil's third temptation of wealth and the kingdoms of this world. Paul didn't teach a prosperity Gospel. Neither did Peter, or James or John.

1Th 1:6 And ye became followers of us, and of the Lord, having received the word in much affliction, with joy of the Holy Ghost:
7 So that ye were ensamples to all that believe in Macedonia and Achaia.
8 For from you sounded out the word of the Lord not only in Macedonia and Achaia, but also in every place your faith to God-ward is spread abroad; so that we need not to speak anything.
9 For they themselves shew of us what manner of entering in we had unto you, and how ye turned to God from idols to serve the living and true God;
10 And to wait for his Son from heaven, whom he raised from the dead, *even* Jesus, which delivered us from the wrath to come.

The way of ministry is not to be a means of personal gain and recognition, but personal sacrifice and obedience.

Mat 20:25 But Jesus called them *unto him,* and said, Ye know that the princes of the Gentiles exercise dominion over them, and they that are great exercise authority upon them.
26 But it shall not be so among you: but whosoever will be great among you, let him be your minister;

**27 And whosoever will be chief among you, let him be your servant:
28 Even as the Son of man came not to be ministered unto, but to minister, and to give his life a ransom for many.**

As you step into ministry, you must realize that the ministry was a privilege that was entrusted to you by God, and that it must always be Christ Who is glorified. Satan is subtle. He will try to sidetrack you any way he can from your effectiveness in the Kingdom of God.

In your own words, discuss the four areas in which every minister of God can be misled or sidetracked from their purpose in ministry _____

_____
_____
_____
_____
_____
_____
_____
_____
_____
_____
_____
_____
_____
_____
_____
_____
_____
_____
_____
_____
_____
_____
_____
_____
_____
_____
_____
_____
_____
_____

No sort of defense is needed for preaching outdoors, but it would take a very strong argument to prove that a man who has never preached beyond the walls of his meetinghouse has done his duty. A defense is required for services within buildings rather than for worship outside of them

William Booth

Notes:

Chapter 11
The Authority of the Believer

WE HAVE LEARNED THE *First Principles* of our faith.

We have learned about the characteristics that define a true disciple of Christ.

We have studied the temptations that are common to every minister of the Gospel.

Assuming that we have successfully absorbed the aforementioned lessons, we are now ready to "*Go on to perfection*"; to walk in the Authority that Christ has given to us as able ministers of the Gospel.

I would suggest that the student and the teacher take time to study the following chapters before they go any farther:

If in a classroom setting, take a session period to read Matthew 5 - 10, and in the next session, discuss what you may learn during this time of study. If you are studying this by yourself, then I would suggest you read those chapters, and spend the rest of your time today thinking about what you learned.

You can continue with this book tomorrow.

Ready to go on? Here is a simple overview of what you just read:

When Jesus called His disciples, He first instructed them in the Way of effective ministry. Matthew 5-7 gives an account of how He did that.

Then after He instructed them, they accompanied Him and had on the job training as they watched Him minister healing and deliverance to the people, and taught them in the Way of faith in Matthew 8-9.

Then in Matthew 10, He sent them out to do the same.

And in Matthew 28, he told the disciples to make disciples, and to teach their disciples to do the same that Jesus had taught them to do. What is the purpose? *To further the Kingdom of God on this earth.* In order to do this we must learn to walk in His Authority and His Power.

Luk 4:35 And Jesus rebuked him, saying, Hold thy peace, and come out of him. And when the devil had thrown him in the midst, he came out of him, and hurt him not.
36 And they were all amazed, and spake among themselves, saying, What a word *is* this! for with authority and power he commandeth the unclean spirits, and they come out.

Just before this event took place, Jesus had been in the synagogue and read from the scroll of Isaiah. We are told that He opened the scroll, and found where it was written,

Luk 4:18 The Spirit of the Lord *is* upon me, because he hath anointed me to preach the gospel to the poor; he hath sent me to heal the brokenhearted, to preach deliverance to the captives, and recovering of sight to the blind, to set at liberty them that are bruised,
19 To preach the acceptable year of the Lord.

Jesus quoted this verse in the synagogue and He declared "This day is this scripture fulfilled".

What is the operative word here in Isaiah 61:1?

"Because".

The word translated as "Because" is the Hebrew word "Ya'an", and by implication means "*for the purpose of*". Understanding that, we can see that the Spirit of the Lord was upon Jesus *FOR THE PURPOSE OF FULFILLING THE WILL OF GOD.*

The Spirit of the Lord was upon Jesus *because* God had anointed Him to preach good tidings to the meek.

By order of importance, the first thing we can see is God *anointed* Jesus to *preach* the Gospel to those who are humble enough to hear it.

Kings and priests were *anointed* as they were instituted into their office. They were anointed for a specific purpose. A King is anointed to rule, to subdue the enemies of his kingdom, and to expand his kingdom.

Kings are expected to be victors and overcomers. Kings are not expected to be overcome. Jesus is the King of kings. The Spirit of the Lord was upon Him *because* He was anointed in the office of the Messiah, the expected King of

Israel. He came proclaiming that the Kingdom of God was at hand. Those who were humble enough would hear and recognize the truth of that statement.

As a King, the Spirit of God was upon Him to *proclaim* Liberty to the captives. A king has the authority to release those who are in prison. In the passage in Luke, Jesus says he was to preach Liberty to the captives, but in Isaiah, the Hebrew word is translated "proclaim", and actually carries with it the idea of *accosting* a person who is met.

When a person accosts another person, they address them aggressively. "Accost" describes a confrontation, one that is generally aggressive in nature. When Jesus proclaimed liberty to the captives, He accosted the spirit or spirits that had them bound, and commanded them to give up their possession.

If you are in a bad side of town, you may be accosted by thugs who demand your money from you. Generally they will accost someone they believe they can overpower. They won't politely ask you to give up your money. They will forcefully demand that you do so, in such a way that you will feel threatened if you don't. It is not just a vain show. They have confidence in their ability to overpower you.

If you happen to be a police officer, the chances are that they won't mess with you because of the authority you have. In fact if you see them messing with someone, you will likely accost them, arrest them and lock them up.

Preaching in the public square is a very real way of accosting the devil. Open air preaching is like the herald who proclaims the decree of the king.

When Jesus walked the earth, those who were bound by sickness and disease would meet the King Who had authority to accost the demon that was holding them captive, and to bring them freedom from their bondage. This King of kings, this conquering

_____
_____
_____
_____
_____
_____
_____
_____
_____
_____
_____
_____
_____
_____
_____
_____

Rev 1:6 And hath made us kings and priests unto God and his Father; to him *be* glory and dominion for ever and ever. Amen.

_____
_____
_____
_____
_____
_____
_____
_____
_____
_____
_____
_____
_____
_____
_____
_____
_____
_____

Messiah would bring them liberty, healing and deliverance.

The Spirit of God wasn't upon Him to acquire things for Himself, or to get rich, or to run a lap around the temple or to have a "Glory fit", or to give a forty minute speech once a week. The Spirit of the Lord was upon Him to advance the Kingdom of God in the world, one soul at a time, and to see them set free from their captivity. Why do you suppose the anointing is upon you, if you have received the baptism of the Holy Spirit?

Priests were also anointed, and Jesus not only operated in the capacity of a King, but as a priest. As a priest, He was able to bind up the broken hearted. to comfort those who mourn, to move them from the spirit of heaviness to a place of joy and praise before God.

The Spirit of the Lord was upon Jesus *because* He had been anointed in the office of a Conquering King, and a Priest of the Most High God.

The Spirit of the Lord is upon us who are in Christ as well. Why? Because Revelation 1:6 declares that God has made us kings *and* priests, not kings *or* priests!

Peter 2:9 declares that we are a ROYAL priesthood. According to 1 John 2:27, we have been anointed. And the Spirit of God is upon us *because* He has anointed us as kings and priests to carry on the Work of Jesus. Think of your anointing as an appointing by the Holy Spirit.

Why is the Spirit of God upon you? To build your own little (or mega) church congregation? To have a glory run around the church, to shake uncontrollably with a Glory fit? To get a personal financial blessing? Are you walking in your anointing?

The Spirit of the LORD is upon you to enable you to fulfill *your* Calling as a King and a Priest of the Most High God. Jesus walked in His anointing as a

Three Greek Words Commonly Translated As "Power"

EXOUSIA

G1849 ἐξουσία exousia *ex-oo-see'-ah*

From G1832 (in the sense of *ability*); *privilege*, that is, (subjectively) *force, capacity, competency, freedom,* or (objectively) *mastery* (concretely *magistrate, superhuman, potentate, token of control*), delegated *influence:* - authority, jurisdiction, liberty, power, right, strength.

DUNAMIS

G1411 δύναμις dunamis *doo'-nam-is*

From G1410; *force* (literally or figuratively); specifically miraculous *power* (usually by implication a *miracle* itself): - ability, abundance, meaning, might (-ily, -y, -y deed), (worker of) miracle (-s), power, strength, violence, mighty (wonderful) work.

KRATOS

G2904

κράτος kratos *krat'-os*

Perhaps a primary word; *vigor* ["great"], (literally or figuratively): - dominion, might [-ily], power, strength.

Notes:

_____
_____
_____
_____
_____
_____
_____

lifestyle. You are anointed for a lifestyle as well, not for an occasional outreach or mission trip.

Act 1:7 And he said unto them, It is not for you to know the times or the seasons, which the Father hath put in his own power.
8 But ye shall receive power, after that the Holy Ghost is come upon you: and ye shall be witnesses unto me both in Jerusalem, and in all Judaea, and in Samaria, and unto the uttermost part of the earth.

Mat 28:18 And Jesus came and spake unto them, saying, All power is given unto me in heaven and in earth.
19 Go ye therefore, and teach all nations, baptizing them in the name of the Father, and of the Son, and of the Holy Ghost:
20 Teaching them to observe all things whatsoever I have commanded you: and, lo, I am with you alway, even unto the end of the world. Amen.

The English word "power" that we see in the New Testament is actually translated from three different Greek words: *Exousia, Dunamis,* and *Kratos.* When we begin to read the English text in the light of the proper definition of these words, our perspective of our position in Christ may radically change.

Power as defined by AUTHORITY: *Exousia*

Jesus put it in perspective when the disciples returned after He sent them out:

Luk 10:19 Behold, I give unto you power (exousia= authority) to tread on serpents and scorpions, and over all the power (dunamis = force) of the enemy: and nothing shall by any means hurt you.
20 Notwithstanding in this rejoice not, that the spirits are subject unto you; but rather rejoice, because your names are written in heaven.

The first thing a minister of the Gospel must understand is that authority (exousia) overrules force (*dunamis*). In the military, a company commander is just one person, yet he is in charge of a multitude of trained fighting men. The men compose the force or the strength of the commander's military unit, but the commander has authority over the company. What he says goes.

Though Satan may have supernatural power, the believer is given *authority* over that power. *It is important to understand that demonic influences are subject to the believer, and not the other way around.* What *you* say goes.

Mat 10:1 And when he had called unto *him* his twelve disciples, he gave them power (*Exousia = AUTHORITY*) *against* unclean spirits, to cast them out, and to heal all manner of sickness and all manner of disease.

The believer who is active in the service (ministry) to his Father has the authority to cast out unclean spirits.

He or she also has the authority given to them from God to heal all manner of sickness and all manner of disease. You may ask, "How does that work?" Sickness and disease are not of God. Some people attribute sickness as a way that God is punishing them, or that He is teaching them something through the sickness. You need to understand that sickness is *not* God's Will.

Everything God made, He pronounced as good. But when Adam and Eve sinned against God, they gave the devil authority over this world.

Jesus said the devil comes to kill, steal and destroy. But Jesus destroyed the works of the devil on the cross, and in doing so, He received all authority in heaven and in earth, and when He told His disciples to "Go ye, therefore", He has entrusted His followers and all those who would come after them with the same authority.

Mat 28:18 And Jesus came and spake unto them, saying, All power (AUTHORITY) is given unto me in heaven and in earth.
19 Go ye therefore, and teach all nations, baptizing them in the name of the Father, and of the Son, and of the Holy Ghost:
20 Teaching them to observe all things whatsoever I have commanded you: and, lo, I am with you alway, *even* unto the end of the world. Amen.

What does that authority consist of? Those who believe in Jesus have the same authority He had given the disciples in Matthew 10:1.

Mar 16:15 And he said unto them, Go ye into all the world, and preach the gospel to every creature.
16 He that believeth and is baptized shall be saved; but he that believeth not shall be damned.
17 And these signs shall follow them that believe; In my name shall they cast out devils; they shall speak with new tongues;

18 They shall take up serpents; and if they drink any deadly thing, it shall not hurt them; they shall lay hands on the sick, and they shall recover.
19 So then after the Lord had spoken unto them, he was received up into heaven, and sat on the right hand of God.
20 And they went forth, and preached every where, the Lord working with *them,* and confirming the word with signs following. Amen.

Jesus said that those who believed in Him would do the same things that He did:

Joh 14:12 Verily, verily, I say unto you, He that believeth on me, the works that I do shall he do also; and greater *works* than these shall he do; because I go unto my Father.

Yet despite the fact that Jesus made these promises, we really don't see too much of the Power of God being demonstrated today. Why?

The operative words here are *Belief and obedience.*

Mat 21:21 Jesus answered and said unto them, Verily I say unto you, If ye have faith, and doubt not, ye shall not only do this *which is done* to the fig tree, but also if ye shall say unto this mountain, Be thou removed, and be thou cast into the sea; it shall be done.
22 And all things, whatsoever ye shall ask in prayer, believing, ye shall receive.

A parallel passage is found in Mark, and may give us a little more insight in the belief that is required to do the Work of God.

Mar 11:23 For verily I say unto you, That whosoever shall say unto this mountain, Be thou removed, and be thou cast into the sea; and shall not doubt in his heart, but shall believe that those things which he saith shall come to pass; he shall have whatsoever he saith.
24 Therefore I say unto you, What things soever ye desire, when ye pray, believe that ye receive *them,* and ye shall have *them.*

"And shall not doubt in his heart". Belief is a heart issue. Heart issues are *trust* issues. The real question at hand is whether the disciple actually believes that the Bible *is* the Word of God.

Biblical Faith Is The Key to Walking In Authority

If we waver on any issue in the Word of God, then we will waver on other areas pertaining to Faith. And there are a whole lot of voices that have contributed to the question of whether or not the Bible can be trusted to be the actual Word of God.

Many people refer to "Blind Faith". But that is not the Faith that the Word of God refers to.

The Bible tells us that Faith is the "Substance", or the "essence" of a thing that you confidently are assured of (Heb 11:1).

Many people say "I believe the Bible is the inspired infallible word of God". The person who says this, is saying that they believe the Bible is 100% true. And then many of the same people who make that statement begin to explain away the things in the Bible, by taking away from or adding to what it says.

Do you believe the Word of God is true?

Mormons declare they believe the Word of God is true - "insofar as it is correctly translated".

Cessationists say they believe the Word of God is true - but a lot of it doesn't apply to us today.

Many Charismatics say they believe the Word of God is true, but scoff at the idea of a literal 7 day creation or the concept of a young earth. They point to men's theories and say there is a gap of time (perhaps billions of years) between Genesis 1:1 and Genesis 1:2. They speculate that there was once another earth before this earth, and that, in fact, sin existed on the earth before Adam and Eve.

But the Bible never refers to this previous race of men, and they exist only in the imaginations of those who have some other doctrinal agenda that that they want to bring forth. Advocates of the "gap theory" say that science proves that the universe is billions of years old, and so they strive to make the Bible conform to their understanding.

I don't think it is unreasonable to understand that when God created Adam and Eve, He created them as fully mature individuals, probably equivalent to at least 20 or 30 years old. When He created the trees and the plants and the animals, he created them as fully mature, as well. If Adam and Eve had the inclination to, they could probably have determined the age of a tree in the Garden by our standards today as being hundreds or thousands of years old.

When God said let there be light, He created the light before he created the stars and the planets. The light permeated the universe at His Word, and then He created the stars, the sun and the moon. When He created the Light, He set it in place, and it didn't take millions of years to reach its' destination. It simply was. But we understand "light years" as a method of measuring time or distance. What finite man understands as millions or billions of years, an Infinite God accomplished with His Word in just a day.

I am not a scientist. I won't pretend to be one. But I do understand that those things that seem to be foolishness to the atheistic scientific community and are written off as superstition are the very things that become a stumbling block to professing Christians who lean more on their understanding than their trust in God.

1Co 1:20 Where *is* the wise? where *is* the scribe? where *is* the disputer of this world? hath not God made foolish the wisdom of this world?
21 For after that in the wisdom of God the world by wisdom knew not God, it pleased God by the foolishness of preaching to save them that believe.
22 For the Jews require a sign, and the Greeks seek after wisdom:

23 But we preach Christ crucified, unto the Jews a stumblingblock, and unto the Greeks foolishness;
24 But unto them which are called, both Jews and Greeks, Christ the power of God, and the wisdom of God.

To the scientist, faith in God defies logic and reason, because God can't be seen or explained. To the Christian, Faith in God is the only reasonable and logical Way of life.

1Co 1:25 Because the foolishness of God is wiser than men; and the weakness of God is stronger than men.
26 For ye see your calling, brethren, how that not many wise men after the flesh, not many mighty, not many noble, *are called*:
27 But God hath chosen the foolish things of the world to confound the wise; and God hath chosen the weak things of the world to confound the things which are mighty;
28 And base things of the world, and things which are despised, hath God chosen, *yea*, and things which are not, to bring to nought things that are:
29 That no flesh should glory in his presence.

Jesus warned repeatedly about a future Judgment and the consequence of Hell. Yet many teachers today downplay the Judgment of God and the idea of a literal Hell. "After all, God is Love. I can't imagine a loving God who would condemn someone to an eternity in torment."

There are a hundred more ways in which men who say they believe the Bible is true actually spend their lives explaining it away, and as a result echo the serpent's whisper; "Yea, has God really said...?" Those whispers are potential Faith destroyers.

Jesus said unless you are converted and become as a little child, you won't enter the Kingdom of heaven. That the Kingdom of heaven and the Kingdom of God are the same, one can see by a careful study of the Word:

Mat 18:3 And said, Verily I say unto you, Except ye be converted, and become as little children, ye shall not enter into the kingdom of heaven. 4 Whosoever therefore shall humble himself as this little child, the same is greatest in the kingdom of heaven.

Luk 18:16 But Jesus called them unto him, and said, Suffer little children to come unto me, and forbid them not: for of such is the kingdom of God. 17 Verily I say unto you, Whosoever shall not receive the kingdom of God as a little child shall in no wise enter therein.

A child's love bears all things, believes all things, hopes all things, and endures all things. Mistrust, doubt, confusion and instability comes later. Jesus said we need to become converted from our lack of faith, and learn to trust our Father. A child doesn't have to have all the scientific details to believe that a thing exists, or to understand why a thing exists. A child simply enjoys their existence.

God's Promises are Yea and Amen. God is not a liar. Faith in Him is NOT blind, or based on a whimsical hope. Faith is *unwavering confidence* that what He has promised He will perform.

The doctor may say you have pneumonia, but God's Word says that by the stripes of Jesus you are healed.

Whose report has the most substance?

According to your faith, so be it.

Or you may see someone who has pneumonia who does not have the faith to be healed.

Yet you know that the Word says that you can lay hands on the sick and they will recover.

Whose faith has the most substance?

Lay your hand on them.

Command them to be healed in the Name of Jesus.

According to your faith so be it.

The outcome of applied Biblical Faith is a *tangible* reality.

Tangible: Tangible TAN'GIBLE, a. [from L. tango, to touch.]
1. Perceptible by the touch; tactile.
2. That may be possessed or realized.

The woman who had been plagued with the issue of blood had a faith that knew if she could but touch the hem of His garment, she would be healed.

That wasn't a blind faith, based on a whimsical hope.

The object of her faith was tangible. The Messiah was in the crowd. His Power to heal was present.

The result of her faith was a tangible reality. She had pressed in, and touched His garment, and she was made whole.

Heb 11:3 Through faith we understand that the worlds were framed by the word of God, so that things which are seen were not made of things which do appear.

We see the evidence of a Creator, and we understand that when God spoke, that which was not became a tangible reality.

Faith is understanding that One Greater than your circumstance is present.

When God created the heavens and the earth, the immaterial became material, and we can see the result of His Word that spoke those things into being.

Abraham's Faith rested in that One Who called those things which be not as though they were, and when He called them into being, *they were*.

There is a school of teachers who twist the Word of God, and say that *you* can call those things that be not as though they were. But the Word of God doesn't say that.

**Rom 4:16 Therefore it is of faith, that it might be by grace; to the end the promise might be sure to all the seed; not to that only which is of the law, but to that also which is of the faith of Abraham; who is the father of us all,
17 (As it is written, I have made thee a father of many nations,) before him whom he believed, even God, who quickeneth the dead, and calleth those things which be not as though they were.**

As is evident from the context, it is God who quickens (or brings to life) the dead, and who calls those things which be not as though they were, not Abraham, and not you. The truth is, you are not God.

While you are a child of God, you are a child of God through adoption.

An adopted child has the same privileges and rights as a natural born child. But they don't have the DNA of the natural child.

As an adopted child, you move from a state of utter poverty and hopelessness into a position of Provision and Promise. You moved from darkness to Light. You become an heir just as if you were a natural son or daughter, but your DNA makeup remains the same.

Abraham believed God, Who does the impossible. Abraham couldn't do the impossible. He could not speak things into existence, but He knew the One Who could, and he had confidence that He would. Faith in the Name of Jesus which is above every name in heaven or in earth, is sufficient for the problem at hand. Multiple Sclerosis is a name. Congestive heart failure is a name. The Name of Jesus is above those names.

The woman with the issue of blood beheld Jesus, Who had done the impossible, and she knew if she could but touch the hem of His garment, she would be made whole.

Great faith looks beyond the circumstance to the One Who is Greater than the circumstance.

Once the adopted child comprehends the fact that his or her Father's estate is theirs as well, they can walk in the assurance that whatsoever they ask according to their Father's Will, will be done.

If you are in Christ, and Christ is in you, you are an heir. The Will and the terms of your inheritance is written in the Bible.

You are not God, or "a god". You are flesh, just like Abraham was. But you can have the same faith as Abraham who believed in the only God Who brings the dead to life, and calls those things that be not as though they were.

You don't have to have faith in your faith.

You don't have to pretend like you are something you are not.

You don't have to confess until the confession materializes.

Faith is an unwavering *assurance* that goes beyond the natural reasoning.

No doctors could heal her. All they could do was take her money. Yet she *knew* this One not only could heal her, but what He had was free for the taking. She simply had to press in through the crowd.

Sometimes you have to press beyond that crowd of reasoning, doubt, and logic that tries to hinder your faith, and simply trust your Father. That means you have to unlearn a lot of what you have accepted as true, and trust God, and take Him at His Word.

If you can receive it, that takes a lot of pressure off you.

When Jesus was crucified, the leadership of the Jews mocked Him, and said **"Let Christ the King of Israel descend now from the cross, that we may see and believe. And they that were crucified with him reviled him"** (Mark 15:32).

"That we may see and believe". That is the difference between religion and faith. Religion consists of philosophical notions that may or may not be true. Today there are a lot of people who say "Well, that is *your* truth. *My* truth is different than yours". But for the Christian there is only One Truth, and that is found in the Word of God. His Name is Jesus. Faith accepts the Word of God as truth, and acts accordingly.

Faith acts and then sees the results. Religion and philosophy tells you "When I see results, I will act". But with that kind of attitude, you will never have the required faith to do the work of God.

Simply put, you have to *believe* you have authority before you can walk in authority.

Mar 13:32 But of that day and *that* hour knoweth no man, no, not the angels which are in heaven, neither the Son, but the Father.
33 Take ye heed, watch and pray: for ye know not when the time is.
34 *For the Son of man is* as a man taking a far journey, who left his house, and gave *authority*

to his servants, and to every man his work, and commanded the porter to watch.
35 Watch ye therefore: for ye know not when the master of the house cometh, at even, or at midnight, or at the cockcrowing, or in the morning:
36 Lest coming suddenly he find you sleeping.
37 And what I say unto you I say unto all, Watch.

This verse serves two purposes, the first of which is to assure those who serve the Lord that we have been given *authority* (verse 34). The second is that we have a responsibility to be found exercising that authority when Jesus comes back. Unfortunately a lot of those who are servants of God today are caught up in a slumber of unbelief.

What does exercising our authority entail? We have already looked at the passage in Mark 16:15-20; let's look at a few more verses which speak of the believer's authority:

Mar 3:14 And he ordained twelve, that they should be with him, and that he might send them forth to preach,
15 And to have power (AUTHORITY) to heal sicknesses, and to cast out devils:

Mar 6:7 And he called *unto him* the twelve, and began to send them forth by two and two; and gave them power (AUTHORITY) over unclean spirits;

The reader who is having a problem believing in his or her position of authority may well protest and say "Well, that was the disciples who he gave that authority to, not me." But read again in Mark 16, where we are told that *whosoever* believes in Him ◀ *will do these very same things.*

Joh 1:12 But as many as received him, to them gave he power (AUTHORITY) to become the sons of God, *even* to them that believe on his name:
13 Which were born, not of blood, nor of the will of the flesh, nor of the will of man, but of God.

Notes:

Mar 16:15 And he said unto them, Go ye into all the world, and preach the gospel to every creature.
16 He that believeth and is baptized shall be saved; but he that believeth not shall be damned.
17 And these signs shall follow them that believe; In my name shall they cast out devils; they shall speak with new tongues;
18 They shall take up serpents; and if they drink any deadly thing, it shall not hurt them; they shall lay hands on the sick, and they shall recover.

Have you received Him? Do you believe in Him? Then He has given you authority to walk as the Son of God walked.

Joh 14:12 Verily, verily, I say unto you, He that believeth on me, the works that I do shall he do also; and greater *works* than these shall he do; because I go unto my Father.

People today should be amazed at how sons and daughters of God walk in their God-given authority, just as they were amazed at how Jesus walked in His God-given Authority.

Mar 1:25 And Jesus rebuked him, saying, Hold thy peace, and come out of him.
26 And when the unclean spirit had torn him, and cried with a loud voice, he came out of him.
27 And they were all amazed, insomuch that they questioned among themselves, saying, What thing is this? what new doctrine is this? for with authority commandeth he even the unclean spirits, and they do obey him.

The Authority that comes from the Throne room of Heaven is no longer a new doctrine.

Jesus gave all believers that authority when He resurrected from the dead. Your authority includes the ability to act as an ambassador sent from the King of Heaven and earth, ministering healing, deliverance, salvation and forgiveness to those you encounter.

Mat 9:4 And Jesus knowing their thoughts said, Wherefore think ye evil in your hearts?
5 For whether is easier, to say, *Thy* sins be forgiven thee; or to say, Arise, and walk?
6 But that ye may know that the Son of man hath power (AUTHORITY) on earth to forgive sins, (then saith he to the sick of the palsy,) Arise, take up thy bed, and go unto thine house.
7 And he arose, and departed to his house.
8 But when the multitudes saw *it*, they marvelled, and glorified God, which had given such power (AUTHORITY) unto men.

Some Christians believe the lie that they are not worthy to be given such a privilege of being an ambassador of Christ. Paul, who referred to himself as the chief of all sinners received that authority from Christ when he was converted.

Act 26:16 But rise, and stand upon thy feet: for I have appeared unto thee for this purpose, to make thee a minister and a witness both of these things which thou hast seen, and of those things in the which I will appear unto thee;

17 Delivering thee from the people, and *from* the Gentiles, unto whom now I send thee,
18 To open their eyes, *and* to turn *them* from darkness to light, and *from* the power (AUTHORITY) of Satan unto God, that they may receive forgiveness of sins, and inheritance among them which are sanctified by faith that is in me.

If God bestowed that favor upon Paul, He will do the same for you.

As I pointed out earlier, Satan has Authority over those who are of the world.

Eph 2:1 And you *hath he quickened,* who were dead in trespasses and sins;
2 Wherein in time past ye walked according to the course of this world, according to the prince of the power (exousia) of the air, the spirit that now worketh in the children of disobedience:
3 Among whom also we all had our conversation in times past in the lusts of our flesh, fulfilling the desires of the flesh and of the mind; and were by nature the children of wrath, even as others.

It would be good for the disciple to call to mind the previous chapter of this book and the various temptations that entice ministers to abuse the authority that God has given them as representatives of His Kingdom. The degree to which you are conformed to the ways of this world will determine the degree of authority you have. Jesus said you cannot serve two masters. Jesus was totally committed to the Will of the Father. The apostles and the early Church was totally committed to the Will of the Father. The Holy Spirit has free reign to work in and through the life of the one who is surrendered to Him.

Impossible, you say? There are too many distractions in this world that prevent you from being committed to Christ to that degree? According to your Faith, so be it. 1 John 1:6 says we cannot have intimate fellowship with God if we walk in darkness. But if you walk in His Light (yielded to His Will), you can ask what you desire, and it will be given you. The truth is God has given us all things that pertain to life and godliness. You have the privilege of walking in the Authority of a child of the Most High God. It really is a matter of what *you* want in life.

2Pe 1:3 According as his divine power hath given unto us all things that *pertain* unto life and godliness, through the knowledge of him that hath called us to glory and virtue:
4 Whereby are given unto us exceeding great and precious promises: that by these ye might be partakers of the divine nature, having escaped the corruption that is in the world through lust.

Money and personal gain is usually at the root of all hindrances. Flee that temptation. Keep your eyes on Christ alone.

Act 8:18 And when Simon saw that through laying on of the apostles' hands the Holy Ghost was given, he offered them money,
19 Saying, Give me also this power (AUTHORITY), that on whomsoever I lay hands, he may receive the Holy Ghost.
20 But Peter said unto him, Thy money perish with thee, because thou hast thought that the gift of God may be purchased with money.
1Co 9:16 For though I preach the gospel, I have nothing to glory of: for necessity is laid upon me; yea, woe is unto me, if I preach not the gospel!
17 For if I do this thing willingly, I have a reward: but if against my will, a dispensation *of the gospel* is committed unto me.
18 What is my reward then? *Verily* that, when I preach the gospel, I may make the gospel of Christ without charge, that I abuse not my power (AUTHORITY) in the gospel.
19 For though I be free from all *men,* yet have I made myself servant unto all, that I might gain the more.

Eph 3:9 And to make all *men* see what *is* the fellowship of the mystery, which from the beginning of the world hath been hid in God, who created all things by Jesus Christ:
10 To the intent that now unto the principalities and powers (AUTHORITY) in heavenly *places* might be known by the church the manifold wisdom of God,

What does it mean to walk in a position of Authority for a Believer?
_____
_____
_____

What is the purpose of Authority?
_____
_____
_____

In Isaiah 61:1, we are told that the Lord had anointed Jesus to proclaim liberty to the captives. What is the primary meaning of that word "proclaim"? _____

How much Authority was Jesus given after His Resurrection? _____
_____

Who is qualified to walk in the Authority of the Kingdom of God? _____
_____

"Now then we are _____ for Christ" (2Co 5:20).

An _____ carries the _____ of the country he or she
represents.

What is the meaning of the word "accost"? _____

_____

When someone is accosted by another, what does that tell you about the
one that is doing the accosting? _____

_____

Biblical _____ Is The Key to Walking In _____

Give an example of how a Servant of God can accost the devil _____
_____
_____

According to Romans 4:17, Abraham had faith in _____, Who
_____and _____
_____

1Jn 4:4 Ye are of _____, little children, and have _____ them:
because _____ is he that is in you, than he that is _____.

1Jn 5:14 And this is the _____ that we have in him, that, if we ask
any thing _____, he heareth us:

15 And if we know that he hear us, whatsoever we ask, we _____ that
we have the petitions that we desired of him.

1Jn 5:4 For whatsoever is _____ overcometh the world: and
this is the victory that _____ the world, *even* our _____.

5 Who is he that _____the world, but he that
_____ Jesus is the _____?

What is the common theme in the letters to all the messengers of the seven churches in Revelation chapters 2 and 3? "He that
_____" receives the reward.

Application: Your assignment until the next session is to walk in the Authority that the Lord has called you to. Record some instances to share with others how that was done.

_____
_____
_____
_____
_____
_____
_____
_____
_____
_____
_____
_____
_____
_____
_____
_____
_____
_____
_____
_____
_____
_____
_____
_____
_____
_____
_____
_____
_____
_____
_____
_____
_____
_____
_____
_____

"I do not consecrate myself to be a missionary or a preacher. I consecrate myself to God to do His will where I am, be it in school, office, or kitchen, or wherever He may, in His wisdom, send me."

— Watchman Nee, The Normal Christian Life

Notes:

_____

Chapter 12
The Power Of Ministry

POWER AS DEFINED BY *FORCE* or *MIGHT*: *Dunamis*

Whereas Exousia speaks of authority, Dunamis speaks of force, or might. The word "dynamite" is illustrative of the power that defines dunamis. Dunamis is the stuff of miracles.

Mar 9:39 But Jesus said, Forbid him not: for there is no man which shall do a miracle (*DUNAMIS*) in my name, that can lightly speak evil of me.

Act 8:13 Then Simon himself believed also: and when he was baptized, he continued with Philip, and wondered, beholding the miracles (*DUNAMIS*) and signs which were done.

**Act 19:11 And God wrought special miracles (*DUNAMIS*) by the hands of Paul:
12 So that from his body were brought unto the sick handkerchiefs or aprons, and the diseases departed from them, and the evil spirits went out of them.**

1Co 12:10 To another the working of miracles (*DUNAMIS*); to another prophecy; to another discerning of spirits; to another *divers* kinds of tongues; to another the interpretation of tongues:

In several instances, *dunamis* is interpreted as "mighty works" when speaking of the miracles of Jesus.

Mat 11:23 And thou, Capernaum, which art exalted unto heaven, shalt be brought down to hell: for if the *mighty works*, which have been done in thee, had been done in Sodom, it would

have remained until this day. (See also Matt 13:54; Matt 14:2; Mark 6:2,5,14; Luke 19:37)

Before His Resurrection, the disciples ministered in the *Authority* they were given by Jesus.

Mat 10:1 And when he had called unto *him* his twelve disciples, he gave them power (EXOUSIA) *against* unclean spirits, to cast them out, and to heal all manner of sickness and all manner of disease.

The scope of the authority that the disciples had before the death, burial and resurrection of Christ *was limited* in that Jesus told them to only minister to those who were of the lost sheep of the house of Israel. During His earthly ministry, Jesus' mission was to reconcile Israel to God.

After His resurrection, Jesus declared that *all* authority was given to Him in Heaven and on earth.

If believers understood the scope and the significance of the authority they have over the works of the enemy because of the Name of Jesus, this world would be a different place today.

Just as Christ gave His disciples the authority to cast out unclean spirits, and to heal sickness and disease that afflicted the people Israel, every believer today has authority to cast out unclean spirits and to heal all manner of sickness in every person they encounter, because *all* authority in heaven and earth has been given to Christ.

But when authority is combined with the stuff of miracles (dunamis), the Kingdom of God advances with a force that cannot be stopped.

Dunamis may be described as the gun in the hand of the thief, but the police man who walks with the authority of the civil government and is armed with a weapon that he has become proficient at using, trumps the thief. He not only has *dunamis* power on his side, but he has the legal authority (*exousia*) to arrest or stop the thief and lock him away so he is no longer a threat to society.

Luk 4:36 And they were all amazed, and spake among themselves, saying, What a word *is* this! for with authority (Exousia) and power (Dunamis) he commandeth the unclean spirits, and they come out.

The Principle of Binding and Loosing

With authority and power comes the ability for the minister of the Gospel to Bind and Loose.

Bind:

Thayer Definition: G1210
δέω deō
1) to bind tie, fasten
1a) to bind, fasten with chains, to throw into chains1b) metaphorically
 Satan is said to bind a woman bent together by means of a demon, as his messenger, taking possession of the woman and preventing her from standing upright
1b2) to bind, put under obligation, of the law, duty etc.
1b2a) to be bound to one, a wife, a husband
1b3) to forbid, prohibit, declare to be illicit

Loose

Thayer Definition: G3089
λύω luō
1) to loose any person (or thing) tied or fastened
1a) bandages of the feet, the shoes
1b) of a husband and wife joined together by the bond of matrimony
1c) of a single man, whether he has already had a wife or has not yet married
2) to loose one bound, i.e. to unbind, release from bonds, set free
2a) of one bound up (swathed in bandages)
2b) bound with chains (a prisoner), discharge from prison, let go
3) to loosen, undo, dissolve, anything bound, tied, or compacted together
3a) an assembly, i.e. to dismiss, break up
3b) laws, as having a binding force, are likened to bonds
3c) to annul, subvert
3d) to do away with, to deprive of authority, whether by precept or act

**Mat 16:17 And Jesus answered and said unto him, Blessed art thou, Simon Barjona: for flesh and blood hath not revealed _it_ unto thee, but my Father which is in heaven.
18 And I say also unto thee, That thou art Peter, and upon this rock I will build my church; and the gates of hell shall not prevail against it.
19 And I will give unto thee the keys of the kingdom of heaven: and whatsoever thou shalt bind on earth shall be bound in heaven: and whatsoever thou shalt loose on earth shall be loosed in heaven.**

As a child of God, you have been given authority over demonic forces that are in this world.

If you don't understand the authority you have over the unclean spirits who have usurped the Authority of God, and if you don't understand the _Power_ that is at your disposal, then you won't be able to effectively walk in your Calling as a minister of the Gospel.

**Mat 12:28 But if I cast out devils by the Spirit of God, then the kingdom of God is come unto you.
29 Or else how can one enter into a strong man's house, and spoil his goods, except he first bind the strong man? and then he will spoil his house.
30 He that is not with me is against me; and he that gathereth not with me scattereth abroad.**

The Law of the Kingdom of God is on your side.

Principalities and powers are subject to you because of what Jesus Christ has accomplished through His death, burial and resurrection. _The child of God has been commissioned to further the Kingdom of God on this earth with Authority and Power to back it up._

Command that thing that is at work in that person's life to _stop_ in the Name of Jesus. "You foul demon, I bind you and your influence over this person in the Name of Jesus" are some powerful words, if the person who speaks those words understands and believes in the authority that they have been given to do so.

3e) to declare unlawful
3f) to loose what is compacted or built together, to break up, demolish, destroy
3g) to dissolve something coherent into parts, to destroy
3h) metaphorically, to overthrow, to do away with

Isa 58:6 *Is* not this the fast that I have chosen? to loose the bands of wickedness, to undo the heavy burdens, and to let the oppressed go free, and that ye break every yoke?

Mat 18:18 Verily I say unto you, Whatsoever ye shall bind on earth shall be bound in heaven: and whatsoever ye shall loose on earth shall be loosed in heaven.
9 Again I say unto you, That if two of you shall agree on earth as touching any thing that they shall ask, it shall be done for them of my Father which is in heaven.
20 For where two or three are gathered together in my name, there am I in the midst of them.

Notes:
_____
_____
_____
_____
_____
_____
_____
_____
_____
_____
_____
_____

But your authority isn't dependent on a formula or the "proper use of words".

Your authority is in Jesus Christ. You can tell a devil to "shut up in the Name of Jesus and come out of him or her", and you have effectively bound it from speaking, and loosed the person from the demon's hold.

**Mar 1:23 And there was in their synagogue a man with an unclean spirit; and he cried out,
24 Saying, Let *us* alone; what have we to do with thee, thou Jesus of Nazareth? art thou come to destroy us? I know thee who thou art, the Holy One of God.
25 And Jesus rebuked him, saying, Hold thy peace, and come out of him.
26 And when the unclean spirit had torn him, and cried with a loud voice, he came out of him.
27 And they were all amazed, insomuch that they questioned among themselves, saying, What thing is this? what new doctrine *is* this? for with authority commandeth he even the unclean spirits, and they do obey him.**

Luk 13:16 And ought not this woman, being a daughter of Abraham, whom Satan hath bound, lo, these eighteen years, be loosed from this bond on the sabbath day?

The principle of Binding and Loosing extends to ministering forgiveness to others.

There are so many people who are under condemnation for past sins in their lives. When you minister deliverance and salvation to someone, they must understand that not only have they been set free and saved; they must also know that they are *forgiven.*

As a child of God, you have the authority to loose those who have been under the weight of guilt and shame from their burden of sin, and to declare to the repentant heart that they are forgiven.

Mat 10:5 These twelve Jesus sent forth, and commanded them, saying, Go not into the way of the Gentiles, and into *any* city of the Samaritans enter ye not:
6 But go rather to the lost sheep of the house of Israel.
7 And as ye go, preach, saying, The kingdom of heaven is at hand.
8 Heal the sick, cleanse the lepers, raise the dead, cast out devils: freely ye have received, freely give.

Notes:

_____
_____
_____
_____
_____
_____
_____
_____
_____
_____
_____
_____
_____
_____
_____
_____
_____
_____
_____
_____
_____
_____

Joh 20:22 And when he had said this, he breathed on *them,* and saith unto them, Receive ye the Holy Ghost:
23 Whose soever sins ye remit, they are remitted unto them; *and* whose soever *sins* ye retain, they are retained.

What a responsibility and a privilege you have been given as an Ambassador for Christ!

Luk 9:1 Then he called his twelve disciples together, and gave them power and authority over all devils, and to cure diseases.
2 And he sent them to preach the kingdom of God, and to heal the sick.

At the risk of repeating myself, let me point out once again that Jesus gave His disciples power and authority over ALL devils, and to cure diseases. But the scope of their ministry was limited to God's Chosen people, the Jews. Jesus had instructed them not to go to the Gentiles, but only to the "lost sheep of Israel" (Matt 10:5).

These were people who knew God, or at least were taught and instructed in the ways of God.

After His Resurrection, and just before He ascended into heaven, He commissioned those same disciples to go into *all* the world to make disciples, and to teach them the things He had commanded them.

If you have been Born Again, you are a disciple. As a disciple, *you* should be taught that you have all power and authority over *all* devils, and are able to minister healing and deliverance to the sick and the oppressed.

Mat 28:18 And Jesus came and spake unto them, saying, All power (Authority) is given unto me in heaven and in earth.
19 Go ye therefore, and teach all nations, baptizing them in the name of the Father, and of the Son, and of the Holy Ghost:
20 Teaching them to observe all things whatsoever I have commanded you: and, lo, I am

with you alway, *even* unto the end of the world. Amen.

As a disciple, the anointing is upon you, *because* God has commissioned you to loose the captives from the prison Satan has them in.

"Sanctified Celebrities"

The way of the world is to look at people who are specially gifted or talented in some area as "unique" and someone who should be honored.

Only a few people become kings or presidents or some type of world leader.

Only a few people become billionaires, or corporate executives.

Only a few people invent things that impact the world.

Only a few people achieve fame because of their extraordinary accomplishments, whether they are good or bad.

And the rest of the people of the world are an anonymous mass of humanity whose lives are recorded on a tombstone as a dash between the date they are born and the date of their death. This is the way of the world.

And despite the admonition in Romans 12:1 that we who are in Christ are not to be conformed to the way of the world, we carry that same mentality as the rest of the world carries.

In the religious world of the church, we have the few who seem to have a special gift from God, and the rest of the masses remain anonymous and insignificant in the scheme of things.

But that is not the Way of Christianity. It is certainly the way of humanity, but not the Way of Christianity.

**1Co 1:26 For ye see your calling, brethren, how that not many wise men after the flesh, not many mighty, not many noble, *are called:*
27 But God hath chosen the foolish things of the world to confound the wise; and God hath chosen the weak things of the world to confound the things which are mighty;
28 And base things of the world, and things which are despised, hath God chosen, *yea,* and things which are not, to bring to nought things that are:
29 That no flesh should glory in his presence.**

Jesus chose coarse fishermen, a tax collector, women of ill repute and a thief to impact the world for God's Glory, *not* charismatic graduates from rabbinical seminaries.

The way of the religious world is to flock to the man or the woman who can preach the best, and to esteem such a one as a sanctified celebrity. Those who aspire to become "preachers" will generally emulate some "preacher" who had positively affected them someway. While we are called to be examples to others, and to follow the example of godly men and women, God hasn't called us to be spiritual clones of one another.

It is NOT the style of preaching that impacts lives for the Glory of God, it is the *anointing* that breaks the yoke. And yet one can generally tell what denomination a person belongs to by the way they preach the message. Jonathan Edwards had poor eyesight and held the script of his message "Sinners in the Hand of An Angry God" close to his face, and read it word for word, and the Holy Spirit convicted the hearts of the men and women who heard those words and sparked a revival that became known as the First Great Awakening.

Another preacher of that time, George Whitfield, declared the Word of God to the masses in a thunderous manner in which it is said thousands were able to hear the Word of God with no modern means of amplification.

As the minister of the Gospel learns to be sensitive to the leading of the Holy Spirit, his or her "style" of ministry will be such that will give Glory to God, and not to themselves.

While the disciples continued with Jesus, they were able to operate in the Power (dunamis) and Authority He had given them. After He had ascended to Heaven, he sent another Helper, the Comforter, or the Holy Spirit to be present with them and to work in them and through them with the Power of God manifesting in their ministry.

As long as they were with Christ, they were able to walk in dunamis power and authority over the enemy. But Jesus told them that once He departed from them after His Resurrection, there would be another Who would come in His place, the Comforter, the Holy Spirit who would lead them in the Way they should go. He wouldn't only be *with* them, but He would be *in* them, and would lead them in the Way of all Truth.

Joh 14:12 Verily, verily, I say unto you, He that believeth on me, the works that I do shall he do also; and greater *works* than these shall he do; because I go unto my Father.
13 And whatsoever ye shall ask in my name, that will I do, that the Father may be glorified in the Son.
14 If ye shall ask any thing in my name, I will do *it*.
15 If ye love me, keep my commandments.

16 And I will pray the Father, and he shall give you another Comforter, that he may abide with you for ever;

17 *Even* the Spirit of truth; whom the world cannot receive, because it seeth him not, neither knoweth him: but ye know him; for he dwelleth with you, and shall be in you.

18 I will not leave you comfortless: I will come to you.

19 Yet a little while, and the world seeth me no more; but ye see me: because I live, ye shall live also.

20 At that day ye shall know that I *am* in my Father, and ye in me, and I in you.

21 He that hath my commandments, and keepeth them, he it is that loveth me: and he that loveth me shall be loved of my Father, and I will love him, and will manifest myself to him.

Joh 14:25 These things have I spoken unto you, being *yet* present with you.

26 But the Comforter, *which is* the Holy Ghost, whom the Father will send in my name, he shall teach you all things, and bring all things to your remembrance, whatsoever I have said unto you.

Joh 15:26 But when the Comforter is come, whom I will send unto you from the Father, *even* the Spirit of truth, which proceedeth from the Father, he shall testify of me:

27 And ye also shall bear witness, because ye have been with me from the beginning.

Joh 16:7 Nevertheless I tell you the truth; It is expedient for you that I go away: for if I go not away, the Comforter will not come unto you; but if I depart, I will send him unto you.

8 And when he is come, he will reprove the world of sin, and of righteousness, and of judgment:

9 Of sin, because they believe not on me;

10 Of righteousness, because I go to my Father, and ye see me no more;

11 Of judgment, because the prince of this world is judged.

12 I have yet many things to say unto you, but ye cannot bear them now.

13 Howbeit when he, the Spirit of truth, is come, he will guide you into all truth: for he shall not speak of himself; but whatsoever he shall hear, *that* shall he speak: and he will shew you things to come.

14 He shall glorify me: for he shall receive of mine, and shall shew *it* unto you.

15 All things that the Father hath are mine: therefore said I, that he shall take of mine, and shall shew *it* unto you.

The Name of Jesus has Power or Authority over every Name. In the Name of Jesus, we can cast out devils, and do many wonderful works. But according to

Matthew 7:22, there are many who will do those things, but are not in right relationship with God. Jesus taught that after His Resurrection and return to the Father, He would send the Comforter or the Holy Spirit to His disciples, and they would be endued with Dunamis Power from on high to continue the Work that they were doing when He was present with Him. The Bible speaks of this as the Baptism of the Holy Spirit. Now instead of witnessing only to the Jews, the Gospel would be published to the Gentiles as well.

Act 1:8 But ye shall receive power (dunamis), after that the Holy Ghost is come upon you: and ye shall be witnesses unto me both in Jerusalem, and in all Judaea, and in Samaria, and unto the uttermost part of the earth.

It is through the Baptism of the Holy Spirit that Mark 16:15-18 would become a reality:

Mar 16:15 And he said unto them, Go ye into all the world, and preach the gospel to every creature.
16 He that believeth and is baptized shall be saved; but he that believeth not shall be damned.
17 And these signs shall follow them that believe; In my name shall they cast out devils; they shall speak with new tongues;
18 They shall take up serpents; and if they drink any deadly thing, it shall not hurt them; they shall lay hands on the sick, and they shall recover.

It is through the Baptism of the Holy Spirit that the Gifts spoken of in 1 Cor 12, 13, and 14 are given. As we will see later, the Gifts are given primarily for the edification of the Church.

Jesus would be no longer there to personally teach and guide and encourage the disciples in their witness to the world. After His death, they were scattered because of fear of what would happen to them. But after the indwelling of the Holy Spirit came on Pentecost, He was present with them again, and they were given a boldness to be His Witnesses throughout the world.

His Name still carries Authority to preach the Gospel and to cast out demons and to lay hands on the sick and see them recover. His Presence through the indwelling Holy Spirit enables us to manifest His dunamis miracle working Power to an unbelieving world.

The Baptism of the Holy Spirit is given so we can be empowered and emboldened to continue the Work that Christ had started with His disciples.

Act 4:29 And now, Lord, behold their threatenings: and grant unto thy servants, that with all boldness they may speak thy word,

30 By stretching forth thine hand to heal; and that signs and wonders may be done by the name of thy holy child Jesus.

31 And when they had prayed, the place was shaken where they were assembled together; and they were all filled with the Holy Ghost, and they spake the word of God with boldness.

32 And the multitude of them that believed were of one heart and of one soul: neither said any *of them* that ought of the things which he possessed was his own; but they had all things common.

33 And with great power gave the apostles witness of the resurrection of the Lord Jesus: and great grace was upon them all.

34 Neither was there any among them that lacked: for as many as were possessors of lands or houses sold them, and brought the prices of the things that were sold,

35 And laid *them* down at the apostles' feet: and distribution was made unto every man according as he had need.

According to Acts 1:8, what is the primary purpose of being baptized with the Holy Spirit? _____

Before His _____, the disciples ministered primarily in the _____ they were given by Jesus.

The scope of their ministry was _____ to the people of _____

After the resurrection of Jesus, the disciples were told to wait in _____ until they were endued with _____ from on high.

1Co 1:26 For ye see your _____, brethren, how that not many _____ after the _____, not many _____, not many _____, *are called:*

27 But God hath chosen the _____ of the _____ to _____ the wise; and God hath chosen the _____ of the world to _____ the things which are _____;

28 And _____ of the world, and things which are _____, hath God _____, *yea,* and things _____, to bring to nought things that are:

29 That _____ should _____ in his _____.

Is there any reason God could not use you to further His Kingdom here on earth? _____

Practical Application:

Write down some testimonies of how you applied your Authority to demonstrate the Dunamis Power that is in you between now and the next session:

_____

_____
_____
_____
_____
_____
_____
_____
_____
_____
_____
_____
_____
_____
_____
_____
_____
_____
_____
_____

Chapter 13
Taking Dominion

We are not sent to minister to a congregation and be content if we keep things going. We are sent to make war and to stop short of nothing but the subjugation of the world to the sway of the Lord Jesus.

-William Booth

G2904

κράτος kratos

Thayer Definition:

1) force, strength
2) power, might: mighty with great power
2a) a mighty deed, a work of power
3) dominion

G2963

κυριότης kuriotēs

Thayer Definition:

1) dominion, power, lordship

2) in the NT: one who possesses dominion

Notes:

_____
_____
_____
_____
_____
_____
_____
_____
_____
_____
_____

POWER AS DEFINED BY DOMINION (Kratos) or the Governing Authority of Christ.

Dunamis is a power that can operate through the believer as he or she is yielded to the Holy Spirit. Kratos, or "dominion", is the Power that only comes from the One Who reigns supreme over all. The devil used to have *kratos* over death. But Christ did away with his dominion.

Heb 2:14 Forasmuch then as the children are partakers of flesh and blood, he also himself likewise took part of the same; that through death he might destroy him that had the power (*kratos*) of death, that is, the devil;

Eph 1:19 And what *is* the exceeding greatness of his power (Dunimis) to us-ward who believe, according to the working of his mighty power (Kratos),
20 Which he wrought in Christ, when he raised him from the dead, and set *him* at his own right hand in the heavenly *places*,
21 Far above all principality, and *power* (exousia - authority), and *might* (dunamis - miracle working power), and *dominion* (kuriotes - one who possesses dominion), and every name that is named, not only in this world, but also in that which is to come:

Before we go any farther, we should look at the word translated above in verse 21 as "dominion". It is a different word than "kratos", which this chapter will primarily deal with. This word is kuriotes, or "lordship" and speaks of one who possesses dominion over someone or some place.

A governor, a king or a president would be described as one who walks in the power of *Kuriotes*.

A good illustration of this can be found in reading Jude, where we see that there are those who despise *kuriotes, and speak evil of dignities.* The next verse speaks of Michael the archangel, who did not bring a railing accusation against the devil (who walks in the power of kuriotes - he is acknowledged as the *god* of this age in 2nd Corinthians 4:4), but instead, used his *authority* which he had in the Name of Christ:

Jud 1:8 Likewise also these *filthy* dreamers defile the flesh, despise dominion, and speak evil of dignities.
9 Yet Michael the archangel, when contending with the devil he disputed about the body of Moses, durst not bring against him a railing accusation, but said, The Lord rebuke thee.

There are many who are in ministry who talk about the devil as if he is some chump that has no power. They say things like the devil is some little insignificant dumb imp who can do nothing against a child of God. They say that he is like a toothless lion, all roar and no bite. If that was true, there would have been no reason for Peter to warn the Body of Christ against the dangers of the devil.

1Pe 5:8 Be sober, be vigilant; because your adversary the devil, as a roaring lion, walketh about, seeking whom he may devour:

Toothless lions can't devour anyone.

Don't let anyone deceive you. Satan is armed and dangerous. And he is not looking for someone to gum to death. He is looking to devour those who are unprepared to withstand him.

While we do have all authority over the enemy, that authority comes from Christ, and *not* from ourselves.

It is important for the minister of the Gospel to understand that Jesus said we cannot serve two masters. If we are embracing the things of Satan's domain, or compromising in our walk as Christians, we are on his turf, and cannot hope to have authority over him.

Mat 6:23 But if thine eye be evil, thy whole body shall be full of darkness. If therefore the light that is in thee be darkness, how great *is* that darkness!
24 No man can serve two masters: for either he will hate the one, and love the other; or else he will hold to the one, and despise the other. Ye cannot serve God and mammon.

Notes:

The minister who is continually pursuing after the wealth of this world, and is continually trying to figure out how to get more money to "finance his ministry" is a slave of that money. Jesus said you cannot serve God and mammon.

At this point in our studies, we should realize by now that faith in God, and not faith in our abilities is what will see us through.

Likewise, the minister who is caught up in pornography or lust or given to anger or covetousness is a servant of sin as well, and cannot be effective in ministry as long as his or her walk is compromised.

Joh 8:34 Jesus answered them, Verily, verily, I say unto you, Whosoever committeth sin is the servant of sin.
35 And the servant abideth not in the house for ever: *but* the Son abideth ever.

If you are caught up in sin, you can't hope to deliver others who are in sin. You can't cast out devils if there is a devil living inside of you. Authority and the Power of Christ only work effectively if you are walking in obedience to Christ.

While the Gifts and the Calling of God are without repentance, we can find ourselves outside of the Will of God, and ineffective against the kingdom of darkness.

Rom 6:16 Know ye not, that to whom ye yield yourselves servants to obey, his servants ye are to whom ye obey; whether of sin unto death, or of obedience unto righteousness?
17 But God be thanked, that ye were the servants of sin, but ye have obeyed from the heart that form of doctrine which was delivered you.
18 Being then made free from sin, ye became the servants of righteousness.

The key to effectively working as a minister of God, is to know *who you are* in Christ.

Notes:

Col 1:12 Giving thanks unto the Father, which hath made us meet to be partakers of the inheritance of the saints in light:
13 Who hath delivered us from the power of darkness, and hath translated us into the kingdom of his dear Son:

Lest you become plagued with thoughts of unworthiness to be able to stand in the Presence of God or to serve Him in ministry because of your failures and your treason toward the Kingdom of God, or are unable to boldly approach His Throne of Grace with an assurance that He would hear you, take heart!

He has begun a good work in you.

When you bowed your knee to the Name of Jesus, and called upon Him to save you from your sins, and to be the Lord of your life, you became a child of God. He qualified you to partake of the inheritance that a child of the Most High God, as a seed of Abraham would be privileged to partake in.

And what He has begun in you, He will be faithful to complete it.

He has delivered you from the authority of darkness that once ruled over your life, and has removed you from the Kingdom of this world into the Kingdom of God.

You simply need to stop giving the devil authority and begin to walk in the Authority of Christ.

He has *redeemed* you. He has paid for Your sins. He has done the Work you could not do.

The devil can no longer stand before the Throne of God and accuse you of who you once were and what you have done. The Throne of Grace is *yours* to approach, and the devil is nowhere to be found there. Now all he can do is tempt you and whisper in your ear words of discouragement, defeat, and doubt.

Oh, Christian, were you to understand the inheritance that is yours *now* in this life, and the

Joh 15:1 I am the true vine, and my Father is the husbandman.
2 Every branch in me that beareth not fruit he taketh away: and every *branch* that beareth fruit, he purgeth it, that it may bring forth more fruit.
3 Now ye are clean through the word which I have spoken unto you.
4 Abide in me, and I in you. As the branch cannot bear fruit of itself, except it abide in the vine; no more can ye, except ye abide in me.
5 I am the vine, ye *are* the branches: He that abideth in me, and I in him, the same bringeth forth much fruit: for without me ye can do nothing.
6 *If* a man abide not in me, he is cast forth as a branch, and is withered; and men gather them, and cast *them* into the fire, and they are burned.
7 *If* ye abide in me, and my words abide in you, ye shall ask what ye will, and it shall be done unto you.
8 Herein is my Father glorified, that ye bear much fruit; so shall ye be my disciples.
9 As the Father hath loved me, so have I loved you: continue ye in my love.
10 *If* ye keep my commandments, ye shall abide in my love; even as I have kept my Father's commandments, and abide in his love.
11 These things have I spoken unto you, that my joy might remain in you.
12 This is my commandment, That ye love one another, as I have loved you.

limitless depths of the riches of the Kingdom of God, you would realize that you have been but a prodigal feeding from the slop of this world's husks, wallowing through life, rather than walking as a child of the Most High God.

Turn a deaf ear to the devil's lies, and begin to walk as a child of God should walk. Submit to God. Resist the devil, and he will truly flee from you. God's Mercies are *new* every morning. What you did yesterday has no bearing on what you will do today, if you simply repent.

What you *were* is *NOT* who you *are*.

Col 1:21 And you, that were sometime alienated and enemies in your mind by wicked works, yet now hath he reconciled
22 In the body of his flesh through death, to present you holy and unblameable and unreproveable in his sight:
23 If ye continue in the faith grounded and settled, and be not moved away from the hope of the gospel, which ye have heard, and which was preached to every creature which is under heaven; whereof I Paul am made a minister;...

The word "*if*" is a big word. It carries with it a condition to the Promises of God. Here, we see that you will be holy, and unblameable and unreproveable in the sight of God *if* you continue in the faith. The implication is if we don't remain in the faith we won't be holy, unblameable, or unreproveable in the sight of God.

It is remaining in Christ that brings forth fruit, because of Christ working in us and through us. Notice in the dialogue of Jesus to His disciples in John 15 (in the sidebar on this and the next page) how many times Jesus used the word "if".

IF we remain in His Will, we will bear much fruit. That is a promise that you can hold on to. Just as Jesus came to do the Will of the Father, and never deviated from that Purpose, so we too are to do the

13 Greater love hath no man than this, that a man lay down his life for his friends.
14 Ye are my friends, *if* ye do whatsoever I command you.

Jud 1:20 But ye, beloved, building up yourselves on your most holy faith, praying in the Holy Ghost,
21 Keep yourselves in the love of God, looking for the mercy of our Lord Jesus Christ unto eternal life.

Notes:

_____
_____
_____
_____
_____
_____
_____
_____

Rev 11:15 And the seventh angel sounded; and there were great voices in heaven, saying, The kingdoms of this world are become *the kingdoms* of our Lord, and of his Christ; and he shall reign for ever and ever.

_____
_____
_____
_____
_____
_____
_____
_____
_____
_____
_____
_____
_____
_____

Will of the Father through the Work of Jesus within us.

As we abide in Jesus, we are able to walk in His Authority (exousia) with confidence. We are able to operate in His Miracle working Power (dunamis) with confidence. We are able to effectively function as ambassadors of His Kingdom, establishing the Power of His Governing Authority (kuriotais) in the earth, thereby taking Dominion for the Kingdom of God.

As we *abide* in Him, we *will* bear much fruit for the Glory of the Kingdom of God.

If you are reading this book, I believe it is safe to assume that your heart's desire is to fulfill the Will of God in your life, and that you view yourself as a disciple of Christ.

There are two kingdoms at work in this life; the kingdoms of this world, and the Kingdom of God. Satan has dominion over the kingdoms of this world. God has the ultimate dominion, and He uses His people to expand His Kingdom in this world.

Kratos speaks of political power, especially of sovereignty. Christ's Work continues today through His people who walk in the revelation of their Calling, advancing the Kingdom of God and His Dominion in this earth. It is important to understand that darkness cannot overtake the light.

A lot of pulpiteers would have you to believe that the darkness is greater than the Light and there is no hope for this world. You need to get away from that mindset. The light dispels the darkness, not the other way around. An eclipse happens because the moon gets between the sun and the earth. Darkness prevails when the world gets between you and the Son. Jesus said we are the light of the world. If we don't hide it, it will spread and overtake the darkness.

You will never see the Power of God at work in your

Notes:

ministry unless you step out in faith and do what you have been told.

Jude instructs us to "build ourselves up on our most holy faith." Sometimes when a carpenter is building a house, he will bend a few nails before he can get the boards together. He doesn't stop just because he bent the nail. He pulls that faulty nail and attempts to drive a new one home. If that one bends, he gets another one until he succeeds. Eventually he will get more proficient at driving nails.

If you lay your hands on a sick person and they don't recover, do it again. If there still is no change, do it again. Jesus said you could do it, so do it. He is the Truth. Have the faith to step out and see it through. If you continually fail, don't fall into condemnation. Check your faith. Examine yourself to see if you are in the faith. There are things (the world) that will hinder the Power of God from manifesting itself through you. For the disciples, it was that they had "little faith".

Maybe you need to regroup and engage in some serious prayer and fasting before the Lord, seeking His Face as to what the hindrance could be. But whatever the case may be, *don't give up.* If you fail a hundred times, the 101st time may be the one.

The Word of God says that we are changed from glory to glory into the image of Christ. The more we walk in obedience to His Commission, the more we begin to act like Him, and to do what He did.

The more yielded we are to His Will, the more the Holy Spirit is able to work in us and through us to further the Kingdom of God and dispel the kingdom of darkness in this world.

2Co 3:18 But we all, with open face beholding as in a glass the glory of the Lord, are changed into the same image from glory to glory, *even* as by the Spirit of the Lord.

This book is instructional and informational. It is designed to encourage the believer to step out of their comfort zone and into the Calling the Lord has called them to. But the believer has to step beyond the information, and walk in the application. You need to get out of the boat before you can hope to walk on the water! A baby doesn't walk the first time he attempts it. More often than not the learning process involves failing before success.

Brother William is the founder of The Elijah Challenge. He travels the world teaching the authority of the believer. He has some excellent resources for those who want to learn more about the practical application of walking in the Authority of the believer, and to see the Kingdom of God advanced through preaching the Gospel and confirming it with signs following. I would encourage the reader to go to his website and learn what he has to teach the disciple of Christ.

In 2010 I had the privilege of inviting him to teach the Body of Christ in Vicksburg, Mississippi. At the time I was having a degree of success in seeing people healed and delivered, but something that Brother William taught brought new revelation to me, and with it greater effectiveness.

William recounted the story of when Jesus cursed the fig tree on His way into Jerusalem, and how the disciples were amazed the next day on their way out of Jerusalem to find the fig tree withered.

Mar 11:19 And when even was come, he went out of the city.
20 And in the morning, as they passed by, they saw the fig tree dried up from the roots.
21 And Peter calling to remembrance saith unto him, Master, behold, the fig tree which thou cursedst is withered away.
22 And Jesus answering saith unto them, Have faith in God.
23 For verily I say unto you, That whosoever shall say unto this mountain, Be thou removed, and be thou cast into the sea; and shall not doubt in his heart, but shall believe that those things which he saith shall come to pass; he shall have whatsoever he saith.

Notes:

_____
_____
_____
_____
_____
_____
_____
_____
_____
_____
_____
_____
_____

G5547
Χριστός Christos
Thayer Definition:
Christ = "anointed"
1) Christ was the Messiah, the Son of God
2) anointed
Part of Speech: adjective

G5546
Χριστιανός
Christianos
Thayer Definition:
1) Christian, a follower of Christ
Part of Speech: noun proper masculine
A Related Word by Thayer's/Strong's Number:
from G5547

Heb 13:8 Jesus Christ the same yesterday, and to day, and for ever.

24 Therefore I say unto you, What things soever ye desire, when ye pray, believe that ye receive *them,* and ye shall have *them.*

The Greek of verse 22 would be more properly interpreted as "**Have faith *of* God**". God's Faith creates. God's Faith heals. God's Faith delivers. With God, nothing is impossible. We are the temple of the Holy Spirit, Who is God dwelling inside us.

It is not our holiness or our ability that accomplishes the miraculous. It is Christ in us.

If you would like to know more about Brother William's ministry you can find it online at: iTheElijahChallenge .org

The Anointing That Breaks the Yoke

I realize that we have already covered much of this, but it is essential that the disciple gets what is being said. Sometimes repetition is the best teacher.

Christ wasn't Jesus' last name. It was a term that described Who He was. "The Christ" referred to the Messiah, the anointed One. In and of itself, the word meant "anointed". Samuel anointed Saul and then later David as kings of Israel. Jesus was anointed of God as the Messiah Who would come and save His people from their sins.

We have been anointed as His Kings and Priests (Rev. 1:5). We are not Christ, but we are *Christians,* followers of Christ who walk in that anointing.

Having been anointed as a king, the individual Christian should walk in the authority (exousia) and dominion (kratos) that a king possesses. As a Priest, he or she can walk in the divine Power (dunamis) that a priest is given as a representative (ambassador) of God.

But simply knowing that is not enough. I can know that I inherited ten million dollars, and it is in the bank waiting for me to tap into it, but unless I actually act on that knowledge, the ten million

Notes:

dollars is of no use to me.

The Bible speaks of our inheritance in Christ. As *Christians* we have access to all that is Christ's. The question really is whether we believe what God has Promised, or if we believe the words of those who say those promises are not for us today.

The Bible warns us that in the last days there would be those who had a form of godliness, but who deny the power thereof.

We read that Jesus Christ is the same today as He was yesterday and forever. He is unchanging. His Word is unchanging. He is the Word.

Mar 16:14 Afterward he appeared unto the eleven as they sat at meat, and upbraided them with their unbelief and hardness of heart, because they believed not them which had seen him after he was risen.
15 And he said unto them, Go ye into all the world, and preach the gospel to every creature.
16 He that believeth and is baptized shall be saved; but he that believeth not shall be damned.
17 And these signs shall follow them that believe; In my name shall they cast out devils; they shall speak with new tongues;
18 They shall take up serpents; and if they drink any deadly thing, it shall not hurt them; they shall lay hands on the sick, and they shall recover.

If you have the Faith of God, you will ask anything in Christ's Name, and it will be done. God spoke before it was, but when He spoke it came into being. That God dwells within you through the Holy Spirit. His anointing is in you. You are not *the Christ,* but you are a *Christian,* an anointed one.

Mk 11:24 Therefore I say unto you, What things soever ye desire, when ye pray, believe that ye receive *them,* and ye shall have *them.*

Filled With the Fullness of God

Eph 3:14 For this cause I bow my knees unto the Father of our Lord Jesus Christ,
15 Of whom the whole family in heaven and earth is named,
16 That he would grant you, according to the riches of his glory, to be strengthened with might by his Spirit in the inner man;
17 That Christ may dwell in your hearts by faith; that ye, being rooted and grounded in love,
18 May be able to comprehend with all saints what *is* the breadth, and length, and depth, and height;
19 And to know the love of Christ, which passeth knowledge, that ye might be filled with all the fulness of God.

The phrase "*that ye might be filled with all the fullness of God*" is not merely a rhetorical saying. That phrase was written with purpose and significance for those who can comprehend and who will respond to Christ's Will for their lives.

What is significant for the minister of God to understand is that we see elsewhere that Christ was filled with all the fullness of God, and now Paul is telling us that we also can be filled with the fullness of God.

Col 1:19 For it pleased *the Father* that in him *(in Christ)* should all fulness dwell;

Col 2:9 For in him *(Christ)* dwelleth all the fulness of the Godhead bodily.

Eph 3:19 And to know the love of Christ, which passeth knowledge, that ye might be filled with all the fulness of God.

To a religious mind, the unspoken (as yet) ramifications of where this line of thought may be taking us would be seen as bordering on heresy.

Notes:

_____
_____
_____
_____
_____
_____
_____
_____
_____
_____
_____
_____
_____
_____
_____
_____

198

G4138

πλήρωμα plērōma *play'-ro-mah*

From G4137; *repletion* or *completion*, that is, (subjectively) what *fills* (as contents, supplement, copiousness, multitude), or (objectively) what is *filled* (as container, performance, period): - which is put in to fill up, piece that filled up, fulfilling, full, fulness.

G4137
πληρόω plēroō *play-ro'-o*

From G4134; to *make replete*, that is, (literally) to *cram* (a net), *level* up (a hollow), or (figuratively) to *furnish* (or *imbue, diffuse, influence*), *satisfy, execute* (an office), *finish* (a period or task), *verify* (or *coincide* with a prediction), etc.: - accomplish, X after, (be) complete, end, expire, fill (up), fulfil, (be, make) full (come), fully preach, perfect, supply.

Yet the Word of God plainly states that we ourselves can be filled with *all* the fullness of God, just as Christ was.

Jesus Himself declared that those who believe in Him would be able to do the same things He did and even greater things. Religion tries to explain those things away, because religion cannot truly comprehend the things of God.

Religion consists of dead works, philosophical musings, and little faith, and as we have seen, little faith gets few results.

Colossians 2:10 confirms what Paul wrote in Ephesians 3:19:

Col 2:10 And ye are *complete* in him, which is the head of all principality and power:

Let's look at this in context with the preceding verses:

Col 2:8 Beware lest any man spoil you through philosophy and vain deceit, after the tradition of men, after the rudiments of the world, and not after Christ.
9 For in him dwelleth all the fulness of the Godhead bodily.
10 And ye are complete in him, which is the head of all principality and power:

Verse 8 says "Beware". Basically, Paul is saying "don't let anyone fool you through their philosophical musings that they derive from their carnal understanding."

Don't let your faith get stagnated in religion. The word "spoil" in verse 8 means to lead one away from the Truth, or to rob someone.

← The minister of God needs to understand that in Christ, all the fullness (*pleroma - Strong's 4138*) of the Godhead dwells. And the word "complete" (*pleroo - Strong's 4137*) in the next verse is a variation of the same word translated as "fullness" in verse 9.

Notes:

Don't miss this:

Just as it pleased God that in Christ should all His fullness dwell, *it also pleases God that the fullness of Christ should dwell in you through His Holy Spirit.*

Just as the fullness of the Godhead dwelt in Christ bodily, the fullness of Christ dwells in *you.*

You *are* the temple of the Holy Spirit. The Holy Spirit dwells within you. God wants to work in and through you. As you yield to Him, He is able to accomplish His Will in this world.

He has delivered you from the authority of darkness that once ruled over your life, and has removed you from the kingdom of this world into the Kingdom of God.

He has *redeemed* you. He has paid for Your sins. He has done the Work you could not do. The devil can no longer stand before the Throne of God and accuse you of who you were - the Throne of Grace is *yours* to approach, and the devil is nowhere to be found there. Now all he can do is tempt you and whisper in your ear words of discouragement and defeat, and doubt.

Oh, Christian, were you to understand the inheritance that is yours NOW in this life, and the limitless depths of the riches of the Kingdom of God, you would realize that you have been but a prodigal feeding from the slop of this world's husks, wallowing through life, rather than walking as a child of the Most High God.

Turn a deaf ear to the devil's lies, and begin to walk as a child of God should walk. What you were is *not* who you are, if Christ dwells in you through the Holy Spirit.

**Col 1:21 And you, that were sometime alienated and enemies in your mind by wicked works, yet now hath he reconciled
22 In the body of his flesh through death, to present you holy and unblameable and unreproveable in his sight:**

Joh 15:16 Ye have not chosen me, but I have chosen you, and ordained you, that ye should go and bring forth fruit, and *that* your fruit should remain: that whatsoever ye shall ask of the Father in my name, he may give it you.

Notes:

_____
_____
_____
_____
_____
_____
_____
_____
_____
_____
_____
_____
_____
_____
_____
_____
_____
_____
_____
_____
_____
_____
_____
_____
_____
_____
_____
_____
_____
_____
_____
_____

23 If ye continue in the faith grounded and settled, and be not moved away from the hope of the gospel, which ye have heard, and which was preached to every creature which is under heaven; whereof I Paul am made a minister;

Paul's mission was that he would not only preach the Gospel, but also that through his ministry, all men would understand the *Authority* and the *Power* that is theirs in Christ.

It is because of what Christ accomplished on the cross that we can have boldness and confidence to access the Throne of Grace for all that our work for the Kingdom of God requires.

We can do that because of Christ, Who dwells within us through the Holy Spirit. It is *God at work in us, and not us who accomplishes the furtherance of the Kingdom.* Our part is to yield to Him so He can use us effectively in His Kingdom here on earth.

Eph 3:9 And to make all *men* see what *is* the fellowship of the mystery, which from the beginning of the world hath been hid in God, who created all things by Jesus Christ:
10 To the intent that now unto the principalities and powers in heavenly *places* might be known by the church the manifold wisdom of God,
11 According to the eternal purpose which he purposed in Christ Jesus our Lord:
12 In whom we have boldness and access with confidence by the faith of him.

Paul prayed that Christians would understand the Power of God that is at our disposal.

Col 1:9 For this cause we also, since the day we heard *it,* do not cease to pray for you, and to desire that ye might be filled with the knowledge of his will in all wisdom and spiritual understanding;
10 That ye might walk worthy of the Lord unto all pleasing, being fruitful in every good work, and increasing in the knowledge of God;

Notes:

11 Strengthened with all might (*Dunamis*), according to his glorious power (*Kratos*), unto all patience and longsuffering with joyfulness;
12 Giving thanks unto the Father, which hath made us meet to be partakers of the inheritance of the saints in light:
13 Who hath delivered us from the power (*Exousia*) of darkness, and hath translated *us* into the kingdom of his dear Son:
14 In whom we have redemption through his blood, *even* the forgiveness of sins:
15 Who is the image of the invisible God, the firstborn of every creature

Oh, that believers would *UNDERSTAND* the Power and Authority that is theirs! That Power and Authority is *your inheritance* as a believer in Christ, as a child of the Most High God Who has *ALL* dominion (*Kratos*) over *all* things.

But we must be single mindedly about the Business of the Kingdom of God, if we are to walk in the Power and Authority that God has ordained for us.

Jesus said we can't serve two masters. It is when we become single minded for the Kingdom of God, that God can use us most effectively.

Repent of your affection for the things of this world. Become single mindedly concerned with living for the furtherance of the Kingdom of God. If you do not allow yourself to get caught up in covetousness, lust, idolatry, jealousy, or those other enticements of the world, you will be able to effectively further the Kingdom of God.

Don't allow your carnal mind to try to explain it away. Begin to exercise that authority that is yours in Christ. You need to get out of your comfortable pew in your church, and go forth and proclaim the Good News of the Kingdom of God. Heal the sick. Cast out devils. Raise the dead. You will never see any of this happening in your life until you begin to apply it to your life.

Jud 1:24 Now unto him that is able to keep you from falling, and to present you faultless before the presence of his glory with exceeding joy,
25 To the only wise God our Saviour, be glory and majesty, dominion (kratos) and power (exousia), both now and ever. Amen

Notes:

_____
_____
_____
_____
_____
_____
_____
_____
_____
_____
_____
_____
_____
_____
_____
_____
_____
_____
_____
_____
_____
_____
_____
_____
_____
_____
_____
_____
_____
_____
_____
_____
_____
_____

At the risk of being accused of being redundant, let me encourage you now to reread Colssians 2:8-10:

Col 2:8 Beware lest any man spoil you through philosophy and vain deceit, after the tradition of men, after the rudiments of the world, and not after Christ.
9 For in him dwelleth all the fulness of the Godhead bodily.
10 *And ye are complete in him*, which is the head of all principality and power:

What does it mean when we are told that we are *complete* in Him?

_____
_____
_____
_____

Col 2:8 Beware lest any man _____ you through _____ and vain _____, after the _____ of men, after the _____ of the world, and not after _____.

9 For in him dwelleth all the _____ of the Godhead bodily.

10 And ye are _____ in him, which is the head of all principality and power:

What should you do if you lay hands on a sick person and they don't recover?

_____
_____
_____
_____
_____
_____

What is the meaning of "Christ"?

_____
_____

_____

_____

What does it mean to be a "Christian"?_____

_____

_____

In your own words, what is the difference between having faith _in_ God, and the Faith _of_ God?

_____

_____

If you are in a group setting, make this a point of discussion with the group.

> "Men will trust in God no further than they know Him; and they cannot be in the exercise of faith in Him one ace further than they have a sight of His fulness and faithfulness in exercise."
>
> — Jonathan Edwards, The Religious Affections

Notes:

_____
_____
_____
_____
_____
_____
_____
_____
_____
_____
_____
_____
_____
_____
_____
_____
_____
_____
_____
_____
_____
_____
_____
_____
_____
_____
_____
_____
_____
_____

CHAPTER 14
Dominionism.
Biblical or not?

IN SOME CHRISTIAN CIRCLES, there is actually a pretty large split over the concept of "Dominion theology", and whether it is valid or not.

Some people refer to Dominionism as "Kingdom Now" theology, and if you were to ask me whether I believe in "Dominionism" or "Kingdom Now", I would have to tell you unequivocally that I do.

Of course, I believe there would have to be some caveats with that statement. I will get to those caveats later. The more relevant question would be "are my beliefs in line with what is commonly accepted as 'Kingdom Now' theology in today's world?" And I would have to answer, "Yes", and "No".

It is my firm conviction that God's original intent was to give man dominion over all that He created in the beginning.

Gen 1:26 And God said, Let us make man in our image, after our likeness: and let them have dominion over the fish of the sea, and over the fowl of the air, and over the cattle, and over all the earth, and over every creeping thing that creepeth upon the earth.

Psa 8:4 What is man, that thou art mindful of him? and the son of man, that thou visitest him?
5 For thou hast made him a little lower than the angels, and hast crowned him with glory and honour.
6 Thou madest him to have dominion over the works of thy hands; thou hast put all things under his feet:
7 All sheep and oxen, yea, and the beasts of the field;
8 The fowl of the air, and the fish of the sea, and

whatsoever passeth through the paths of the seas.
9 O LORD our Lord, how excellent is thy name in all the earth!

Psa 145:13 Thy kingdom is an everlasting kingdom, and thy dominion endureth throughout all generations.

God foretold the Dominion of the coming Son of Man:

Dan 7:13 I saw in the night visions, and, behold, one like the Son of man came with the clouds of heaven, and came to the Ancient of days, and they brought him near before him.
14 And there was given him dominion, and glory, and a kingdom, that all people, nations, and languages, should serve him: his dominion is an everlasting dominion, which shall not pass away, and his kingdom that which shall not be destroyed.

He said that the Dominion would be given to His saints:

Dan 7:27 And the kingdom and dominion, and the greatness of the kingdom under the whole heaven, shall be given to the people of the saints of the most High, whose kingdom is an everlasting kingdom, and all dominions shall serve and obey him.

It is God's intent that we would understand the extent of the Dominion which we have been given in this life. Paul prayed that God would give His people the spirit of wisdom and revelation in the knowledge of Him:

Eph 1:18 The eyes of your understanding being enlightened; that ye may know what is the hope of his calling, and what the riches of the glory of his inheritance in the saints,
19 And what is the exceeding greatness of his power (Dunamis) to us-ward who believe, according to the working of his mighty power (Kratos),

Notes:

20 Which he wrought in Christ, when he raised him from the dead, and set him at his own right hand in the heavenly places,
21 Far above all principality, and power (Exousia), and might (Dunamis), and dominion (Kuriotace), and every name that is named, not only in this world, but also in that which is to come:
22 And hath put all things under his feet, and gave him to be the head over all things to the church,
23 Which is his body, the fulness of him that filleth all in all.

Of Jesus it was said that the government would be upon His shoulder, and that of the *increase of His government and peace there would be no end*:

Isa 9:6 For unto us a child is born, unto us a son is given: and the government shall be upon his shoulder: and his name shall be called Wonderful, Counsellor, The mighty God, The everlasting Father, The Prince of Peace.
7 Of the increase of his government and peace there shall be no end, upon the throne of David, and upon his kingdom, to order it, and to establish it with judgment and with justice from henceforth even for ever. The zeal of the LORD of hosts will perform this.

The question is this: What does "*from henceforth even forever*" mean? From when to when is the increase of His government to happen? Obviously from the day the Child who was foretold in the prophecy was born, until forever. And we know that Child was Jesus.

History proves the truth of that prophecy. Jesus' ministry began with 12 disciples. Now there are over 2 billion who profess faith in Christ worldwide. Some project that by 2020 there will be 2.6 billion professing Christians worldwide. Those statistics are based on current patterns of growth. I personally believe that if the Church begins to rise up and fulfill the Great Commission as the

Body of Christ in a corporate manner instead of on an individual congregational basis, there will be twice that amount.

Jesus declared that *all* authority had been given Him. When was *all* authority given to Jesus? At His resurrection or sometime in the future? What did He mean, then, when He commanded His Disciples to "Go ye therefore"? What is the significance of the "therefore?"

Mat 28:18 And Jesus came and spake unto them, saying, All power is given unto me in heaven and in earth.
19 Go ye therefore, and teach all nations, baptizing them in the name of the Father, and of the Son, and of the Holy Ghost:
20 Teaching them to observe all things whatsoever I have commanded you: and, lo, I am with you alway, even unto the end of the world. Amen.

"Go ye therefore" is a command that follows the statement that "ALL POWER" had been given to Jesus. The word POWER is better translated as AUTHORITY. Dominion comes as a result of authority. Jesus' command to us is that since He has *all* authority in heaven and in earth, we are to go in that authority as well.

When Jesus gave authority to the disciples over *all* the power of the enemy, He expected them and every disciple after them (that means you, if you are in Christ) to exercise their God-given Dominion over satanic forces.

Luk 10:19 Behold, I give unto you power (exouusia - authority) to tread on serpents and scorpions, and over all the power (dunamis - force, strength) of the enemy: and nothing shall by any means hurt you.
20 Notwithstanding in this rejoice not, that the spirits are subject unto you; but rather rejoice, because your names are written in heaven.

In Luke 10:19, Jesus gave the disciples authority or dominion over all the power of the enemy. In Matthew 28, He commissioned the disciples to teach others about that dominion, and how to exercise that dominion (teaching them to observe all things I have commanded you).

Mat 28:18 And Jesus came and spake unto them, saying, All power is given unto me in heaven and in earth.
19 Go ye therefore, and teach all nations, baptizing them in the name of the Father, and of the Son, and of the Holy Ghost:
20 Teaching them to observe all things whatsoever I have commanded you: and, lo, I am with you alway, even unto the end of the world. Amen.

What is the purpose of that dominion?

That one day all the kingdoms of the world would be brought in subjection to God.

Rev 11:15 And the seventh angel sounded; and there were great voices in heaven, saying, The kingdoms of this world are become the kingdoms of our Lord, and of his Christ; and he shall reign for ever and ever.

Personally, I hate to see what the devil's power has done to this world.

I hate to see that many who profess Christ have given up their God given authority in exchange for the devil's lies and sidetracks, and his devices and methods are many.

I hate to see so called leaders of the Church concede victory to the enemy, and convince others that the devil in the world is too strong for us, but in the four walls of the church, he's not. *Such leaders are traitors to the Cause of Christ.*

To not actively engage in war against the devil and his agenda across all spectrums of our society is to commit treason against God.

To decry the horror of abortion inside the four walls of your church, while never lifting your voice outside an abortion mill is the stuff of a traitor's or a coward's heart, it is akin to the millions of professing Christians in Germany who refused to speak against the extermination of the Jews while serving in Hitler's army.

Hypocrites point to Homosexuals and condemn their behavior, yet never demonstrate the Love of Christ to them that says God is not willing that any should perish.

I do believe that Christ was given all dominion at His resurrection.

I believe that He entrusted that Authority to His Church, and that as the early Church exercised that Dominion, thousands were added to the Church daily, and multitudes were healed and delivered from the power (*Exousia, Dunamis and Kuriotace*; Kratos was never his) of Satan as a result.

But eventually, the devil crept in and distorted the gospel and the purpose of the Church.

And for centuries occasional men and women of God who understood God's Purpose for His Church would rise up and fight against the religious trappings of Churchianity and shout "***AWAKE***" to the slumbering Church.

The devil would have to concede ground to those who walked in the Authority of Christ. But in the concession, he would convince man to hold on to this or that aspect of his lie or his compromise.

God is the same today as He was yesterday. His Plan from the beginning was that man would have dominion over all that He created. That Plan never changed.

True Revival of the Church will take place once the leadership of the church realizes that the business of the Church is to take place outside the four walls of the Church, and seriously begins to equip the Body of Christ to do the work of the ministry.

Revival does not consist of a series of meetings that keep the church behind the four walls, regardless of how good the meetings are. What we need is less meetings, and more outreach. Outreach is learned through application. The sad truth is that most of the leadership in the church today don't know how to disciple others in the way of ministry. All they know is how to prepare a sermon for the next meeting. Jesus taught His disciples by personal application. They watched Him do the work, and He taught them as they watched. Then they themselves were encouraged to do the work of the ministry. 100% of Jesus' disciples were trained for ministry. That isn't happening in most fellowships today.

The leadership needs to understand this, and start equipping the saints of God to go out and rescue those that are perishing, not to invite others to be a part of their meetings. What we need today is less meetings, and more outreach. Today the church is largely composed of those who are bound to sin who generally just exchange one social clique for another.

They become part of a group that doesn't do this or that, who compare themselves to the groups that do. Some Christians go from one meeting to another so they can maintain their sobriety, and often they fall. After they fall, they continue a while in their backslidden state, then return to the meeting, and confess their weakness to a group of others who wallow in their weakness as well, and who can sympathize with their powerlessness over sin.

If they would go from one street corner to another, proclaiming the Kingdom of God, and ministering freedom to the captives, the contrast between Light and Darkness would be a continual reminder to them, and the Power that is in Christ to overcome the works of the devil would be their mainstay, and not their mantra.

If reaching out to the lost becomes a lifestyle instead of an occasional outreach, one is less likely to fall. The more I am occupied with furthering the Kingdom of God, the less I will have to do with the kingdom of darkness. I won't have time to backslide, if my lifestyle is 24/7 about the Kingdom. Hypocrisy thrives in the cliques who forget where they came from, and have no compassion for those who are perishing in the world. Those who are outside want no part with the hypocrites who say one thing, but live another.

Notes:

_____
_____
_____
_____
_____
_____
_____
_____
_____
_____
_____
_____
_____
_____
_____
_____
_____
_____
_____
_____
_____
_____
_____
_____
_____
_____
_____
_____
_____
_____
_____
_____
_____
_____
_____

When I am equipped minister to an addict that is out there in the world, I can demonstrate the Love of Christ to him or her as they behold the one who has been rescued from the power of sin now going out and saying, "you can do it!"

There are more who are perishing on the streets in the world than will ever come into the building. Once we get them to see that they need the Saving Grace of Jesus Christ, then we can bring them into the building to be equipped to turn the world upside down for Jesus.

True revival will consist of sons and daughters who will prophesy on the streets, proclaiming the Kingdom of God. The sick will be made whole, the lame will be healed, blind eyes will be opened. As a result thousands will be added to the Church daily.

One Glorious Day there will be a proclamation made in the heavenlies that the kingdoms of this world are become the kingdoms of our Lord (Rev 11:15).

The Christian must be doing all he or she can do to see this become a reality.

We are called to take the world for Christ, not to hide in our sanctuaries with our respective cliques, waiting for Christ to rapture us out.

It takes nine weeks in the army to prepare a soldier for war. That is called Basic Training. In the church it takes a lifetime of attendance, and even then many have never fulfilled their calling.

I said earlier I would mention some caveats that should go with the statement that I believe in Dominionism or a "Kingdom Now" doctrine.

Evangelism Is The First Priority Of The Church

The Kingdom of God is FIRST to be populated with souls through the life changing power of the Gospel of the Kingdom of God.

Notes:

An unpopulated kingdom is no kingdom at all. Christ's first purpose was that He came into the world to save those who believe in Him. He came to seek and save those who are lost, and to reconcile humanity to God. Every soul saved populates the Kingdom of God, and depopulates the kingdom of Satan.

Modern day Dominionists speak of "seven mountains of culture" that must be brought in line with the Kingdom of God. These seven mountains are Religion, Family, Education, Government, Media, Arts & Entertainment, and Business. The concept of the seven mountains of culture are taken from the Book of Revelation, where the harlot (the world system) is said to sit on seven mountains (*Rev 17:9*).

According to Dominionists, the purpose of the Church is to redeem these seven mountains for the Glory of God. While I hold a different belief regarding what the seven mountains are (I believe they are the seven continents of the world, and others believe they are the seven mountains that surround Rome), I agree with the premise of transforming our culture for the Kingdom of God. As the Kingdom of God advances, the culture will change. It is how that is accomplished where we may disagree.

Dominionists generally rely on social activism to affect change. Get out the vote. Boycott products. Buy American. While these are our responsibility as people of conscience, according to the Bible, *the primary catalyst for change is the Gospel of the Kingdom of God.*

I believe the proclamation of the unadulterated Gospel of the Kingdom of God in the public arena of society will affect change.

One of the assumptions held by many, if not most of those who ascribe to the "Kingdom Now" or "Dominionist theology" today is that Dominionism naturally brings material prosperity to all who walk in the true precepts of the "Kingdom Now" theology. "It takes money to bring about change", they believe.

1. A strong or inordinate desire of obtaining and possessing some supposed good; usually in a bad sense, and applied to an inordinate desire of wealth or avarice.

Out of the heart proceedeth covetousness. Mark 7.
Mortify your members--and covetousness which is idolatry. Col 3.

2. Strong desire; eagerness.

2Ti 3:12 Yea, and all that will live godly in Christ Jesus shall suffer persecution.

Notes

_____
_____
_____
_____
_____
_____
_____
_____
_____
_____
_____
_____
_____
_____
_____
_____
_____
_____
_____
_____

"I can't make good Christian movies that will effectively compete with secular movies without an abundance of money".

The natural inference is that since we are a nation of kings and priests, and that our God owns the cattle on a thousand hills, then we should expect to prosper materially as well, and therein lies the danger. While in pursuit of those riches that will enable us to further the Kingdom of God, we can become so consumed with the cares of this world (bills, investments, debt, material gain, secular obligations, schedules) and the pride of life that the Gospel of the Kingdom of God becomes secondary to our daily lifestyle. Remember our earlier chapter on temptations to those who are in ministry. Jesus said we are to make the Kingdom of God our priority.

The Word of God says that we are not to set our affections on things below.

Col 3:1 If ye then be risen with Christ, seek those things which are above, where Christ sitteth on the right hand of God.
2 Set your affection on things above, not on things on the earth.

Just a few verses later, Paul equates covetousness with idolatry.

Satan tempted Jesus with all the prosperity of all the kingdoms of the world. But Jesus rejected it, and lived a simple life of obedience to the Word of God. In the end, as a result of that obedience even unto death He obtained *everything*.

Paul says that whether he was abased, or whether he abounded, he learned to be content in whatever his state was. In exercising his God-given authority and dominion, he was shipwrecked, stoned, persecuted, beaten and left for dead.

That is not a picture that a lot of the Health and Wealth Dominionist Kingdom Now prosperity teachers of today like to paint for their disciples. Paul informed Timothy that *ALL* who live godly will suffer persecution.

Somewhere in the midst of all that he went through, Paul also left letters to tell us about the warfare we are engaged in, and to assure us that our battle is ultimately to bring the Kingdom of God to this world to rule first in our lives, and then in those who we encounter.

Rom 14:16 Let not then your good be evil spoken of:
17 For the kingdom of God is not meat and drink; but righteousness, and peace, and joy in the Holy Ghost.
18 For he that in these things serveth Christ *is* acceptable to God, and approved of men.
19 Let us therefore follow after the things which make for peace, and things wherewith one may edify another.

The Faith chapter (Hebrews 11) tells about men and women who were shining examples of Faith. We read about overcomers and mighty men and women of God. But then we read this about some of those pillars of Faith:

Heb 11:36 And others had trial of *cruel* mockings and scourgings, yea, moreover of bonds and imprisonment:
37 They were stoned, they were sawn asunder, were tempted, were slain with the sword: they wandered about in sheepskins and goatskins; being destitute, afflicted, tormented;
38 (Of whom the world was not worthy:) they wandered in deserts, and *in* mountains, and *in* dens and caves of the earth.

1Co 4:19 But I will come to you shortly, if the Lord will, and will know, not the speech of them which are puffed up, but the power.
20 For the kingdom of God *is* not in word, but in power.

The majority of Christians in the Western world have exchanged the power and authority that is theirs in Christ for the things of the world. In pursuing after the things of this world, we forfeit our ability to walk with the Power of kings, and the Authority of priests.

To focus on transforming the "seven cultural mountains" of the world generally results in repackaging Christianity by emulating the ways of the world in order to win others for Christ.

The Kingdom of God is not sanctified capitalism.

Rev 1:5 And from Jesus Christ, who is the faithful witness, and the first begotten of the dead, and the prince of the kings of the earth. Unto him that loved us, and washed us from our sins in his own blood,

6 And hath made us kings and priests unto God and his Father; to him be glory and dominion for ever and ever. Amen.

What does being a king and a priest entail? Walking in Authority and in the supernatural demonstration of Power.

The focus of many who embrace Dominionist theology is to *Christianize* the seven cultural mountains. For instance, one of the seven mountains of culture is the entertainment industry.

From a Dominionist perspective, the Christianized entertainment industry will consist of movies and art forms that are family friendly, rather than those that prevail today that are centered on lust and violence.

Joh 18:36 Jesus answered, My kingdom is not of this world: if my kingdom were of this world, then would my servants fight, that I should not be delivered to the Jews: but now is my kingdom not from hence.

Those who have been transformed by Christ discover they don't need a movie or a play or a concert to entertain them. The focus of Paul or the early Christians was not to Christianize the arts and entertainment of the world. *They simply preached Christ and His Kingdom, and the focus of those who were being saved changed from a worldly perspective to that of the Kingdom of God.*

Watch what takes place when the Kingdom of God is preached with authority and Power:

Act 19:8 And he went into the synagogue, and spake boldly for the space of three months, disputing and persuading the things concerning the kingdom of God.
9 But when divers were hardened, and believed not, but spake evil of that way before the multitude, he departed from them, and separated the disciples, disputing daily in the school of one Tyrannus.
10 And this continued by the space of two years; so that all they which dwelt in Asia heard the word of the Lord Jesus, both Jews and Greeks.
11 And God wrought special miracles by the hands of Paul:
12 So that from his body were brought unto the sick handkerchiefs or aprons, and the diseases departed from them, and the evil spirits went out of them.

Act 19:18 And many that believed came, and confessed, and shewed their deeds.
19 Many of them also which used curious arts brought their books together, and burned them before all *men:* and they counted the price of them, and found *it* fifty thousand *pieces* of silver.
20 So mightily grew the word of God and prevailed.

21 After these things were ended, Paul purposed in the spirit, when he had passed through Macedonia and Achaia, to go to Jerusalem, saying, After I have been there, I must also see Rome.
22 So he sent into Macedonia two of them that ministered unto him, Timotheus and Erastus; but he himself stayed in Asia for a season.
23 And the same time there arose no small stir about that way.

The silversmiths didn't change their manufacturing techniques from building idols of Dianna to building statues of Jesus and Mary. They had to close up shop because people were no longer interested in the idols they made.

The Kingdom of God had come to the region, and as a result, those who made their money through deception and the kingdom of darkness were threatened, because no one wanted to waste their money on the products they sold.

It wasn't the result of a call for a boycott. It was the result of changed lives and changed lifestyles that took place after the Gospel was publicly proclaimed with demonstration of power.

The god of this world and his followers are not going to just sit still and allow this to happen without a fight.

Acts 19:24 For a certain _man_ named Demetrius, a silversmith, which made silver shrines for Diana, brought no small gain unto the craftsmen;
25 Whom he called together with the workmen of like occupation, and said, Sirs, ye know that by this craft we have our wealth.
26 Moreover ye see and hear, that not alone at Ephesus, but almost throughout all Asia, this Paul hath persuaded and turned away much people, saying that they be no gods, which are made with hands:
27 So that not only this our craft is in danger to be set at nought; but also that the temple of the great goddess Diana should be despised, and her magnificence should be destroyed, whom all Asia and the world worshippeth.
28 And when they heard _these sayings_, they were full of wrath, and cried out, saying, Great _is_ Diana of the Ephesians.
29 And the whole city was filled with confusion: and having caught Gaius and Aristarchus, men of Macedonia, Paul's companions in travel, they rushed with one accord into the theatre.

When the Gospel is preached with Power (_exousia, dunamis, kratis_), society will be supernaturally transformed, not assimilated or reshaped into a capitalistic Christian package. It is important to grasp the fact that Paul and Silas did not go about trying to change culture, organizing boycotts, picketing businesses, and "getting out the vote". Jesus taught His disciples how to change the world, and it was through preaching the Gospel, casting out demons and healing the sick. Man may have changed that model, but I don't believe God has.

I am not saying that boycotting businesses and getting out the vote is wrong. But it is the Gospel that they preached and which was confirmed with supernatural Power that changed the culture, and that Gospel brought with it persecution from the world, because the economy of the Kingdom of God is contrary to that of the world.

Act 16:19 And when her masters saw that the hope of their gains was gone, they caught Paul and Silas, and drew *them* into the marketplace unto the rulers,
20 And brought them to the magistrates, saying, These men, being Jews, do exceedingly trouble our city,
21 And teach customs, which are not lawful for us to receive, neither to observe, being Romans.
22 And the multitude rose up together against them: and the magistrates rent off their clothes, and commanded to beat *them*.

As the Gospel is boldly proclaimed in the marketplace *with the demonstration of the Power of God*, it will bring change. Not everyone will welcome that change.

Act 17:6 And when they found them not, they drew Jason and certain brethren unto the rulers of the city, crying, These that have turned the world upside down are come hither also;

When an individual comes to a saving knowledge of Christ, his or her perspective changes. It is the Gospel that transforms a person from an idolater to a worshipper of God. It is the Gospel that transforms a person from a fornicator, an adulterer, a homosexual, a thief, a liar, a drunkard, into a saint of God.

1Pe 4:1 Forasmuch then as Christ hath suffered for us in the flesh, arm yourselves likewise with the same mind: for he that hath suffered in the flesh hath ceased from sin;
2 That he no longer should live the rest of *his* time in the flesh to the lusts of men, but to the will of God.
3 For the time past of *our* life may suffice us to have wrought the will of the Gentiles, when we walked in lasciviousness, lusts, excess of wine, revellings, banquetings, and abominable idolatries:
4 Wherein they think it strange that ye run not with *them* to the same excess of riot, speaking evil of *you*:

A king or a president or a dictator who finds Christ and whose heart is changed from the sin of self to the Will of God will change the way his kingdom is run. But how will he hear the gospel, unless someone preaches?

I don't need money to preach the Gospel.

I don't need strobe lights and repackaged music to attract people for the Kingdom of God.

I don't need programs to help people find deliverance.

All I need is the Power of God.

When people hear that the Power of God is present to heal, save and deliver, they will come. When they come and see the reality of the Kingdom of God at work, they will repent. When they repent, their desires will change. Less money will be invested in the things of this corrupt world. Their focus will be in investing their resources in furthering the Kingdom of God in their sphere of influence.

The kingdoms of this world change one soul at a time as individuals repent and come to a saving knowledge of Christ.

In the Kingdom of God, there is no homosexual agenda. There are no thieves, liars and adulterers or fornicators. In the Kingdom of God unwanted pregnancy is not an issue. In the Kingdom of God, drug abuse or alcoholism is nonexistent. In the Kingdom of God there is no racism or elitist mindset.

And all of that is not accomplished through the social activism of Christians seeking to change existing laws for new laws. It is accomplished through hearts that are changed by the Power of Christ through the proclamation of the Gospel of the Kingdom of God. When this Gospel of the Kingdom is preached, not only behind the four walls of the "church", but in the market place and in the public forum, blind eyes see, deaf ears are opened, the lame walk and those who are held captive to sin are delivered.

The Word of God plainly teaches us that we are not wrestling against flesh and blood, but against powers and principalities, against spiritual wickedness in high places. We cannot defeat these with carnal means.

Repentance, Prayer and Evangelism are the only effective tools we have as the Church. We are to call humanity to repentance as we proclaim the Gospel of the Kingdom of God, but we ourselves are also obligated to walk in a state of repentance before God, bathing all of our daily affairs in prayer as we seek for opportunities to proclaim the Kingdom of God to those we encounter.

Sin has no more dominion over those of us who have come to Christ.

Rom 6:13 Neither yield ye your members as instruments of unrighteousness unto sin: but yield yourselves unto God, as those that are

Notes:

alive from the dead, and your members as instruments of righteousness unto God.
14 For sin shall not have dominion over you: for ye are not under the law, but under grace.

The writer of Hebrews reminds us that we are to walk in the authority that God has given us, to bring the world into submission (subjection) to the Kingdom of God.

Heb 2:1 Therefore we ought to give the more earnest heed to the things which we have heard, lest at any time we should let *them* slip *(carelessly pass by)*.
2 For if the word spoken by angels was stedfast, and every transgression and disobedience received a just recompence of reward;
3 How shall we escape, if we neglect *(make light of)* so great salvation; which at the first began to be spoken by the Lord, and was confirmed unto us by them that heard *him;*
4 God also bearing *them* witness, both with signs and wonders, and with divers miracles, and gifts of the Holy Ghost, according to his own will?
5 For unto the angels hath he not put in subjection *(to submit to one's control)* the world *(the globe)* to come *(that which is to be expected)*, whereof we speak.
6 But one in a certain place testified, saying, What is man, that thou art mindful of him? or the son of man, that thou visitest him?
7 Thou madest him a little lower than the angels; thou crownedst him with glory and honour, and *didst set him (appointed, designated) over the works of thy hands*:
8 Thou hast put *all things* in subjection under his feet. For in that he put all in subjection under him, he left nothing *that is* not put under him. But now we see not yet all things put under him.

The preceding verses are speaking plainly of God's Plan for humanity. That all things would be subject to man (*vs 8*). Dominion is clearly taught here. *There is nothing that has not been put under man's authority.*

Joh 14:15 If ye love me, keep my commandments.
16 And I will pray the Father, and he shall give you another Comforter, that he may abide with you for ever;
17 *Even* **the Spirit of truth; whom the world cannot receive, because it seeth him not, neither knoweth him: but ye know him; for he dwelleth with you, and shall be in you.**
18 I will not leave you comfortless: I will come to you.
19 Yet a little while, and the world seeth me no more; but ye see me: because I live, ye shall live also.
20 At that day ye shall know that I *am* **in my Father, and ye in me, and I in you.**
21 He that hath my commandments, and keepeth them, he it is that loveth me: and he that loveth me shall be loved of my Father, and I will love him, and will manifest myself to him.

Notes:
_____
_____
_____
_____
_____
_____
_____
_____
_____
_____
_____
_____
_____
_____
_____
_____
_____
_____
_____
_____
_____
_____

But the writer goes on to say that while that is absolutely a true statement, the reality is that not all things are under his authority. Death is still a reality. Suffering is still a reality. But we who are Christ's are called to the same ministry that Christ was called to (*verse 11*). We are One with Him. We are co-laborers with Christ. We are the priests, He is the High Priest.

Heb 2:11 For both he that sanctifieth and they who are sanctified *are* **all of one: for which cause he is not ashamed to call them brethren,**
12 Saying, I will declare thy name unto my brethren, in the midst of the church will I sing praise unto thee.
13 And again, I will put my trust in him. And again, Behold I and the children which God hath given me.

Remember in our previous chapter, we learned that the fullness of Christ lives in us. As we realize our calling, we are able to walk in the authority He has given us. We are able to endure the things that the world throws at us as we yield to His Instruction because He is working in us and through us by the Holy Spirit, that Comforter He promised to send in John 14 (see the sidebar here).

Heb 2:9 But we see Jesus, who was made a little lower than the angels for the suffering of death, crowned with glory and honour; that he by the grace of God should taste death for every man.
10 For it became him, for whom *are* **all things, and by whom** *are* **all things, in bringing many sons unto glory, to make the captain of their salvation perfect through sufferings.**
11 For both he that sanctifieth and they who are sanctified *are* **all of one: for which cause he is not ashamed to call them brethren,**
12 Saying, I will declare thy name unto my brethren, in the midst of the church will I sing praise unto thee.
13 And again, I will put my trust in him. And again, Behold I and the children which God hath given me.

14 Forasmuch then as the children are partakers of flesh and blood, he also himself likewise took part of the same; that through death he might destroy him that had the power of death, that is, the devil;
15 And deliver them who through fear of death were all their lifetime subject to bondage.
16 For verily he took not on *him the nature of* angels; but he took on *him* the seed of Abraham.
17 Wherefore in all things it behoved him to be made like unto *his* brethren, that he might be a merciful and faithful high priest in things *pertaining* to God, to make reconciliation for the sins of the people. 18 For in that he himself hath suffered being tempted, he is able to succour *(help)* them that are tempted.

The next chapter (Hebrews 3) begins with "*Wherefore*".

Don't lose sight of the fact that chapter 2 is initially speaking of the authority mankind has been given to bring the world into subjection to the Kingdom of God. Then later, the admission is that it is apparent that not everything has yet been brought into subjection.

But Christ has accomplished the Work, whether we realize it or acknowledge it or not ("It is finished"). Since that is true, we should "consider" or *set our minds fully* on Christ, the Apostle and High Priest of that which we profess to be - a kingdom of priests, Christians, *anointed* ones.

Heb 3:1 Wherefore, holy brethren, partakers of the heavenly calling, consider the Apostle and High Priest of our profession, Christ Jesus;

Verse 6 tells us that we are His house. He dwells in us, *if* we remain in Him.

Heb 3:5 And Moses verily *was* faithful in all his house, as a servant, for a testimony of those things which were to be spoken after;
6 But Christ as a son over his own house; whose house are we, if we hold fast the confidence and the rejoicing of the hope firm unto the end.

And then follows another "wherefore". Since we are Christ's house, we are not to walk in unbelief as the Israelites (who were also called to be a nation of kings and priests, and who were to take the land that was promised them) did:

Heb 3:7 Wherefore (as the Holy Ghost saith, To day if ye will hear his voice,
8 Harden not your hearts, as in the provocation, in the day of temptation in the wilderness:
9 When your fathers tempted me, proved me, and saw my works forty years.

10 Wherefore I was grieved with that generation, and said, They do alway err in *their* heart; and they have not known my ways.
11 So I sware in my wrath, They shall not enter into my rest.)
12 Take heed, brethren, lest there be in any of you an evil heart of unbelief, in departing from the living God.

Note here that unbelief is the opposite of faith, and unbelief is evil in the eyes of God. The subject at hand was that the generation who left Egypt could not inherit the Promise and enter into the land that was reserved for them because of their unbelief.

It was the responsibility of Israel to go into the Promised land and take dominion over it. But the majority only saw giants, and didn't think they could accomplish what the Lord had called them to do. They couldn't enter in because of unbelief.

Hebrews 3:7-9 is telling those who believe in Christ that they are to take dominion over the land for the furtherance of the Kingdom of God. Much of the leadership are telling Christians from the pulpit that it's not doable in this life time, because the devil and evil have the upper hand, and the majority of those Christians are believing them.

Don't miss this: To allow this world to slip into decay and to refuse to do your part in furthering the Kingdom of God is to act in rebellion against God. God says that it is an evil heart of unbelief that causes that:

Heb 3:10 Wherefore I was grieved with that generation, and said, They do alway err in their heart; and they have not known my ways.
11 So I sware in my wrath, They shall not enter into my rest.)
12 Take heed, brethren, lest there be in any of you an evil heart of unbelief, in departing from the living God.

The word "departing" carries with it the idea of a revolt, as in Acts 5:37, where we see that Judas of Galilee "drew away" many after him in an apparent act of rebellion against the authorities.

The biggest hindrance to the furtherance of the Gospel of the Kingdom of God in this world is the inability or unwillingness of those who are in the five fold ministry to equip the saints for the work of the ministry. The second biggest hindrance is the unwillingness of the Body of Christ to step into their calling. Either way, it is evil in the Eyes of God, and akin to rebellion against the Will of God.

The concept of a clergy/laity divide has served two purposes. It has ensured that hirelings will maintain their position of support from their audience, and it has effectively hindered the Power of God from working through the Body of Christ while confining the work of the church to the four walls of an ambitious individual's personal kingdom. The four walls are not bad, *if* the focus is to train and equip the Body of Christ to be disciples who are commissioned to go forth and to further the Kingdom of God in their sphere of influence.

Most of the time, what takes place behind the four walls stays there as the clergy teach their flock to be "rapture ready" because of all the giants in the land. According to the author of Hebrews, that kind of mindset is that of an evil heart of unbelief.

The responsibility of the "clergy" if you wish to call them that, is to train every member of the Church to walk in their Gift, and to further the Kingdom of God in the world.

Remember this:

The disciples were not seminarians. When Jesus called them, most of them were unschooled fishermen. Some of the "clergy" of the time perceived that these disciples were ignorant and unlearned men, and yet they could not deny the Power of God that worked through them. If you have been Born Again, and are studying this book because you have accepted the Call of Jesus Christ for your life, you are qualified to do the work of the ministry.

If Christ is in you, the same anointing that resides in that preacher resides in you. He might know more than you right now, but you both are the temple of God.

You just need to learn what your calling is, and respond to it.

Let me just say right now that there is no New Testament calling to be some minister's "armor bearer".

There is no New Testament calling to clean the toilets or the sanctuary.

You may have the gift of helps that works in you and through you, and you may assist another in the Work of the Ministry he or she has been called in while you are being discipled into your own personal Calling, and you may choose to exercise that Gift of Helps to clean the toilets or the sanctuary. Someone has to do that.

But you need to understand that you are a minister of the Kingdom of God just as much as the "preacher" is. You are responsible to further the Kingdom of God in your own sphere of influence, whether that is your work place or in the grocery store or among your neighbors or on the street corners or in front of multitudes. You are called to be a disciple, and once you have been discipled, to go out and make disciples yourself.

It is not too late to change our focus. It is not too late to further the Kingdom of God in demonstration of power and authority by sending out an army of transformed saints of God with the intent of changing society for the Glory of God. Hopefully this book will help to serve that purpose.

Gen 1:26 And God said, Let us make man in our image, after our _____: and let them have _____ over the fish of the sea, and over the fowl of the air, and over the cattle, and over all the earth, and over every creeping thing that creepeth upon the earth.

Psa 8:4 What is man, that thou art mindful of him? and the son of man, that thou visitest him?
5 For thou hast made him a little lower than the angels, and hast crowned him with glory and honour.
6 Thou madest him to have _____ over the works of thy hands; thou hast put all things under his feet:
7 All sheep and oxen, yea, and the beasts of the field;
8 The fowl of the air, and the fish of the sea, and whatsoever passeth through the paths of the seas.
9 O LORD our Lord, how excellent is thy name in all the earth!

Psa 145:13 Thy kingdom is an _____kingdom, and thy _____ endureth throughout all generations.

What does the Word of God declare concerning Christ's Government? (Is 9:7) _____

Dan 7:13 I saw in the night visions, and, behold, one like the Son of man came with the clouds of heaven, and came to the Ancient of days, and they brought him near before him.
14 And there was given him _____, and _____, and a _____, that _____ people, nations, and languages, should _____ him: his _____ is an everlasting _____, which shall not _____, and his kingdom that which shall not be _____.

When did this take place? _____

Mat 28:18 And Jesus came and spake unto them, saying, All _____ is given unto me in _____ and in _____.
19 Go ye therefore, and teach all _____, baptizing them in the name of the Father, and of the Son, and of the Holy Ghost:
20 Teaching them to observe all things whatsoever I have commanded

you: and, lo, I am with you alway, *even* unto the _____.
Amen.

Dan 7:27 And the _____ and _____, and the greatness of the kingdom under the whole heaven, shall be given to _____

_____of the most High, whose kingdom is an everlasting kingdom, and all _____ shall serve and obey him.

According to the above verse, what is the Purpose of the Church?_____
_____
_____
_____

Seek the Lord as to what your part in the Kingdom of God is. Write down your thoughts as to how you can contribute to the furtherance of His Kingdom in your sphere of influence.

_____
_____
_____
_____
_____
_____
_____
_____
_____
_____

If your fellowship doesn't have an equipping program, consider asking your pastor to implement one. Give him a copy of this book, and ask him if it would be possible to spend a number of Wednesday nights focusing on helping the Body of Christ in your fellowship to become effective ministers of the Gospel.

"One hundred religious persons knit into a unity by careful organization do not constitute a church any more than eleven dead men make a football team. The first requisite is life, always."- A. W. Tozer

Jesus came to give us LIFE, and life more abundantly. That abundant life comes as a result of being engaged in the things concerning the Kingdom of God, and experiencing the Liberty from the snares of this world that Christ brings to those who are in Him - Lance Rowe

"The spirit of Christ is the spirit of missions. The nearer we get to Him, the more intensely missionary we become."
— Henry Martyn

"You can go to hell with the "gifts of the Spirit" but not the fruit of the Spirit."
- David Popovici,

Notes:
_____
_____
_____
_____
_____
_____
_____
_____
_____
_____
_____
_____
_____
_____
_____

Chapter 15
The Church and Ministry

THROUGHOUT THIS BOOK we have explored the characteristics of the minister of God, and the supernatural power that should accompany the preaching of the Gospel beyond the four walls of the man made edifice that is generally referred to as a "church".

Too often those who minister in the highways and the byways of our cities, or who are gifted with the prophetic become critical of those who don't, and withdraw from the "organized church", and are then viewed as "Lone Rangers", unaccountable, and unsubmissive to authority.

This hinders the ability and the opportunity to encourage the Body of Christ to step out and do the work of the ministry.

We are to be a part of the Body of Christ, and not to be separate from the Body.

The sad truth of the matter is that many fellowships today do not function with the five-fold ministry in place that the early Church did (Eph 4:11-16), namely apostles, prophets, evangelists, pastors and teachers.

A lot of pastors don't yet have a revelation of the need for equipping the church for the work of the ministry. Or they don't know how to go about it. But that doesn't give those of us who function in the role of apostle, prophet, or evangelist a reason to forsake fellowshipping with those who don't have that in place.

The Church today is in need of reformation. That reformation won't come if those who know the truth forsake it. You don't need to push your agenda or strive for recognition. Just be what the Lord has

"One hundred religious persons knit into a unity by careful organization do not constitute a church any more than eleven dead men make a football team. The first requisite is life, always."- A. W. Tozer

Jesus came to give us LIFE, and life more abundantly. That abundant life comes as a result of being engaged in the things concerning the Kingdom of God, and experiencing the Liberty from the snares of this world that Christ brings to those who are in Him - Lance Rowe

"The spirit of Christ is the spirit of missions. The nearer we get to Him, the more intensely missionary we become."
— Henry Martyn

Notes:

_____
_____
_____
_____
_____
_____
_____
_____
_____
_____
_____
_____
_____
_____
_____
_____
_____
_____
_____
_____
_____
_____

called you to be. He will reward you for your faithfulness.

In every congregation I believe there is the potential to realize each of those ministries (Apostle, Prophet, Evangelist, Pastor and Teacher) in any given Body. Alienating ourselves from them will not contribute to building the Church or bringing needed reform to the Church.

Hopefully we have established the fact that every Christian is called and commissioned to go out into the world to preach the Gospel, and is able to cast out devils, lay hands on the sick, and see them healed. Whether they do those things or not is dependent on their belief system.

Mar 16:15 And he said unto them, Go ye into all the world, and preach the gospel to every creature.
16 He that believeth and is baptized shall be saved; but he that believeth not shall be damned.
17 And these signs shall follow them that believe; In my name shall they cast out devils; they shall speak with new tongues;
18 They shall take up serpents; and if they drink any deadly thing, it shall not hurt them; they shall lay hands on the sick, and they shall recover.

There are some who would say that the apostles alone were given the authority by Jesus to cast out unclean spirits and to heal sickness and disease.

Mat 10:1 And when he had called unto *him* his twelve disciples, he gave them power *against* unclean spirits, to cast them out, and to heal all manner of sickness and all manner of disease.

But in Mark 16 and Matthew 28, the disciples are told to make disciples and that they were to teach *those* disciples to obey all things that Jesus had commanded them, and then those disciples would make disciples, and teach their disciples to make disciples - and on to the present day.

The *only way* the Commission changed was that before the death, burial and resurrection of Christ, the disciples were only to go to the lost sheep of Israel.

After the resurrection of the Lord, the disciples were now apostles (sent out ones), commissioned to train and equip other disciples to go into *all* the world, and to do on a global scale what they had been taught to do on a more localized scale. They had trained for three and a half years with the Master. Now they were qualified to train others. Not only were their disciples to go to the lost sheep of Israel, but to the Gentiles as well.

The saying is true: "Sheep beget sheep." Disciples are to make disciples. If you have been born from above and received the Gift of eternal life through Jesus Christ, you are called to be a disciple (student), in the way of ministry. After you have been taught and equipped in the Way of Ministry, you should be "sent out" and commissioned to make disciples yourself.

Somehow the responsibility of "discipling" has been left to the pastor or to the Sunday School teacher, and even then the discipling that is generally being done is not to train the Body to be able ministers who are to make disciples themselves, but to instruct them how to be good members in the church or in society.

The sad truth is that because of our religious traditions, most Christians in the Church of America never get beyond the milk of the basic principles of Christian doctrine to become ministers themselves. If the Christian has sat for thirty years under the teaching of his or her pastor and has never learned to minister to others and to make disciples, regardless of how good the preaching is, they have simply been bottle-fed milk all their Christian life. ◄ A disciple is a student. They learn from a teacher. We are all called to one day become teachers of our own disciples.

Heb 5:12 For when for the time ye ought to be teachers, ye have need that one teach you again which *be* the first principles of the oracles of God; and are become such as have need of milk, and not of strong meat.
13 For every one that useth milk *is* unskilful in the word of righteousness: for he is a babe.
14 But strong meat belongeth to them that are of full age, *even* those who by reason of use have their senses exercised to discern both good and evil.

Notes:

Notes:

There is no getting around the fact that the Gospel of the Kingdom of God is meant to be preached outside the four walls of the Church buildings, and it is to be preached with the demonstration of the Power of God. The purpose of the Gospel is to further the Kingdom of God in the earth. That is "Going on to Perfection", or maturity in our Christian walk. Every Christian needs to get beyond the pew of a disciple, and get outside the walls to make their own disciples. My first book "The First Principles" is a course in discipleship concerning the Basic Doctrines of the Christian Faith, which are mentioned in Hebrews 6:1-2. You can purchase that book at https://www.createspace.com/5877934

But while we are all called to advance the Kingdom of God in this world through exercising our God given Authority as kings and priests of the Kingdom of God with mighty signs and wonders confirming the Gospel, there are passages of Scripture that tell us that there are specific Gifts that are dispersed among the members of the Body of Christ through the Holy Spirit:

**1Co 12:4 Now there are diversities of gifts, but the same Spirit.
5 And there are differences of administrations, but the same Lord.
6 And there are diversities of operations, but it is the same God which worketh all in all.
7 But the manifestation of the Spirit is given to every man to profit withal.
8 For to one is given by the Spirit the word of wisdom; to another the word of knowledge by the same Spirit;
9 To another faith by the same Spirit; to another the gifts of healing by the same Spirit;
10 To another the working of miracles; to another prophecy; to another discerning of spirits; to another divers kinds of tongues; to another the interpretation of tongues:
11 But all these worketh that one and the selfsame Spirit, dividing to every man severally as he will.
12 For as the body is one, and hath many**

members, and all the members of that one body, being many, are one body: so also is Christ.

13 For by one Spirit are we all baptized into one body, whether we be Jews or Gentiles, whether we be bond or free; and have been all made to drink into one Spirit.

14 For the body is not one member, but many.

15 If the foot shall say, Because I am not the hand, I am not of the body; is it therefore not of the body?

16 And if the ear shall say, Because I am not the eye, I am not of the body; is it therefore not of the body?

17 If the whole body were an eye, where were the hearing? If the whole were hearing, where were the smelling?

18 But now hath God set the members every one of them in the body, as it hath pleased him.

19 And if they were all one member, where were the body?

20 But now are they many members, yet but one body.

21 And the eye cannot say unto the hand, I have no need of thee: nor again the head to the feet, I have no need of you.

22 Nay, much more those members of the body, which seem to be more feeble, are necessary:

23 And those members of the body, which we think to be less honourable, upon these we bestow more abundant honour; and our uncomely parts have more abundant comeliness.

24 For our comely parts have no need: but God hath tempered the body together, having given more abundant honour to that part which lacked:

25 That there should be no schism in the body; but that the members should have the same care one for another.

26 And whether one member suffer, all the members suffer with it; or one member be honoured, all the members rejoice with it.

27 Now ye are the body of Christ, and members in particular.

28 And God hath set some in the church, first apostles, secondarily prophets, thirdly teachers, after that miracles, then gifts of healings, helps,

Notes:

governments, diversities of tongues.
29 Are all apostles? are all prophets? are all
teachers? are all workers of miracles?
30 Have all the gifts of healing? do all speak
with tongues? do all interpret?
31 But covet earnestly the best gifts: and yet
shew I unto you a more excellent way.

The natural (read carnal) way to interpret these verses is in the general context of what is commonly misconstrued as that which takes place in the four walls of the local ministry commonly referred to as "church"; but it is important to understand the Church in all instances to be the *universal* Body of Christ, comprising all fellowships who are in Christ.

We will deal with the local fellowship here, since chapters 11, 12, 13, and 14 are instructions concerning order in the local fellowship of the universal Church, but it must be understood that "church" as you have probably been conditioned to view it is *not* the Church that Jesus spoke of when He said the gates of Hell would not prevail against it.

As long as your local fellowship remains centered on a person who insists on being known or referred to as "Pastor" or "Evangelist" or "Prophet" or "Bishop" or "Apostle" or "Reverend", and you are no more than a weekly spectator of their antics on center stage, the gates of hell *have* prevailed and have succeeded in limiting the Kingdom of God's advancement.

Do you realize that "Reverend" is not even a Biblical designation for one who is in ministry? It is a product of the man centered clergy/laity division that religion has substituted for true Christianity; another way that the "gates of hell" have prevailed against the counterfeit that has been so flippantly referred to as "church".

But the gates of Hell will not and cannot prevail against the Church that is being equipped to be a mighty force to go out and further the Kingdom of God.

1Co 3:3 For ye are yet carnal: for whereas *there is* among you envying, and strife, and divisions, are ye not carnal, and walk as men?
4 For while one saith, I am of Paul; and another, I *am* of Apollos; are ye not carnal?
5 Who then is Paul, and who *is* Apollos, but ministers by whom ye believed, even as the Lord gave to every man?
6 I have planted, Apollos watered; but God gave the increase.
7 So then neither is he that planteth any thing, neither he that watereth; but God that giveth the increase.
8 Now he that planteth and he that watereth are one: and every man shall receive his own reward according to his own labour.
9 For we are labourers together with God: ye are God's husbandry, *ye are* God's building.

Notes:

_____
_____
_____
_____
_____
_____
_____
_____
_____
_____
_____
_____
_____
_____
_____
_____
_____
_____
_____
_____

Concerning the Church, and Paul's instruction regarding it and the order of the local congregation, we read:

1Co 12:4 Now there are diversities of gifts, but the same Spirit.

"Diversities" and "Differences" in the next few verses are both translated from the same Greek Word. As we continue in our study, we will see what these Gifts are. We also see that while there may be "differences", there is the *same* Spirit, the *same* Lord, and the *same* God Who is at work through these Gifts manifesting themselves in us. Regardless of the gifts that are at work in the local congregation, we can be assured that it is the same Spirit that is operating through each individual, and one is not more blessed or more "anointed" than the other.

One person in the congregation may operate in the Gift of healing and one may operate in the Gift of helps. It is natural for our carnal mind to esteem one as being more spectacular or blessed than the other, but that isn't true. It is the *same* Spirit that is at work in both individuals to Will and to Do what He pleases through these yielded vessels.

To esteem one above the other is to say that the Spirit of God is in some way less significant in one person than in the other. The gifted preacher gets more recognition than the church janitor. But is that really the Way of God? No, that is just man's carnal inclination to glorify men.

Paul briefly addressed this issue when he pointed out that some were saying that they were of Apollos, and some were saying they were of Paul, and allowing preferences and division to come into the Church through that kind of carnal reasoning.

1Co 12:5 And there are differences of administrations, but the same Lord.

Administrations = ministries

The truth is that there are different ministries that should be operating under the same roof of a local

Apostle:
652 ἀπόστολος apostolos *ap-os'-tol-os*
From G649; a *delegate*; specifically an *ambassador* of the Gospel; officially a *commissioner* of Christ (apostle), (with miraculous powers): - apostle, messenger, he that is sent.

1 Co 1:10 Now I beseech you, brethren, by the name of our Lord Jesus Christ, that ye all speak the same thing, and *that* there be no divisions among you; but *that* ye be perfectly joined together in the same mind and in the same judgment.
11 For it hath been declared unto me of you, my brethren, by them *which are of the house of Chloe*, that there are contentions among you.
12 Now this I say, that every one of you saith, I am of Paul; and I of Apollos; and I of Cephas; and I of Christ.
13 Is Christ divided? was Paul crucified for you? or were ye baptized in the name of Paul?

1Co 3:3 For ye are yet carnal: for whereas *there is* among you envying, and strife, and divisions, are ye not carnal, and walk as men?
4 For while one saith, I am of Paul; and another, I *am* of Apollos; are ye not carnal?

Notes:
_____
_____
_____
_____
_____
_____

Church body. I am of the opinion that the fivefold ministry as defined in Ephesians 4 (Apostles, Prophets, Evangelists, Pastors and Teachers) should be active in every congregation in order to equip the Church for the Work of the ministry. I think there is a gross misunderstanding of these "offices" in today's church.

← As we have seen earlier in this chapter, the disciples eventually became "apostles". The word apostle means "sent out ones", or those who have been appointed as delegates.

Strong specified that an apostle is a commissioner of Christ and that they had "miraculous" powers. But according to Mark 16:15-18, all believers are endued with those powers.

It is **my personal conviction** that today's missionaries are the apostles of the church. They have been sent out to establish new ministries. They do the work of the prophet, the evangelist, the pastor and the teacher in the course of their ministry. They train their converts to carry on the work. When their work is finished, they go onto somewhere else. Some religious circles have mystified the "office" of the apostle, and use the title as a special place of honor above the other five fold ministries, while designating a missionary as a special separate work. They like the label without the personal sacrifice a missionary must make. The Bible says there would be false apostles who would creep into the church. Many who have the label are just that. False apostles, men who have not hazarded their lives for the sake of the furtherance of the Gospel.

Again, the Apostle is not greater than the Prophet, or the Prophet is not greater than the Evangelist, and the Evangelist is not greater than the Pastor, and the Pastor is not greater than the Teacher.

It is the same Lord that has appointed each one to their respective Calling. The key is the word "Lord". Jesus is Sovereign over each man's ministry.

It is for the Lord to appoint to each person their particular place in the Kingdom of God. There are a lot of men and women who have appointed themselves to the ministry, and it becomes a job or a vocation rather than a genuine Calling from the Lord. Thus there are pastors who have 9-5 office hours, and they are "hirelings" rather than true shepherds of the Church.

A true shepherd is on hand at all times for his sheep.

There are evangelists who are scheduled to preach from one church to another throughout the year, but who have never lifted their voice in a public square. These are motivational speakers, but they are not evangelists.

1 Cor 12:6 And there are diversities of operations, but it is the same God which worketh all in all.

The word translated as "operations" is the same word (different tense) translated as "worketh" in the same verse. One who walks in the calling of an evangelist and who has been given the Gift of healing by the Spirit of God may operate in that gifting differently than another who also has the Gift of healing. Smith Wigglesworth was an evangelist who operated in the Gift of healing. It is reported that he sometimes violently struck people in the area of their affliction, and they were healed.

John G Lake was an evangelist who also was given the Gift of healing by the Spirit of God. His mode of operation was totally different than that of Smith Wigglesworth's.

What they had in common was that both men of God knew that it was their responsibility to equip the Church to operate effectively in furthering the Kingdom of God. Both men preached messages that told all Christians who cared to hear, "You can do the things that we do, because we serve the same God".

G4851

συμφέρω sumpherō

Thayer Definition:
1) to bear or bring together
2) to bear together or at the same time
2a) to carry with others
b) to collect or contribute in order to help
2c) to help, be profitable, be expedient

Joh 4:15 The woman saith unto him, Sir, give me this water, that I thirst not, neither come hither to draw.
16 Jesus saith unto her, Go, call thy husband, and come hither.
17 The woman answered and said, I have no husband. Jesus said unto her, Thou hast well said, I have no husband:
18 For thou hast had five husbands; and he whom thou now hast is not thy husband: in that saidst thou truly.
19 The woman saith unto him, Sir, I perceive that thou art a prophet.

Joh 4:28 The woman then left her waterpot, and went her way into the city, and saith to the men,
29 Come, see a man, which told me all things that ever I did: is not this the Christ?
30 Then they went out of the city, and came unto him.

Notes:

_____
_____
_____
_____
_____
_____

1Co 12:7 But the manifestation of the Spirit is given to every man to profit withal.

"Profit withal" means "to bear or bring together". The Gifts of the Spirit are meant to edify the Body of Christ, and to contribute to the well being and the Unity of the Church.

The *authority* to heal, and to cast out devils which occurs in the process of evangelizing the nations and furthering the Kingdom of God on earth is different than the Gifts that are at work in the Church.

The Power of God is manifested with the proclamation of the Gospel in the public forum as a confirmation of the Truth of God's Word. The signs and miracles that take place in the market place are meant to bring the unsaved into the Kingdom.

The signs and miracles that take place in the Church are to assist the Body of Christ to grow and walk in the Blessings associated with being a citizen of the Kingdom of God.

The Gifts that are listed in 1 Corinthians 12 are for the Body of Christ.

1 Co 12:8 For to one is given by the Spirit the word of wisdom; to another the word of knowledge by the same Spirit;

Word of Wisdom

Wisdom is the gift of counselors, advisors, and instructors. This Gift is needed in the Body of Christ to help the babe in Christ to overcome daily challenges (read *trials and tribulations*) that he or she may encounter in their Christian walk and to grow in maturity.

Word of Knowledge

Knowledge entails an understanding of Biblical doctrines and Christian duties, as defined by the Word of God. Knowledge speaks of intelligence, or understanding of a thing or circumstance. The Gift of Knowledge will typically work through a teacher who is called to bring the Body of Christ to a place where they can effectively operate in their Gifts and Callings. But there is more to the word of knowledge than mere academia.

The *word of knowledge* will manifest itself in a believer as they minister to those who are outside the faith, in order to prove that the power of God is working through them, for example, Jesus' dialogue with the Samaritan woman at the well in John Chapter 4. He knew that she had had five husbands, and that she was just "shacking up" with the man she was currently with. This conversation resulted in Jesus being able to minister to the whole village.

The Gift of the Word of Knowledge is also at work in the Body of Christ to expose that which is not what it appears to be, or to bring to light some hidden circumstance that needs to be addressed in order to keep the Church from error. We see this Gift manifested in Peter in the case of Ananias and Sapphira:

Act 5:1 But a certain man named Ananias, with Sapphira his wife, sold a possession,
2 And kept back *part* of the price, his wife also being privy *to it,* and brought a certain part, and laid *it* at the apostles' feet.
3 But Peter said, Ananias, why hath Satan filled thine heart to lie to the Holy Ghost, and to keep back *part* of the price of the land?
4 Whiles it remained, was it not thine own? and after it was sold, was it not in thine own power? why hast thou conceived this thing in thine heart? thou hast not lied unto men, but unto God.
5 And Ananias hearing these words fell down, and gave up the ghost: and great fear came on all them that heard these things.
6 And the young men arose, wound him up, and carried *him* out, and buried *him.*
7 And it was about the space of three hours after, when his wife, not knowing what was done, came in.

Notes:

8 And Peter answered unto her, Tell me whether ye sold the land for so much? And she said, Yea, for so much.
9 Then Peter said unto her, How is it that ye have agreed together to tempt the Spirit of the Lord? behold, the feet of them which have buried thy husband *are* at the door, and shall carry thee out.
10 Then fell she down straightway at his feet, and yielded up the ghost: and the young men came in, and found her dead, and, carrying *her* forth, buried *her* by her husband.
11 And great fear came upon all the church, and upon as many as heard these things.

1Co 12:9 To another faith by the same Spirit; to another the gifts of healing by the same Spirit;

The Gift of Faith

There is a Gift of Faith, and there is the process of growing from one degree of faith to another degree of faith. They are different. Jesus rebuked the disciples on a few occasions for having "little faith". When the disciples were fearful in the storm, Jesus rebuked them for having little faith.

A person with a Gift of Faith would have just rested in his or her security in the midst of the storm, like Jesus did.

Mat 8:24 And, behold, there arose a great tempest in the sea, insomuch that the ship was covered with the waves: but he was asleep.
25 And his disciples came to *him*, and awoke him, saying, Lord, save us: we perish.
26 And he saith unto them, Why are ye fearful, O ye of little faith? Then he arose, and rebuked the winds and the sea; and there was a great calm.

Peter started walking on the water, but when he became aware of the circumstances, he began to sink. He had asked Jesus to call him to that situation, just as there are many who ask Jesus to

Notes:

call them to ministry. Those with little faith become fearful or discouraged when their circumstances begin to look bleak, and they either fall away or give up on ministry. Those with a Gift of Faith will continue to walk in their calling, no matter what the situation looks like.

Mat 14:28 And Peter answered him and said, Lord, if it be thou, bid me come unto thee on the water.
29 And he said, Come. And when Peter was come down out of the ship, he walked on the water, to go to Jesus.
30 But when he saw the wind boisterous, he was afraid; and beginning to sink, he cried, saying, Lord, save me.
31 And immediately Jesus stretched forth *his* hand, and caught him, and said unto him, O thou of little faith, wherefore didst thou doubt?

A person with a Gift of Faith doesn't worry about provision. He or she understands that their Father will take care of them. The thought of "what might happen" doesn't concern them. Those who grow from faith to faith have to learn to stop leaning on their own understanding and to trust in Him.

Mat 6:30 Wherefore, if God so clothe the grass of the field, which to day is, and to morrow is cast into the oven, *shall he* not much more *clothe* you, O ye of little faith?
31 Therefore take no thought, saying, What shall we eat? or, What shall we drink? or, Wherewithal shall we be clothed?
32 (For after all these things do the Gentiles seek:) for your heavenly Father knoweth that ye have need of all these things.
33 But seek ye first the kingdom of God, and his righteousness; and all these things shall be added unto you.
34 Take therefore no thought for the morrow: for the morrow shall take thought for the things of itself. Sufficient unto the day *is* the evil thereof.

Notes:

1 Cor 12:9 mentions that there are Gifts of healing, not a "Gift of Healing".

There are different kinds of healing that are in operation in the Body of Christ. The *primary* form of healing that we immediately think of is that which takes place when people need a physical touch from God. We are instructed in the Bible to anoint them with oil and pray for them, and the prayer of faith shall heal them. An individual or individuals with a Gift of Healing are in the Body of Christ to minister to those members of the Body who need a physical touch from God.

Just as there is a difference between the Gift of Faith and growing in faith, there is also a difference between having the *Authority* to heal and the *Gift* of healing.

The Authority to heal and to cast out demons is given to every servant of God who is intent on fulfilling the Great Commission of furthering the Kingdom of God on this earth. The Power of God is present when the proclamation of the Gospel of the Kingdom of God is made, in order to confirm the Word of God.

Mar 16:20 And they went forth, and preached every where, the Lord working with *them*, and confirming the word with signs following. Amen.

While every Christian can walk in the authority to heal in the course of proclaiming the Kingdom of God, the *Gifts of healing* mentioned in 1 Corinthians 12 are distributed in the Body of Christ *severally* (individually) according to the Will of the Holy Spirit, and intended primarily for the edification of the Body of Christ. There is a difference between healing a non-believer of his or her infirmity, and healing a believer of his or her infirmity.

For the non-believer, that healing touch will be the proof that Jesus Christ is Who we proclaim Him to be. For the believer, it is a benefit of being a citizen of the Kingdom of God.

Isa 61:1 The Spirit of the Lord GOD *is* upon me; because the LORD hath anointed me to preach good tidings unto the meek; he hath sent me to bind up the brokenhearted, to proclaim liberty to the captives, and the opening of the prison to *them that are* bound;

But there are often different factors involved concerning healing in the Church.

A person who had not yet received Jesus may be healed of emphysema even while they still abuse their lungs with cigarettes. Yet another person who is a Christian will not receive a healing until they repent of the abuse they are subjecting their lungs to.

The difference is the non-Christian is still in bondage to sin. God's Grace will extend to that one in order to reveal His Goodness. It is the Goodness of God that leads men to repentance.

The Christian, on the other hand, is not to continue in his or her bondage once they come to Christ. To continue in your sin as a professed child of God is to make the Cross of Christ of none effect. The Holy Spirit dwells in a child of God. Those who are Christ's become His temple. We have a responsibility to maintain the integrity of that temple. Whatever sin you indulge in as a Christian, you are bringing God into that sin as well.

One of the purposes of the indwelling of the Holy Spirit is to bring deliverance to those who were once held captive to their sins.

Walking in willful sin can result in a Christian suffering sickness.

1Co 11:30 For this cause many *are* weak and sickly among you, and many sleep.
31 For if we would judge ourselves, we should not be judged.
32 But when we are judged, we are chastened of the Lord, that we should not be condemned with the world.

It is very important to understand this:

Sometimes sickness in a Christian can be the result of sin in his or her life. Quit smoking those cigarettes, if you want to be healed of your C.O.P.D. or emphysema. God may save the heathen even while he or she is yet in their sin, **but you have not been saved to continue in your sin.**

You should underline, highlight and put big quotation marks around that last paragraph, and reference it often.

1Co 6:15 Know ye not that your bodies are the members of Christ? shall I then take the members of Christ, and make *them* the members of an harlot? God forbid.
16 What? know ye not that he which is joined to an harlot is one body? for two, saith he, shall be one flesh.

17 But he that is joined unto the Lord is one spirit.
18 Flee fornication. Every sin that a man doeth is without the body; but he that committeth fornication sinneth against his own body.
19 What? know ye not that your body is the temple of the Holy Ghost *which is* **in you, which ye have of God, and ye are not your own?**
20 For ye are bought with a price: therefore glorify God in your body, and in your spirit, which are God's.

My wife once ministered under our tent to a woman who was on oxygen. She came up to be prayed for her healing, but she had just been outside smoking. My wife told her we don't come to God to be healed so we can continue in our sin.

Two years later the woman came under our tent and gave a testimony of how she had almost died in the hospital, and she finally quit smoking. My wife prayed for her, and the next night she gave testimony of the Lord's healing touch on her. She said she was breathing better than she could before.

She wasn't completely healed, because years of abusing her body had taken their toll. As a child of God, she needs to be correctly discipled in order to walk in her healing. The problem with a lot of Christians today is that they are not being discipled in the Way of possessing their bodies in sanctification. Many false teachers are perpetrating a doctrine that says God understands that you are just a sinner and powerless to live a life according to His Will.

I have a saying that helps me to distinguish between how God deals with sinners and with His children. The saying is this: "Dogs do what dogs do. You can't expect a dog to do what a saint does, because they don't know any better. The real tragedy is when saints live as dogs, and do what dogs do."

1Co 11:26 For as often as ye eat this bread, and drink this cup, ye do shew the Lord's death till he come.
27 Wherefore whosoever shall eat this bread, and drink *this* **cup of the Lord, unworthily, shall be guilty of the body and blood of the Lord.**
28 But let a man examine himself, and so let him eat of *that* **bread, and drink of** *that* **cup.**
29 For he that eateth and drinketh unworthily, eateth and drinketh damnation to himself, not discerning the Lord's body.
30 For this cause many *are* **weak and sickly among you, and many sleep.**
31 For if we would judge ourselves, we should not be judged.
32 But when we are judged, we are chastened of the Lord, that we should not be condemned with the world.

Notes:

"**Let a man examine himself-**" In James, the passage on ministering healing, we are told to confess our faults one to another.

Jas 5:14 Is any sick among you? let him call for the elders of the church; and let them pray over him, anointing him with oil in the name of the Lord:
15 And the prayer of faith shall save the sick, and the Lord shall raise him up; and if he have committed sins, they shall be forgiven him.
16 Confess *your* faults one to another, and pray one for another, that ye may be healed. The effectual fervent prayer of a righteous man availeth much.

There are also people who need emotional healing, which is just as real as the need for physical healing. *Counseling* is a Gift of healing. The person who does this kind of healing would be a person who has patience and a ready ear, and a willingness to bear the burdens of others. Some physical sicknesses are the result of stress or bitterness. A counselor can minister healing to people by helping them to let go of their bitterness and their stress.

Sometimes Christians can be "oppressed of the devil". Those who are in the ministry of deliverance can be classified as operating in the Gift of Healing. Smith Wigglesworth claimed to be able to see the demon at work in a person's life, and he would violently strike that devil to get it to come out. And it would, while the individual would be unharmed.

Act 10:38 How God anointed Jesus of Nazareth with the Holy Ghost and with power: who went about doing good, and healing all that were oppressed of the devil; for God was with him.

There are also people who are wise in how a change in diet or environment may result in one's healing. This is a gift of healing, as well. A physician as well as a therapist could fall under this category.

I don't believe the wide spread prescription of drugs

for every ailment or disorder fits in the category of a "Gift of healing". The Bible refers to the last days when widespread drug use would be prevalent in the world. The word translated as "Sorcery" in Revelation 9:21 is the word "*pharmekeia*" in the Greek, from which we get our word "pharmaceutical" or "pharmacy".

Rev 9:20 And the rest of the men which were not killed by these plagues yet repented not of the works of their hands, that they should not worship devils, and idols of gold, and silver, and brass, and stone, and of wood: which neither can see, nor hear, nor walk:
21 Neither repented they of their murders, nor of their sorceries, nor of their fornication, nor of their thefts.

I hope this has helped to clear up the issue of healing. It is important for the purpose of this study to remember that while there are those who operate in the *Gifts* of healing in the Church, every Christian is authorized to operate with the *Power* to heal in the world as they preach the Gospel of the Kingdom of God.

1Co 12:10 To another the working of miracles; to another prophecy; to another discerning of spirits; to another *divers* kinds of tongues; to another the interpretation of tongues:

The Working Of Miracles:

The word "miracles" here is the Greek word *dunamis*, which we looked at earlier (see chapter 12). There is another Greek word which is translated as "miracles", and that word is "*semeion*". Semeion is also translated as "signs", as in a wicked and adulterous generation seeks after a sign".

"Semeion" miracles are like Jesus turning the water into wine (Jn 2:11), speaking a word to the nobleman in Galilee that his son who was in Capernaeum was healed (Jn 4:50,54), feeding five thousand with a few loaves and fishes (Jn 6:14), raising the dead back to life (Jn 11:47, 12:18); Peter and John speaking a

Mat 16:4 A wicked and adulterous generation seeketh after a sign; and there shall no sign be given unto it, but the sign of the prophet Jonas. And he left them, and departed.

Notes:

_____
_____
_____
_____
_____
_____
_____
_____
_____
_____
_____
_____
_____
_____
_____
_____
_____
_____
_____
_____
_____
_____
_____
_____
_____
_____
_____
_____
_____
_____
_____
_____
_____
_____

word and the man who was crippled from his mother's womb being made whole (Acts 4:16, 22).

Casting out devils, speaking in new tongues, drinking poison and not being harmed, taking up serpents, laying hands on the sick are all signs, or miracles that are meant to confirm the Gospel.

These types of miracles are supposed to follow after those who believe.

Mar 16:17 And these signs (semeion) shall follow them that believe; In my name shall they cast out devils; they shall speak with new tongues; 18 They shall take up serpents; and if they drink any deadly thing, it shall not hurt them; they shall lay hands on the sick, and they shall recover.

Signs should follow the believer, but never should the believer follow the signs. Leave that to the unbeliever, so they can become convinced of the reality of the Kingdom of God, and be saved. God's Power is not to be misused like a carnival side show, and yet many who walk in His Power do that very thing, as if they are something special, and thus taking the Glory from God.

Semeion are not for the believer, they are for the unbeliever.

The miracles that are mentioned in 1 Cor 12:10 as a Gift for the Church is not semeion, but *dunamis*; *power*, and as we have seen concerning the Gifts of faith and healing, the *Gift* of Dunamis which is given for the edification and benefit of the Church is different than the dunamis power we are all to walk in as messengers of the Gospel. Dunamis power was demonstrated through the disciples as they walked in the Authority Jesus had given to them to preach the gospel in Judea.

Luk 9:1 Then he called his twelve disciples together, and gave them power (dunamis) and

Notes:

244

authority (exousia) over all devils, and to cure diseases.
2 And he sent them to preach the kingdom of God, and to heal the sick.

As children of God, we have power and authority over all devils. That is our inheritance as saints (or those who have been set apart) of the Most High God. The child of God is called to live an overcoming life.

The Power of God demonstrates the contrast between the Kingdom of God and the kingdoms of this world. While Jesus was with the disciples, they were able to operate under His (Dunamis) Power and Authority to preach the Kingdom of God to the lost sheep of Israel. But then He was crucified, and His disciples where scattered like sheep who had lost their shepherd.

Acts 19:11 gives us a picture of what the Gift of Miracles at work in the Church would look like. We are told that Paul dwelt in Ephesus for the space of two years, having separated the disciples from those religious ones who did not believe and whose hearts were hardened to the Truth (vs 9), by which I believe the Church of Ephesus was founded.

We are told that "special demonstrations of power" were performed by God through Paul:

Act 19:11 And God wrought special miracles (*dunamis*) by the hands of Paul:
12 So that from his body were brought unto the sick handkerchiefs or aprons, and the diseases departed from them, and the evil spirits went out of them.

The Gift of Miracles entails a supernatural work that is unexplainable by man's logic. In this instance, there were sick people who couldn't make it to the fellowship, and so things that belonged to Paul were used to bring healing and deliverance to them.

I find it necessary at this moment to point out that if

245

Notes:

this event had never been recorded in the Word of God, and something like this was done today, many "men of God" would denounce such a thing as not being from God.

The same could be said of Jesus turning water into wine. Had that never been recorded in the Bible, and someone did that today, many modern day "defenders of the Faith" would certainly denounce that as not being from God. They would state the logical argument: "Why would God contribute about 54 gallons of booze to a party?"

A person who operates in the Gift of Miracles may do things a little different than our religious sensibilities may want to accept. Some people scoff at "prayer cloths", or blessing objects to achieve a desired purpose for the Glory of God, but we need be careful in doing so. At the same time, we are told that there would be those who came with a false doctrine, and backing that teaching up by lying signs and wonders (Matt 24:24, Mark 13:22, 1 Thes 2:9-11).

While I certainly am not endorsing such a thing, "gold dust" appearing in a service should not be immediately dismissed as "*Not of God*" - What should be the determining factor is being able to discern whether or not the message being given is contrary to the Word of God. If the message deviates from doctrinal truth as defined in the Bible, then it doesn't matter what is taking place, we can safely say it is not of God. The Word of God should be our standard.

Supernatural occurrences do not in themselves prove that God is at work, or that He is confirming the Word being given.

Deu 13:1 If there arise among you a prophet, or a dreamer of dreams, and giveth thee a sign or a wonder,
2 And the sign or the wonder come to pass, whereof he spake unto thee, saying, Let us go after other gods, which thou hast not known, and let us serve them;

3 Thou shalt not hearken unto the words of that prophet, or that dreamer of dreams: for the LORD your God proveth you, to know whether ye love the LORD your God with all your heart and with all your soul.
4 Ye shall walk after the LORD your God, and fear him, and keep his commandments, and obey his voice, and ye shall serve him, and cleave unto him.

Having said this, we need to understand that supernatural power from God *can* produce supernatural things in the congregation that defy logic. There are those who operate in that Gift, but that Gift will *enhance* or *confirm* the Word of God, not detract from it.

1Th 1:5 For our gospel came not unto you in word only, but also in power (dunamis), and in the Holy Ghost, and in much assurance; as ye know what manner of men we were among you for your sake.
6 And ye became followers of us, and of the Lord, having received the word in much affliction, with joy of the Holy Ghost:
7 So that ye were ensamples to all that believe in Macedonia and Achaia.
8 For from you sounded out the word of the Lord not only in Macedonia and Achaia, but also in every place your faith to God-ward is spread abroad; so that we need not to speak any thing.

Heb 2:1 Therefore we ought to give the more earnest heed to the things which we have heard, lest at any time we should let *them* slip.
2 For if the word spoken by angels was stedfast, and every transgression and disobedience received a just recompence of reward;
3 How shall we escape, if we neglect so great salvation; which at the first began to be spoken by the Lord, and was confirmed unto us by them that heard *him*;
4 God also bearing *them* witness, both with signs and wonders, and with divers miracles, and gifts of the Holy Ghost, according to his own will?

Remember: signs follow the believer, but the believer should never follow after signs. To deny the work of miracles or any other Gift in the Body of Christ is to fall under the category of those who have a form of godliness, but who deny the power (dunamis) thereof (2 Tim 3:5).

The next gift mentioned in 1 Cor 12:10 is the **Gift of Prophecy**. The Gift of Prophecy that is at work in the Body of Christ is different than that which is at work in the marketplace. In the market place, the Prophet proclaims "Repent and turn from your wicked ways! Soon we will all stand before the Judgment seat of God, some to receive the reward of eternal life with the God Who created them for His Glory, and for those who have rejected Him, the damnation of eternal torment. Flee from the wrath of God before it is too late!"

1Co 14:3 But he that prophesieth speaketh unto men *to* edification, and exhortation, and comfort.

The prophetic in the Church is to build the Body of Christ up (*edification*) to realize and to walk in their Gifting and Calling for the furtherance of the Kingdom of God. The prophetic in the Church is to encourage the Church to *draw closer* (exhortation) to God. The Word "*exhortation*" in the Greek is the word "*paraklesis*", which means to draw near.

The prophetic in the Church is to give a word for the purpose of persuading or of arousing or stimulating, or calming and consoling (Thayer's). That is what the word translated as "comfort" in verse 3 ◀ (Gr. p*aramuthia*) really means. That would sound something like this:

"We realize that the times are getting worse and worse, and that it looks like darkness is taking over, but we are the Light of the world (Matthew 5:14-16). Where light is, there can be no darkness. We can dispel the darkness. We need to press in and be what Christ has called us to be. We are called to

G3889
παραμυθία
paramuthia
Thayer Definition:
1) any address, whether made for the purpose of persuading, or of arousing and stimulating, or of calming and consoling
1a) consolation, comfort
Part of Speech: noun feminine

Notes:

overcome, not to walk in defeat (Revelation 2 -3, 'he that overcomes')! It is time to seek God as to what our Gifts and Callings are, and to step out in faith and to begin to make the Kingdom of God our priority, and advance the Kingdom one soul at a time."

Listen well to the message you are receiving from the pulpit. Are you being lulled to sleep, or are you being stirred up to action?

False prophets and false shepherds in the church convey a message of "Our situation here on earth is hopeless, but we know what the end of the Book says"; but that is *not* the message of the Word of God. We are more than conquerors through Him who Loved us (Rom 8:37).

"We are all sinners saved by Grace" is *not* the message of the Word of God. We are called to be saints of the Most High God, not sinners (1 Cor 1:2).

"God loves you just the way you are" is *not* the message of the Word of God. God loves you, but He calls all men everywhere to repent (Acts 17:30).

"Just be faithful to attend this church on Sunday and Wednesday and be sure that you pay your tithe, and you have done your part, and one glad day you will fly away" is *not* the message of the Word of God. God calls us to be doers of the Word and not hearers only (Jas 1:22-25).

"Give a hundred dollar donation and you will receive a hundred fold return" is *not* the message of the Word of God. God calls us to give up all that we have for the sake of the Kingdom of God in order to get a hundred fold return (Mark 10:29, 30).

False prophets and false pastors lead the church to abandon ship; to lay their spiritual weapons down, to live in comfort, and to give up the fight. They have a form of godliness, but deny the Power thereof, unless it is in the four walls of their fellowships. They have their congregation gathering at the altar in a continuous cycle of guilt over their sin, rather than going out and furthering the Kingdom of God.

A true prophet and true pastor will exhort and train the Church to engage in warfare in the world that results in victory. If it ain't about the Kingdom of God being furthered in this world, it ain't about the Gospel that Jesus preached.

This is the victory that overcomes the world, even our faith.

Rev 12:10 And I heard a loud voice saying in heaven, Now is come salvation, and strength, and the kingdom of our God, and the power of his Christ: for the accuser of our brethren is cast down, which accused them before our God day and night.
11 And they overcame him by the blood of the Lamb, and by the word of their testimony; and they loved not their lives unto the death.

Doesn't sound like a defeated Church to me. It sounds like warfare. And they who know their God will do exploits. Some will fall in the battle. There are always casualties in war. But the Church is victorious.

Dan 11:32 And such as do wickedly against the covenant shall he corrupt by flatteries: but the people that do know their God shall be strong, and do exploits.
33 And they that understand among the people shall instruct many: yet they shall fall by the sword, and by flame, by captivity, and by spoil, many days.
34 Now when they shall fall, they shall be holpen with a little help: but many shall cleave to them with flatteries.
35 And some of them of understanding shall fall, to try them, and to purge, and to make them white, even to the time of the end: because it is yet for a time appointed.

When will this happen? It's happening now, and it's time for the Church to stop wondering about tomorrow and fight the battle today. Proclaim the Word. Cast out devils. Take the land for the Kingdom of God in the Name of Jesus.

The Gift of Discernment.

Because of false prophets and lying signs and wonders that creep in the Church, the Lord places those with the Gift of discernment in the Body of Christ. Those with the Gift of discernment will also have an intimate knowledge of the Word of God.

The Gift of tongues and interpretation of tongues.

There is so much controversy in the issue of tongues, that I am just going to make a couple of personal observations, and leave it to the individual to settle in his or her mind what they believe, and I trust that the Lord will lead them into truth if they are mistaken.

There is a Gift of tongues that is given for the individual's personal growth in their Christian walk. They may or may not understand what they are saying, because it is the Spirit of God that is speaking in them for their personal spiritual edification.

1Co 14:2 For he that speaketh in an *unknown* tongue speaketh not unto men, but unto God: for no man understandeth *him;* howbeit in the spirit he speaketh mysteries.

There is also a gift of tongues that manifests itself in a word of encouragement or instruction in the Church. When this particular Gift is in operation, the Gift of interpretation will also follow.

Co 14:4 He that speaketh in an *unknown* tongue edifieth himself; but he that prophesieth edifieth the church.
5 I would that ye all spake with tongues, but rather that ye prophesied: for greater *is* he that prophesieth than he that speaketh with tongues,

except he interpret, that the church may receive edifying.
6 Now, brethren, if I come unto you speaking with tongues, what shall I profit you, except I shall speak to you either by revelation, or by knowledge, or by prophesying, or by doctrine?
7 And even things without life giving sound, whether pipe or harp, except they give a distinction in the sounds, how shall it be known what is piped or harped?
8 For if the trumpet give an uncertain sound, who shall prepare himself to the battle?
9 So likewise ye, except ye utter by the tongue words easy to be understood, how shall it be known what is spoken? for ye shall speak into the air.

The individual giving a message may also give the interpretation. Some teachings in the Church is that there is an individual who will give the message in tongues, and someone else will interpret. And sometimes, that is the case, and 1 Cor 12:10 seems to imply that (**to another *divers* kinds of tongues; to another the interpretation of tongues**), but there are also other times where the one speaking the tongue will also interpret what he or she said.

1Co 14:13 Wherefore let him that speaketh in an *unknown* tongue pray that he may interpret.
14 For if I pray in an *unknown* tongue, my spirit prayeth, but my understanding is unfruitful.
15 What is it then? I will pray with the spirit, and I will pray with the understanding also: I will sing with the spirit, and I will sing with the understanding also.
16 Else when thou shalt bless with the spirit, how shall he that occupieth the room of the unlearned say Amen at thy giving of thanks, seeing he understandeth not what thou sayest?

Again, because of abuse of the Gifts in the Church, discernment is paramount.

As I said at the beginning, because the Gift of tongues is such a controversial subject in the Church, I understand that there are various views as to their function and their purpose in the Church, and I believe it should be left to the individual to determine their doctrinal stance concerning tongues. I would point out, though, that *Biblical* doctrine not mixed with man's traditions or denominational slant is important.

An example of what I mean by this is that there are some fellowships that encourage everyone to "speak in their prayer language" during the service. Yet Paul, in his instruction to the Church in Corinth concerning the Gifts cautions against that very thing. He says if someone happens into a service where everyone is speaking in tongues, and they don't understand what is happening, they will think something weird or crazy is going on.

**1Co 14:18 I thank my God, I speak with tongues more than ye all:
19 Yet in the church I had rather speak five words with my understanding, that *by my voice* I might teach others also, than ten thousand words in an *unknown* tongue.
20 Brethren, be not children in understanding: howbeit in malice be ye children, but in understanding be men.
21 In the law it is written, With *men of* other tongues and other lips will I speak unto this people; and yet for all that will they not hear me, saith the Lord.
22 Wherefore tongues are for a sign, not to them that believe, but to them that believe not: but prophesying *serveth* not for them that believe not, but for them which believe.
23 If therefore the whole church be come together into one place, and all speak with tongues, and there come in *those that are* unlearned, or unbelievers, will they not say that ye are mad?
24 But if all prophesy, and there come in one that believeth not, or *one* unlearned, he is convinced of all, he is judged of all:
25 And thus are the secrets of his heart made manifest; and so falling down on *his* face he will worship God, and report that God is in you of a truth.**

The important thing to remember is that it is the Holy Spirit who gives to each member of the Body of Christ those Gifts that He sees fit to give, and the Gifts are distributed to the Body for the edification of the Body of Christ.

1Co 12:11 But all these worketh that one and the selfsame Spirit, dividing to every man severally as he will.

A true New Testament Church service is never about one man. The Gifts are given to each member for the purpose of ministering one to another. If a fellowship followed the Biblical example of "doing church", it would typically consist of more than just the traditional two hours on a Sunday morning.

**1Co 14:26 How is it then, brethren? when ye come together, every one of you hath a psalm, hath a doctrine, hath a tongue, hath a revelation, hath an interpretation. Let all things be done unto edifying.
27 If any man speak in an *unknown* tongue, *let it be* by two, or at the most *by* three, and *that* by course; and let one interpret.
28 But if there be no interpreter, let him keep silence in the church; and let him speak to himself, and to God.
29 Let the prophets speak two or three, and let the other judge.
30 If *any thing* be revealed to another that sitteth by, let the first hold his peace.**

31 For ye may all prophesy one by one, that all may learn, and all may be comforted.
32 And the spirits of the prophets are subject to the prophets.
33 For God is not *the author* of confusion, but of peace, as in all churches of the saints.

Think about what would take place in this country if the Church followed the Biblical example, and refused to put God in a two hour box once a week. I believe there would be a clear dividing that would take place between the sheep and the goats. Those who were more concerned about the football game than they are about serving the Lord would find another church that would accommodate them.

Those who truly love the Lord would want to be in a place where the Holy Spirit had free reign, and where they could exercise their calling. Time wouldn't matter to them, as each member had a part in the service to minister to one another's needs.

Rom 12:3 For I say, through the grace given unto me, to every man that is among you, not to think *of himself* more highly than he ought to think; but to think soberly, according as God hath dealt to every man the measure of faith.
4 For as we have many members in one body, and all members have not the same office:
5 So we, *being* many, are one body in Christ, and every one members one of another.
6 Having then gifts differing according to the grace that is given to us, whether prophecy, *let us prophesy* according to the proportion of faith;
7 Or ministry, *let us wait* on *our* ministering: or he that teacheth, on teaching;
8 Or he that exhorteth, on exhortation: he that giveth, *let him do it* with simplicity; he that ruleth, with diligence; he that sheweth mercy, with cheerfulness.
9 *Let* love be without dissimulation. Abhor that which is evil; cleave to that which is good.
10 *Be* kindly affectioned one to another with brotherly love; in honour preferring one another;
11 Not slothful in business; fervent in spirit; serving the Lord;
12 Rejoicing in hope; patient in tribulation; continuing instant in prayer;
13 Distributing to the necessity of saints; given to hospitality.

That is going on to perfection, fulfilling the Will of God for your life.

What is the difference between walking in the Authority of God as a child

of God and the Gifts of the Holy Spirit? _____
_____
_____
_____

Explain the Gift of Faith in contrast to going from Faith to Faith _____
_____
_____
_____
_____

Who is qualified to operate in the Gifts of the Holy Spirit? _____
_____
_____
_____

List the Gifts of the Spirit _____
_____
_____
_____
_____

Who determines what your Gifting is? _____

What is the difference between the Prophetic word being given in the Church, as opposed to that being given in the marketplace? _____
_____
_____
_____
_____

What is the purpose of the five fold ministry? _____
_____
_____
_____

What is the Purpose of the Gifts of the Spirit? _____
_____
_____
_____
_____

What Gifts do you have? _____
_____
_____

There is an excellent resource by C. Peter Wagner that can assist the believer to determine what his or her Gifts are. You can search for it on the internet: "Finding Your Spiritual Gifts".

APPENDIX

COUNT THE COST

I have been called by the Lord, and I responded to His Call years ago.

I raised my arms in praise and said "Here I am, Lord, teach me what You would have me do, lead me where You would have me go, use me for the furtherance of Your Kingdom."

He said "You have to deny yourself. Your personal ambitions. Your right to be right, your comfort and your personal agendas. In all you do, you are to seek me first, and prefer me above all. Are you willing?"

I said, "Yes, Lord, but I don't know that I will be everything You expect me to be. I am so weak in so many areas."

He said "All I require is a willing vessel, not a perfect one. Will you yield to my Desires before your own?"

"I will, Lord, and I do. But my imperfections are so many..."

"But MY Grace is sufficient".

"The road I will take you down will be rough," He assured me. "There will be those of your own household who will not understand.

Friends will betray you.

Family will see you as strange.

Religious ones will alienate themselves from you.

Many who you disciple will fall away.

Loneliness will accompany you because few will walk side by side with you.

There will be persecution, ridicule and scorn.

You will give of yourself to many, but not many will give of themselves to you.

You will have to learn to bless those who curse you, and pray for those who despitefully use you.

You will have times of no sleep while others rest comfortably.

You will have to learn contentment in abasement.

Sometimes the only one you will find to encourage you is My Word as you turn to Me, like David encouraged Himself in me.

You will have to invest in others when no one invests in you.

There will be no excuse for you to be offended, and you must strive not to be an offense to others.

Forgiveness and unconditional love toward others must be an important driving force for your life.

A lot of times things and circumstances will not seem to be "fair".

Sometimes the storms will seem to be endless, and it may not seem like I am with you, but I will be. Are you sure you want to go down this road?"

"I want to be where You are, Lord," I replied, and I reached out and grabbed His Yoke, and shouldered His Burden.

For the most part, it's been the easiest thing I have ever done.

Mat 11:28 Come unto me, all ye that labour and are heavy laden, and I will give you rest.
29 Take my yoke upon you, and learn of me; for I am meek and lowly in heart: and ye shall find rest unto your souls.
30 For my yoke is easy, and my burden is light.

Give me this day my daily Bread, Lord.

I hunger for more of You.

1) MY PERSONAL TESTIMONY

Before you begin to read this, let me encourage you as a minister of God to write out your personal testimony. Once you do, you can then condense it into a tract. I find it to be one of the most effective tools in ministering on the streets. If I tell someone it is my personal testimony and that I wrote it, 9.9 times out of 10, they will put it in their pocket and bring it home to read it later. Here is my story. You can find the tract version and download it on my website, crosscountry4jesus. com/index150.html

Drugs. Alcohol. Unrestrained sexual lusts. A criminal mind. Prison time for robbery. Liar. Cheat. Pimp. Deceit. Selfishness.

The Bible says that those who live like I had lived cannot enter the Kingdom of God. But then it says

"AND SUCH WERE SOME OF YOU, BUT YOU ARE WASHED, BUT YOU ARE SANCTIFIED, BUT YOU ARE JUSTIFIED IN THE NAME OF THE LORD JESUS, AND BY THE SPIRIT OF GOD." (1 Cor.6:11)

Too often, I hear of people dwelling more on their life before Christ, than what their life in Christ is now. I don't particularly care to dwell on what I was outside of Jesus. Suffice it to say that JESUS SET ME FREE!

In the fall of 1983 (September 6th) I was headed for Salt Lake City, Utah, after a six month visit to my home town in Northern Minnesota. I had spent a couple of months in jail for trying to outrun a game warden, which resulted in a head-on collision with the game warden (it's a long story), but it didn't stop there. My engine was still running, the game warden's head was on the steering wheel, and I thought I'd killed him. I put my car in reverse, went around him, and soon was facing a road block, which I attempted to run through, but my tire blew before I could do it. Praise the Lord. I would have probably been killed, because the officers had their guns trained on me, just as the tire blew.

Anyway, after some jail time, I headed for Salt Lake City to go to work on a highline tower construction job. I told the girl I had spent the summer with (the part of summer that I wasn't in jail) that I would come back to get her after I got settled in Salt Lake City. I was lying to her. I liked her, but I couldn't stay faithful to one woman.

On the way, I thought I would stop and say good bye to a couple of ex-party friends of mine, Dave and Lorinda N_____. Dave was a big Chippewa Indian who I used to party with, and sometimes he would get very violent when he got drunk. Lorinda was the sister of the girl I was leaving behind. She used to get high all the time. But now they were Christians, and they didn't do the things they used to do. Even though I knew they would preach to me, I stopped anyway, because Christian or no, they were still my friends.

PHILOSOPHY VERSUS THE TRUTH

Sure enough, when I got there, they started telling me about Jesus. My time in prison had given me three and a half years to study philosophy and religion, so I had all sorts of arguments to offer them. Everything they told me went in one ear and out the other, because I figured that they were just too close minded for me to reason with them. After all, I had studied Buddhism, Hinduism, Astrology, Palmistry, witchcraft, and American Indian Religions; I had read the Bhagavad Ghita, the Koran, the Satanic Bible by Anton Lavey, the Life of Buddah, and a number of other books on religion and philosophy; I had studied the writings of Gurdjeiff and Confucious and Mencius, and several other confused teachers who claimed enlightenment. I had practiced yoga, and experimented with meditation and dabbled in the Occult. For someone to tell me that Jesus was the ONLY WAY, was just too unreasonable to me.

Oh, I believed in Jesus. Historically, there was no doubt that He existed. But I thought He was just a good man, a prophet, a sage, a shaman, a yogi, a guru, a man who had reached a higher level of consciousness than most men had ever reached. I thought He was like Buddha, or Muhammad. But no way would I be close minded enough to say He was the ONLY WAY.

But one time, a man held a gun to my head, and outwardly, I defied him to pull the trigger, but inwardly, I prayed to Jesus to get me out of this one. Another time I had spent 48 hours in a Minnesota blizzard with little more than a sweater and a couple of pairs of pants and a thin summer sleeping bag. I called on Jesus then, too. Another time, when I was hitchhiking in Idaho, my packsack was all that was between me and a rattlesnake. I was talking to Jesus then, as well. Several other times, I had been in danger, and each time I called on Jesus, not to mention the many times I spent hugging a commode after a long hard drunken binge, puking my guts out, and swearing to Jesus that I'd never do *THAT* again.

AT THOSE TIMES IN MY LIFE, IT NEVER ENTERED INTO MY MIND TO CALL ON ANYONE BUT JESUS.

Anyway, I stood there arguing and philosophizing with Dave and Lorinda, and Dave's sister for three and a half hours, trying to get them to see my point. During those three and a half hours, Dave would repeat one phrase over and over again. He'd say: *"Now faith is the substance of things hoped for, and the evidence of things not seen."* I didn't know what that meant, it didn't make any sense to me, and after a while, I began to conclude that maybe the reason he had become a Christian was because the drugs had gotten to his mind, because he just kept on repeating that phrase over and over again. It got so that I would know when he was going to say it, because he would get this funny look on his face, and say, "Now...." and inwardly, I would say it with him..."Yeah, yeah, *faith is the substance of things hoped for, and the evidence of things not seen*".

After about three hours, their pastor, Lonnie Lee and his wife, Patty came over and joined them while they witnessed to me. After another half hour, I said, "Look guys, I have a long way to go yet, so I really should be going." Lonnie asked if they could pray with me. I told them sure, they could pray for me all they want. I didn't realize they meant right there. They grabbed hold of my arm, and led me to the kitchen and sat me down on a chair and started to pray for me. My head was down, and it was hard for me to keep from laughing because Dave, that big once-so-violent man was saying "oh, yes, Jesus", and it seemed so out of character with the Dave I had known. I left, after Lonnie explained that they had prayed that God would reveal Himself to me through the Holy Spirit.

About 150-200 miles down the road, I checked into a motel in Fairbault, Minnesota. There was a bar nearby, but I knew that if I went to the bar at 7:00 in the evening, there was a good chance that I would spend too much of my travelling money, so I sat in my room, and a sudden restlessness came over me. I turned on the television, but I always thought the television was a waste of time, so I just went through the channels and turned it off. I noticed a Bible on the bed stand, but I ignored it, and went and took a shower.

When I came out of the shower, as I dried my hair, I noticed that Gideon's Bible again. I picked it up, and said a prayer, something like: "God, you had five of Your best people telling me about Jesus today. If Jesus is the ONLY WAY, if You think I can be a Christian, and if You think you could forgive me for my sins, now's the time to tell me."

When you are alone in a motel room, you can get serious with God, and no one will care, because no one will see you. I opened the Bible, and expected some thunder, a loud voice, an earthquake or an angel to appear, but nothing happened. I laid down on the bed and started to read right where I had opened the Bible to.

TESTIMONY CONTINUED

The Bible had opened to the book of Romans. I naturally started to read at the top left hand corner of the left hand page, and by the time I got to the last verse at the bottom right hand corner of the right page, I was ready to conclude that there was nothing there for me. No thunder, no Voice from heaven, no earthquake, no angel to tell me that Jesus was the *ONLY WAY*.

Not only that, but I couldn't even remember what I had just read. To me, the text had been dry and boring. I figured it was time to go to the bar. But there was a part of me that really knew what the Truth was, and that part of me persuaded me to read just a little more. So I read the rest of the page, and went to turn the page.

Now, I was lying flat on my back, and as I turned the page, I stretched my arms above me and yawned. As I did so, a page came floating out of the Bible and landed on my chest. I picked up that page, and my eyes went instantly to the chapter that was in bold print. "**CHAPTER 11**". I read the first verse under chapter 11, and it said "*Now faith is the substance of things hoped for, and the evidence of things not seen*".

Immediately, I remembered Dave saying that verse over and over again. I looked at the page number. I have the page stored away, and I can't remember the exact page number right now, but we will say it was Page 913.

I used to go to the horse track at Delta Downs in Vinton, Louisiana almost on a weekly basis when I lived in Houston. I understood the odds of that particular page falling out on my chest. When I acknowledged the impossibility of that happening, God touched me with His Sweet Holy Spirit. I gave my heart to Him right then and there. He had answered my questions. Yes, Jesus was the ONLY WAY, Yes, I could be a Christian, and Yes, He would forgive my sins. I forgot about the bar. I stayed there and read the rest of Hebrews 11, and understood what it was saying. I stayed up late into the night, reading and understanding the Word of God.

I was in Salt Lake City for a month, when the Lord put a great desire in my heart for that girl I had left behind. I asked Him to join our hearts together. Then I drove all the way back to Minnesota, and told her about my conversion. Michelle wanted Jesus too. Since that day we have been together, and are happily married, with seven children, and have been on a wonderful journey of faith and growth together in the things of God.

HALLELUJAH! WHAT A WONDERFUL SAVIOUR WE HAVE!

2
HOW OUR MINISTRY DEVELOPED

BLESSED BE THE NAME OF THE LORD JESUS CHRIST

I originally wrote this testimony in 1999 for my website.

After Michelle and I got saved in 1983, the Lord did some mighty things in our lives. There are many testimonies we have accumulated since then, and though I revel in His Grace and Mercy, and love to speak of the wondrous things He has done in our lives, time and space would not allow me the opportunity to speak of them all. But I want to give a testimony of the circumstances that led us to the ministry the Lord has given us. My prayer is that it blesses and encourages those who read it.

The reason I even want to include this account here is not to boast in my accomplishments, but rather to show the reader that you don't need a special degree or title or pledges for financial support to minister in the service of the Lord.

Notice how I stumbled through each phase of the development of the ministry. The Lord sustained me through it all. All He requires is willingness and obedience. These two characteristics He will always bless.

Over the years, I have been privileged to pray one on one with thousands to receive Jesus. This is not to boast...truly, any accomplishments I have had are from the Lord. I am not a great and eloquent speaker, nor am I a scholar or a theologian. I only tell you this to encourage you. If I can do it, ANYONE CAN DO IT! Just be obedient to the call of the Lord in your life.

Our first six months in the Lord Jesus Christ were spent in Salt Lake City. There the Lord blessed us mightily, in teaching us to hear His Voice and to learn of His Love for us.

Circumstances eventually led to us losing our car (it was parked in an alley for too many days, because the battery was dead and it was impounded). As the wrecker was hooking up to the car, I tried to talk the driver into unhooking the car, and I would move it somewhere else. The driver told me he would, if I could pay him 50.00 for the hook up fee.

I didn't have the money. I had given up on the highline job I had gone there to work on. I felt led of the Lord to quit the union that I belonged to (IBEW), so we were scraping by with spot jobs at job service, living basically from day to day, and watching the Lord provide for us.

Our car was important to our work situation - no car meant no work. It was February, and as we watched the tow truck pull the car away, I walked to the apartment, asking the Lord, "Why?" Even at that young age in the Lord, I didn't point a finger at Him, nor was I angry with Him for allowing that to happen. I've had many people testify to me that they have been angry at the Lord. I can't ever remember a time that I was. I understand that He is Sovereign, and my life is in His hands. So I wasn't angry. I was just wondering why He allowed that to happen. It didn't make any sense to me. Soon the rent would be due, it was February, and what would we do?

Once inside the apartment, Michelle and I prayed, asking our Father to help us to understand. As we prayed, I opened the Bible. When I opened the Bible, my eyes landed on Hebrews 10:34 (ASV):

For ye both had compassion on them that were in bonds, and took joyfully the spoiling of your possessions, knowing that ye have for yourselves a better possession and an abiding one.

As I read that, Michelle and I started laughing and "joyfully took the spoiling of our old Vega". We were sure that the Lord was up to something good. A few weeks later, we couldn't pay our rent, so we loaded up my duffel bag and a pack sack, and left Salt Lake City, hitchhiking towards California, but not knowing where we were going.

My pride wouldn't let me ask any one for anything, and as a result, we would make our needs known only to God. Initially, we ate at a couple of missions, but we got violently sick after eating at one, and decided we weren't going to eat at anymore missions, which made us even more dependent on the Lord for His day to day Provision. Beyond that, we didn't have a clue as to where we were going, and what we were going to do.

We hitchhiked for two months, during which time the Lord mightily blessed us with an awareness of His Presence in our lives. Every day brought a testimony that would take us to new levels of Faith in the Lord. He gave us many opportunities to witness of His Grace or to minister to whoever picked us up, and we were blessed daily.

I will relate just a couple of the incidents here, just to give the reader an idea of the things we experienced.

HUMAN TURTLES, WONDERFUL FRITTERS

We were in Auburn, California. We had left a lot of things behind when we left Salt Lake City, but we brought what we could with us, as well. This made for some heavy burdens on our back. I carried the duffel bag, and Michelle carried the back pack.

Our progress through town was at the pace of two blocks at a time, then we would rest for ten minutes or so, and walk another two blocks. As we made our way slowly through the town, we eventually came to a bakery. In the window were all kinds of wonderful looking pastries. What grabbed our attention was a sign that advertised apple fritters, two for a dollar.

The fritters looked huge. We hadn't eaten breakfast yet, and both of us were hungry. We didn't have a dollar, not even fifty cents - I think I counted out thirty-some cents - but we looked in that window and talked about how great those fritters looked to us. Soon, though, we just committed it to the Lord, and knew that we would not go hungry that day. But as we walked away from the bakery, we couldn't help but talk about those fritters and how good they looked.

A couple of blocks farther down the road, we found a large brick planter outside a lawyer's office. It must have been a Saturday or a Sunday, since the office was closed. Either way, that planter provided a perfect place to rest. As we sat there, we spoke some more about the fritters. The Lord was always faithful to bring me work when we needed it; splitting someone's firewood, or cleaning a yard, or unloading a truck. We knew we would eat that day, but boy, didn't those fritters look good! Soon, we decided it was time to go. As I started to help Michelle with her back pack, something caught my eye.

There, right behind where I had been sitting, was a crisp one dollar bill, folded lengthwise!

Our eyes got huge as we rejoiced in the Lord's provision. I took the backpack off Michelle's back, and she ran to the bakery and bought two apple fritters. As I said before, they were HUGE, and they were absolutely delicious. Wonderful Jesus! *Manna fritters*.

For the record: Michelle and I occasionally buy apple fritters as a remembrance of the Lord's provision. We have never found any fritters that were as good or as big as those two we had that day.

Never once did we go without food when we needed it. The Lord has always been faithful to supply our needs. Jesus said not to worry about what we are going to eat. That experience in our lives sealed that scripture in our hearts.

LAKE TAHOE

We got into Lake Tahoe early in the morning. As we stood there in town, it started to snow. Big wet flakes came down. We had a few dollars, so we went into a store and bought a couple of ponchos to keep us dry.

The Lord had enabled us to always have clean clothes; we always were able to afford a Laundromat when we needed one. But this day, we were down to our last change of clean clothes, and we had spent our money on the ponchos.

All day we stood there, trying to get a ride, but to no avail. After several hours we started trying to analyze what the Lord was doing. We knew He would never let us down, but we started eyeing the camp grounds across the street, figuring we could pitch our tent if we had to, and keep each other warm.

The issues we were talking about as we stood there, was the fact that we needed a shower and we needed to wash our clothes. Never once did we question whether God would come through for us - it was more like, "what was He up to?" We figured that there was someone who the Lord wanted us to tell about Him, but they hadn't gotten there yet.

From early in the morning, to about 5:00 that evening, we stood in that spot, trying to get a ride. No one would stop. Finally, a car stopped. The man in the car told us that he had seen us standing there that morning. When he saw us still standing there, he knew he had to pick us up. He was the director of a alcoholic recovery retreat, and he told us that all of his cabins were vacant. We were welcome to stay the night if we wanted to. He also told us that if we had any laundry we needed to do, there was a washer and dryer in the cabin we would be staying in. Wonderful Jesus! The man blessed us with a cabin, laundry facilities, showers, and a large kettle of stew. We were blessed.

The next day he drove us to the out skirts of town. He wasn't even out of sight when a car stopped to pick us up. The man and woman who picked us up explained to us that there had been chain restrictions the day before, and the restrictions had just been lifted. They told us they were picking us up to help with the weight. As we rode, the Lord gave us a great opportunity to witness to them of God's love and the need for Jesus Christ in their lives. We were young Christians, and didn't really know a lot, but the Lord used us on that ride to plant some wonderful seed. The man and woman were thanking us when they let us out of the car. We were learning that *all things work together for good for those who love God, who are called according to His purpose.*

Every day we had a testimony of the Lord working in our lives. We were totally dependent on Him. He always came through for us.

OUT OF OUR COMFORT ZONE

We traveled for two months like that, and eventually ended up in Arizona. We spent four years there. During that time, our two oldest daughters, Talitha and Feather were born.

All of our children were born at home, and I have been privileged and blessed to deliver them all. The majority of the time that we were in Chino Valley, Arizona, I worked as a carpenter. I also worked as a concrete worker, and a landscaper while we were there. We were doing pretty well for ourselves; we had all we needed, owned all that we had (no debt), were settled in, and had a small park model trailer we called home.

Every morning for the three and a half years that we spent in Chino Valley (our first 6 months in Arizona we lived in the Showlow area of the White mountains), I would get up at 5:00, and study the Word of God before I went to work at 7:00. I studied the Word every morning, seven days a week for the three and a half years we were there, using a Strong's concordance, Thayer's, Vine's, and the Englishman's Concordance to help me in my study of the Word. On Saturdays and Sundays I would spend several hours in the study of the Word. I had an insatiable hunger for the Word of God.

One Sunday, I was sitting at the table, studying God's Word, when He spoke to me. "What are you doing for me?" I was witnessing to whoever I worked with. I was living a relatively clean life before the Lord, and I told Him so. He asked again, "What are you doing for me?" He spoke to me from the verse in Hebrews 11:6 that says "without faith it is impossible to please God- ", and immediately, I remembered how totally dependent on Him we were for those two months that we hitchhiked. He reminded me of all the wonderful things He had done during that time.

We were aware that He provided for our needs even then, but it wasn't the same any more. I was growing in knowledge of the things of God, but I had to ask myself, where was I when it came to faith? I suddenly had a crazy thought. I looked at my wife, and asked her: "Do you remember when we hitchhiked through California and Nevada, and how close we were to God, because we had to rely on Him for everything?" She said she did. "Well, what would you say if we sold everything, got a bus, and just traveled for Jesus, and let Him guide us where He wants us, so we can learn more about faith?"

Michelle said "If that's what the Lord wants, that's what we will do." So it was settled. Now all we had to do was make sure this was of God and just not my own idea. So I put it in God's hands.

Later that day, we went out yard-saling. We weren't even looking for a bus, but we found one. It was a 1949 Ford. The man wanted $800.00 for it. I bought it, and the next weekend we had a yard sale of our own and sold most of our stuff, and used the money to convert the bus into a motor home. Some friends of ours, Bob and Annette helped us build the bus.

The last thing we did was put our trailer up for sale. It sold in a week. We left shortly afterwards, having no idea at all where we were going. We just threw ourselves in the arms of our Father.

We had no idea how long we were going to travel (certainly, we did not think we'd be at it for 23 years; 1988-2011), or even what our calling was, or even that we had a calling. All we knew was we were going to travel for a time to learn about faith.

On the back of the bus we painted a huge sign that said "Faithwalkin' ". We painted several scriptures in various easy to read places. We were leaving our city, not knowing where we would end up. We made a covenant with the Lord that we would let no one know of our needs, and I would work with my own two hands to supply our needs. The Lord would have to supply the work as we travelled.

EXCEPT THE FATHER DRAW THEM....

Talitha was 2, and Feather was almost 1 at the time. There are so many testimonies I could share. God is faithful. Many people would approach me, curious about the bus. There aren't too many 1949s out there these days. They'd want to look at the old flathead engine. Each time this would open a door for me to witness to them, and tell them about Jesus. I was leading people to the Lord, and still did not realize my calling as an evangelist, and certainly did not see myself as a minister. Others would approach us because of the scriptures that were written on the bus, and the results were the same.

VAPOR LOCKING FOR THE LORD

On our first day of our new adventure, we were climbing Williams mountain, and the bus just stopped running. I was able to safely roll the bus backwards to the side of the road, and set the emergency brake. It had an electric fuel pump on it, and I crawled under the bus to determine if it was getting gas. It took some time to check the fuel pump, by pulling the fuel line that ran to the engine, and to have Michelle turn the key. Fuel came running freely out of the pump from the tank. I hooked it all up again, and tried to start it, and it started. Glory! I figured the fuel pump would need to be replaced sooner or later. We continued up the mountain with no more problems. I bought a new fuel pump, but that didn't remedy the situation. For the next couple of weeks, every couple of days, the bus would stop in the worst places, and each time I would disconnect that line, tap on the pump, and it would start right up. I wasn't a mechanic, but the routine always worked, and I was beginning to realize there was a pattern to these events. Every time it stalled like that, I would end up witnessing to someone who would stop to help us, and it would always result in them praying to receive Jesus.

After a couple of weeks of this, I was at a wayside rest when a man approached me. He told me his first vehicle was a 1949 Ford. He wanted to look at the old flathead, so I opened the hood and let him revel in his memories a while. He told me about how he had souped his engine up, and how it was the fastest in the town where he grew up. Then he asked me, "Have you had problems with it vapor locking?" I told him I didn't know what that meant.

He explained to me that the fuel lines were so close to the engine, that they would get hot, and the gas would form a "vapor lock" in the line, and cause the engine to stall. So that was the problem! I asked him what he did to fix it. He told me the best thing to do was to put wooden clothes pins along the line; as they would insulate the line and protect it from overheating so often. He said the clothes pins just helped the problem, but they didn't solve it. The only thing I could do was just wait for the line to cool, and the fuel would flow again. I realized then that every time I pulled that line from the electric fuel pump to the engine, that I was allowing the gas to flow out of the line, eliminating the "vapor lock". From that time on, for the next year, the bus would vapor lock in some of the most difficult places, and *every time* it did, I would end up ministering to or praying with someone who stopped to help to receive Lord.

It was then that God firmly cemented Romans 8:28 in my heart.

Rom 8:28 And we know that all things work together for good to them that love God, to them who are the called according to *his* purpose.

To this day, we equate those "all things" that come our way that interrupt our plans or our forward momentum as "Vapor locking for the Lord".

I began to think that the Lord intended me to witness only to the ones who approached me, which were a lot of people. I had no inclination to "go out" to witness to people. I was leading many to the Lord just through them coming to me.

I had the faith to believe each one was a divine appointment, and that the Lord was drawing them into His Kingdom.

DIVINE DIRECTION

About three months after we left Arizona, we were in Sydney Nebraska. My dad was dying of colon cancer in Salt Lake City. It was winter, and the mountains between him and us were treacherous, and the brakes on the bus were not the greatest. But I wanted my Dad to see his granddaughters before he passed into Glory. We sought the Lord for direction. That night I dreamed that I was telling a friend of mine about Jesus. Michelle also dreamed that she was telling a friend of hers about Jesus. Both of our friends who were in our dreams lived in Florida. We took that as the direction from the Lord that we had been seeking. So we started for Florida. We lived in the '49 for one year. It took us seven years to get to Florida. One day I will see my dad in Glory.

Mar 10:29 And Jesus answered and said, Verily I say unto you, There is no man that hath left house, or brethren, or sisters, or father, or mother, or wife, or children, or lands, for my sake, and the gospel's,

30 But he shall receive an hundredfold now in this time, houses, and brethren, and sisters, and mothers, and children, and lands, with persecutions; and in the world to come eternal life.

BASIC TRAINING FOR THE PULPIT

We wintered in Lincoln, Nebraska, parked at the People's City Mission, while I worked for a construction company as a "tender" or a "hoddy" for some brick layers. One evening, I told my wife that I felt that I could relate to the homeless guys better than the people who came in to minister at the chapel services every night, *because we were where they were at...at street level.*

I told her that I would like the opportunity to preach to them. She told me she was sure that if I mentioned it to the workers there, they would probably give me an opportunity to preach in the chapel some night. I told her that I didn't want to make anything happen. If the Lord wanted me to share to the men, He would open the door for me to do so. That way I could know I was in His Will. Two days later, Anita McCracken told me that a person who was scheduled to preach had cancelled, and that they needed someone to preach that night. She asked me if I would. I said "sure". She said the only catch was that chapel was in 15 minutes, so I would have no time to prepare. I threw myself in the arms of my Father, and He mightily blessed me.

That whole month of February people kept on canceling their appointments. I probably preached 20 days out of that month. The Lord was training me for pulpit ministry.

Since then I have committed my ways to the Lord, and have made it an unswerving policy not to open any doors myself, or to promote our ministry, but to walk through the doors that the Lord opens for us.

A NEW HOME

My mother came down to Lincoln to visit us, and Michelle went with her back to Minnesota for a week to visit relatives. While she was up there, she stopped in to see Lonnie Lee, a pastor friend of ours who was instrumental in planting the seeds that eventually led me to coming to the Lord that same night (see my testimony). When she went to his house, Lonnie was praying to the Lord, asking Him what he should do about a bus he had.

When he opened the door to his house, and saw Michelle, he knew the Lord had given him the answer. He asked Michelle how our bus was doing. The '49 was losing power. I got stopped on the freeway once for going too slow! She said it wasn't doing too well, but it would get us where we needed to go. Lonnie told her we could have his bus if we drove up to get it. A couple of months later, we went to Northern Minnesota, and our bus died just as we got to my home town, Margie.

CALLING DEFINED

We spent a year and a half there, building our new bus, and making it livable. The following spring we left Margie to continue our trek to Florida. But first, we went to Warroad, Minnesota, and spent about a month up there, ministering in the way the Lord had taught me, letting people come to the bus for ministry.

In St. Cloud Minnesota, a sister in the Lord named Betty Reardon told me that my calling was that of an evangelist. I never realized that, *although by that time I had ministered to and led lots of people to the Lord.* We were still learning about Faith. She asked me if I ever handed out tracts, I told her that I let the Lord bring people to me. She gave me a box of tracts, and told me to try it some time. Eventually, I did, and ended up discovering a whole new dimension in the ministry the Lord had called me to. We were in St. Cloud for about six months, and led many people to a saving faith in Jesus.

ARMED AND DANGEROUS

The Lord blessed me abundantly in the tract ministry. We spent about two months in Austin Minnesota, and it was at a small church there, that the pastor prophesied to me and said that I was destined to make oaks from saplings. He told me I had a future of discipling others to do the work of the ministry. I didn't even know what that meant, but to this day I have the cassette tape of that prophetic word. We spent a few months in Osage, Iowa, at a ministry called Rennaisance - a Christian community given to ministering to ministers - and about eight months in Waterloo/Cedar Falls, Iowa.

The Lord literally gave me the streets in Waterloo, Iowa...it seemed like every person I spoke to was open and receptive to the things of God. I got to lead many people to the Lord and out of the grasp of Satan each time I went out on the streets.

Our third child, Elijah was born there in our bus on the job site in June of 1992.

TENNESSEE REFINING

I had spent about four years on the road, ministering one-on-one to people with no one but Jesus to show me the ropes. Don't get me wrong - Jesus is the perfect Teacher but sometimes it got pretty frustrating, as I would begin to get the "Elijah Syndrome" (Lord, I'm the only one that's out here, serving you). I never met another street evangelist in all that time.

Actually, I wasn't even sure that there was such a person. I would meet a lot of people who told me they wanted to go out on the streets with me, but I never had any one actually go, with the exception of my brothers and sisters at Renaissance when they came down to Waterloo to work the streets with me a couple of times.

Then we got to Chattanooga. There are so many testimonies that could be included in each one of these sections, but the purpose of this is to just let the reader get a general idea of how we have gotten to the place that we are at now. Out bus broke down on the exit ramp to Gunbarrel Avenue in EastRidge, Tennessee, and as a result of this divine vapor lock, we ended up living in Birchwood, Tennessee, and working in the Chattanooga/Cleveland Tennessee area with a Christian plumbing company, "Mainline Plumbing".

For two and a half years we worked there, and it was an ideal situation. John Latour, the owner of Mainline Plumbing understood and honored my calling as an evangelist, so when the Lord would quicken me to go preach somewhere, he backed me up in it.

In Cleveland, Tennessee, we found a wonderful church which we call "home", **_Living Word Fellowship,_** on Old Tasso Road.

Grace Elizabeth was born Birchwood, Tennessee, in our bus on the Latour's property where we lived for the two and a half years we spent in Tennessee.

I first started open air preaching at the abortion clinic in Chattanooga. The Lord teamed me up with a precious brother who carried a cross as part of his ministry. Mike Siemer and I became regular partners in ministry for the two and a half years we were in Tennessee.

He was already an open air preacher...I was better at one on one. But as I ministered at the abortion clinic, I got more and more confident to preach on the streets. Soon I was sharing the microphone with Mike on the streets. I was convinced that I wouldn't ever carry a cross like Mike did. It seemed so impractical. I liked the freedom of being able to go freely from person to person.

I wrote my first tract there...I found a brother that would print them inexpensively, and had ten thousand printed up.

So far I have passed out somewhere around 100,000 of that tract which was titled "All Things Were Created By Him and For Him".

Eventually we left Tennessee, and finally headed for Florida, the destination the Lord had given us back in the winter of 1988.

PICK UP YOUR CROSS DAILY...

We ended up in Crystal River, Florida in 1995. I was at a Bible Study shortly after we got there, and the Lord spoke to my heart that this would be the place to build a cross. This was not like the cities I was used to - there were no places where there was a lot of foot traffic, where I could pass out tracts. A visual form of evangelism would work here.

Naturally, I had to let Mike know - I knew he would get a kick out of it, since I had said I would never do that kind of ministry. On the way to the lumber company the next day, I figured I would stop at the mall and call Mike and let him know. As I was getting close to the mall, ***I saw a man walking down the road, carrying a cross! Wonderful Jesus! Talk about confirmation!***

When I spoke to Mike on the phone, I told him what I was going to do, and what I saw. Mike said that he knew the guy, and that I should go to meet him. I did, and Brian O'Connell and I became good friends and co-laborers together.

FULL TIME SERVICE

Shortly after I built my cross, the Lord spoke to my heart again, and I asked my wife to make a robe for me. The purpose of the robe was never to imitate Jesus, although many people think that is what I am doing when they see me. The robe was a prophetic tool. To the Christians that stop, I tell them that the Lord is coming for a spotless bride. In Revelation 19:7-8, we are told that the Lamb's bride is dressed in white linen, and the white linen represents the righteousness of the saints. The Word to Christ's bride then as it is now is to make herself ready.

Rev 19:7 Let us be glad and rejoice, and give honour to him: for the marriage of the Lamb is come, and his wife hath made herself ready. 8 And to her was granted that she should be arrayed in fine linen, clean and white: for the fine linen is the righteousness of saints.

Then again, wearing the white robe also serves another purpose. When people see me, whether their reaction is negative or positive, there is no doubt that they think of Jesus. Even if they say *"Look at that nut! Who does he think he is, Jesus?"* They have still thought about Jesus. It doesn't matter what people think of me - that they think about Jesus is important.

One day I was carrying the cross in Crystal River, and the Lord mightily blessed me with lots of opportunities to minister. Then He spoke to my heart, and said *"You can do this all the way to California."* When I shared it with Michelle, she told me if that was what the Lord wanted, we would do it.

The Lord opened a lot of doors, and in August of '96, we left on our journey "Crosscountry". From that time to now, He has blessed us with being able to minister full time.

Our bus broke down in Mobile, Alabama. The Lord blessed us with a nice motor home a short time later. He moved a brother and sister in Christ (Ron and Marian Reese) to buy a 35 foot 1988 Allegro for us. He is our Provider. If He calls us to a work He will see that it prospers. Not for our own selfish needs, but so the work can go on.

I made it as far as Port Arthur, Texas on that walk, and ended up working with Pastor Ralph Foster of Bethel Temple as the church's evangelist and unofficial associate pastor.

During those years, the Lord further defined and refined our ministry. Since 1998, the Lord has caused me to understand how important it is for the Church (consisting of many local fellowships) in the area to come together and to work together for the furtherance of the Kingdom of God, and in the various areas he would have us to minister on that walk, God would have me do outreaches or start ministries that involved multiple fellowships coming together. True unity of the local Body of Christ is a hard thing to establish and to maintain.

In 2001, the Lord called me to carry a cross up both sides of the Mississippi River on a prayer walk for the Church in America. That was a 10 year walk, which got me as far as Twin Lakes Arkansas on one side, and Panther Burn, Mississippi on the other side.

During that ten year period of time, God further refined and defined the ministry He entrusted us with. And from 2011, till the present time, the Lord has planted us in Northeast Alabama, Pastoring a Saturday night fellowship, geared toward discipling and equipping saints to fulfill their Calling, and working toward bringing the Church leadership together to see the Kingdom of God established in this region.

I believe God gave me a word for the Church several years ago (1990) and I have been echoing that Word in various ways through the years... The word was this:

"This is the day of the lay man. No longer is Christianity to be a pulpit-to-pew relationship; it was never intended to be that. The Word of God says that He has made us all kings and priests, and we are to sit and rule in the heavenly places in Christ. The function of the pastors and the evangelists and the teachers, the apostles and the prophets is to equip the saints so that they, too can become pastors, or evangelists, or teachers, or apostles or prophets, or walk in their particular calling of ministry.

Too often pastors have lorded it over their flocks, concerned more with retaining and building their numbers than with sending their people out. It is time for the lay man to arise and to realize their calling. God has given each one of us Gifts so that we can further His Kingdom. It's not in our name, and what we have done, nor is it in our ministry and how influential we are...it is all in Jesus, and that his kingdom would be established on earth, as it is in heaven.

The lay man who is content with sitting in his pew is like the slothful and evil servant who buried his talent in the ground, instead of investing it to further his master's kingdom.

The pastor who condones the complacency of the pew sitter is like the Pharisee who loves the chief places, and who makes his prayers to be heard of men...

Both of these people are in a terrible position.

The time is short. The Kingdom of God is at hand. The harvest is ripe. It's past time to get busy."

The Lord gave me that message in a very large church we were visiting. He told me to stand up and give it while the pastor was in the midst of his sermon. I argued with the Lord.

I said "Lord, I am a stranger here. I don't look like these people and we drive a funky old bus...they won't receive it."

He pressed on me to give the Word. I said, "Lord, if You want me to give this message, You will have to open up the opportunity." Just at that moment in our conversation with each other, the pastor stopped in the middle of his message, and said, "I believe someone has a Word for the Church".

I looked around, secretly hoping someone else would speak. No one stepped up. So I stood up, and gave that message. The pastor seemed like he didn't like what he heard. He didn't acknowledge the word that was given; he just resumed his message. Afterward, several people came up to me and thanked me for what I said. But the pastor didn't say a thing. When we walked out, he just shook my hand and said "It was good to have you here", then looked at the next person, shook their hand and said the same thing.

Since then I have been giving the same message in different ways to the Body of Christ doing my part in helping saplings become mighty oak trees.

In 1988 I had no idea of what "ministry" looked like. If someone would have asked me if I was a minister of the Gospel, I would have told them "No", because religion had blinded me to the fact that we are all called to be ministers.

So many people think they need a seminary degree, or a license or recognition in order to minister. Joe Christian has basically been content to leave "the Work of the Lord" to those with titles or degrees.

If you are willing, the Lord will bless you and use you for the furtherance of His Kingdom, and someday you will look back and stand in awe at the Work He has done in you and through you. He is just looking for a yielded vessel.

I pray the Lord richly blesses you as you seek His face for direction in the ministry He would have for you...

Taking God's Name in Vain

Exo 20:7 Thou shalt not take the name of the LORD thy God in vain; for the LORD will not hold him guiltless that taketh his name in vain.

Satan is the father of lies, and so many lies and traditions have crept into the Church because of his influence on many of those who are in leadership over the Body of Christ. One of the biggest lies that has been encouraged and embraced in the Church is the misinterpretation of the Third Commandment. Because that commandment has been misinterpreted, the Church in general has been rendered powerless in the world.

Some guy walks up to the Christian and purposely utters a series of cuss words that involve a reference to God or the Name of Jesus, and the Christian becomes grieved because this sinner is always taking God's Name in vain.

Christians are continually grieved in their work places because of the blasphemous language that is uttered day in and day out as those ungodly heathens hold their ungodly conversations, taking God's name in vain as casually as they drink their water during a break. The Christian that finds himself or herself in such a place ask others to pray for them, that they would find a better job that isn't so full of heathens.

The irony of all that is the fact that those who are grieved by the offensive language of their co-workers are guilty of the crime that they are accusing the heathen of.

The word "take" is the Hebrew Word "Nasah". It means to lift, to bear, to carry, to bear continuously.

My wife's maiden name used to be Pritchard. But one day Michelle Pritchard exchanged vows with me and took my family name. Now she is Michelle Rowe and has officially been so since 1985. Since January 10, 1985, everyone she encounters knows her as a Rowe. If she cheated on me, and was unfaithful, she could be said to have taken my name in vain.

I have been a Christian since 1983. I took the Name of Jesus Christ as my Lord on September 6, 1983, and became known as a Christian to all I encountered after wards.

The word translated as "vain" means emptiness, vanity, falsehood, emptiness of speech, lying.

The grave implications of what was actually meant by not taking the Lord's Name in vain is hidden and glossed over by the shallow definition of using God's name as a cuss word. It seems that no one poses the question "If that's what it meant, then why didn't God just say you shall not use my name as a profanity, instead of *you shall not receive or bear my Name as a meaningless exercise.*"

The person who calls on the Name of Jesus to save them from the flames of Hell, and yet who gives God little attention outside the 4 walls of the Sunday (or Saturday) and midweek meeting place has taken the Name of the Lord in vain.

The person who calls on Jesus and becomes a tithe paying member of a local congregation so that they will be raptured out before the tribulation, and does no more to further the Kingdom of God has taken the Name of the Lord in vain. The three parables the Lord tells in Matthew 25 illustrate those who have taken the Name of the Lord in vain, contrasted with those who are faithful to Him.

Mat 25:14 For *the kingdom of heaven is* as a man travelling into a far country, *who* called his own servants, and delivered unto them his goods. 15 And unto one he gave five talents, to another two, and to another one; to every man according to his several ability; and straightway took his journey...

Mat 25:24 Then he which had received the one talent came and said, Lord, I knew thee that thou art an hard man, reaping where thou hast not sown, and gathering where thou hast not strawed:
25 And I was afraid, and went and hid thy talent in the earth: lo, *there* thou hast *that is* thine.
26 His lord answered and said unto him, *Thou* wicked and slothful servant, thou knewest that I reap where I sowed not, and gather where I have not strawed:
27 Thou oughtest therefore to have put my money to the exchangers, and *then* at my coming I should have received mine own with usury.
28 Take therefore the talent from him, and give *it* unto him which hath ten talents.
29 For unto every one that hath shall be given, and he shall have abundance: but from him that hath not shall be taken away even that which he hath.
30 And cast ye the unprofitable servant into outer darkness: there shall be weeping and gnashing of teeth.

The person who continues in their sin, excusing it with the popular phrase (another tool of Satan) "I am just a sinner saved by grace" has taken the Name of the Lord in vain because they are declaring that Christ's Work on the Cross didn't accomplish what He was sent to do, to destroy the works of the devil, and to loose those who are bound. His Grace is what frees us from the Power of sin.

Mat 1:21 And she shall bring forth a son, and thou shalt call his name JESUS: for he shall save his people from their sins.

Rom 6:12 Let not sin therefore reign in your mortal body, that ye should obey it in the lusts thereof.
13 Neither yield ye your members *as* instruments of unrighteousness unto sin: but yield yourselves unto God, as those that are alive from the dead, and your members *as* instruments of righteousness unto God.
14 For sin shall not have dominion over you: for ye are not under the law, but under grace.

Mat 7:21 Not every one that saith unto me, Lord, Lord, shall enter into the kingdom of heaven; but he that doeth the will of my Father which is in heaven.
22 Many will say to me in that day, Lord, Lord, have we not prophesied in thy name? and in thy name have cast out devils? and in thy name done many wonderful works?
23 And then will I profess unto them, I never knew you: depart from me, ye that work iniquity.

The Christian who is silent about their faith outside the four walls of the Church has taken the Name of the Lord in vain.

Mat 10:32 Whosoever therefore shall confess me before men, him will I confess also before my Father which is in heaven.
33 But whosoever shall deny me before men, him will I also deny before my Father which is in heaven.

The Christian construction worker I mentioned earlier needs to understand that just as dogs do what dogs do, so will heathens do what heathens do. Every where the Christian goes should be their mission field, their opportunity to be the light that God desires them to be.

Heathens will blaspheme the Name of God. But they are not guilty of taking the name of God in vain. They haven't yet *taken* the Name of God. The Christian worker should take every opportunity to tell them why they have taken the Name of God for themselves, because God's Will is that none of those heathens should perish, but rather that they should come to repentance. If you are a Christian and not walking in obedience to His Great Commission to proclaim His Kingdom and make disciples, you have taken His Name in Vain.

The First Commandment is not to have any gods before God. The one who has taken the Name of the Lord God in vain will pick and choose which parts of the Bible he or she wants to believe and obey.

When the flesh wants to justify itself and hold on to some particular sin, then the one who has transgressed the Third Commandment will be quick to turn to the god that "loves me just the way I am". But that is another god, and NOT the God of the Covenant.

God loves you, but He doesn't necessarily love the way you are.

That is why the first part of that First Commandment is "Exo 20:2 I *am* the LORD thy God, which have brought thee out of the land of Egypt, out of the house of bondage."

He didn't bring you out of bondage so you could return and wallow in it. That is why He sent Jesus, preaching "Repent for the Kingdom of God is at Hand." The one who doesn't strive against sin has taken the Name of God in vain. What's the point in coming to the Deliverer if you don't want to be delivered?

Heb 12:1 Wherefore seeing we also are compassed about with so great a cloud of witnesses, let us lay aside every weight, and the sin which doth so easily beset *us*, and let us run with patience the race that is set before us,
2 Looking unto Jesus the author and finisher of *our* faith; who for the joy that was set before him endured the cross, despising the shame, and is set down at the right hand of the throne of God.
3 For consider him that endured such contradiction of sinners against himself, lest ye be wearied and faint in your minds.
4 Ye have not yet resisted unto blood, striving against sin.

The second commandment is not to make unto you any graven image or any likeness of anything that is in heaven or that is in the earth beneath or that is in the water that is under the earth, to bow down to them nor serve them... So we can easily see that the worship of Buddha or the saints or Hindu statues or any other "graven image" is prohibited by God, and the Christian can say "Praise the Lord! I am not guilty of that one!"

But isn't that coin in your pocket a graven image? Or that dollar bill? The Word of God says that the *Love of money* is the root of all evil (*1 Tim 6:10*). The one who pursues worldly gain more than they do the furtherance of the Kingdom of God is guilty of taking the Name of the Lord in vain, because they are placing more affection on that graven image in their pocket than they are on God.

It's not wrong to be rich. The Word of God doesn't say that money is the root of all evil.

God blesses those He can trust with finances so they can contribute to the Kingdom of God. *Money* isn't the root of all evil, it is the *Love of money* that is the root of all evil. So if a person who professes to be a Christian spends the bulk of his or her life being consumed with getting more and more of this world's goods while cringing at the suggestion they should give a *tenth* of their income to the Work of God, or giving free will offerings over and above that ten percent for the purpose of furthering the Kingdom of God, they are in effect holding a graven image more important than the Kingdom of God, thus having taken the Name of the Lord God in vain.

But of even more concern are those who operate in a position of Ministry who have taken the Name of God in vain, and preach doctrines and traditions of men or denominational philosophies and preferences rather than the Truth of the Word of God.

Paul summed up his epistle to the Romans with these words:

Rom 16:17 Now I beseech you, brethren, mark them which cause divisions and offences contrary to the doctrine which ye have learned; and avoid them.
18 For they that are such serve not our Lord Jesus Christ, but their own belly; and by good words and fair speeches deceive the hearts of the simple.
19 For your obedience is come abroad unto all *men.* I am glad therefore on your behalf: but yet I would have you wise unto that which is good, and simple concerning evil.
20 And the God of peace shall bruise Satan under your feet shortly. The grace of our Lord Jesus Christ *be* with you. Amen.

Preachers that preach man made tradition, doctrines of men and denominational philosophies and preferences instead of the Word of God cause divisions contrary to the doctrine of Christ, and in effect take the Name of God in vain.

It is Christ's desire that His followers should be one. One in purpose, one in love, one in holiness, and in one accord.

Christ's Purpose is that all men would be saved. But how can they be saved unless they hear the Gospel? And how can they hear the Gospel unless one is sent?

If a Pastor, Apostle, Prophet, Evangelist, or Teacher is not teaching their disciples how to do the Work of the ministry, then they have taken the Name of God and His Calling in vain.

Far too many (certainly not all) "men of the cloth" are engaged in vanity, deceiving those who follow them into thinking that their faithful attendance to their particular fellowship is all Christianity is about, and competing with one another to build a bigger and better "church".

They are simply hirelings looking for monetary gain and pursuing their own agendas rather than the Will of God for the Church.

The world would know that we are His disciples by the Love we have for one another. What would happen if pastors would stop being jealous of one another, and begin to work with one another across denominational lines to further the Kingdom of God?

What if every week community outreach was being done by the Body of Christ as a whole? What if instead of the occasional outreach by a particular ministry or the occasional three day "revival meeting", Christians made it a lifestyle practice to reach out every day?

Do you say that is unrealistic? Maybe that's because too many professing Christians have taken the Name of God in vain.

Joh 15:8 Herein is my Father glorified, that ye bear much fruit; so shall ye be my disciples.

It will take you three minutes to read this, and those three minutes may plant a seed to help change your perspective for the rest of your life:

Rom 8:19 For the earnest expectation of the creature waiteth for the manifestation of the sons of God.

Manifestation = Revealing, revelation. This same word is used in a couple of very significant places:

1Co 1:4 I thank my God always on your behalf, for the grace of God which is given you by Jesus Christ;
5 That in every thing ye are enriched by him, in all utterance, and in all knowledge;
6 Even as the testimony of Christ was confirmed in you:
7 So that ye come behind in no gift; waiting for the coming of our Lord Jesus Christ:
8 Who shall also confirm you unto the end, that ye may be blameless in the day of our Lord Jesus Christ.
9 God is faithful, by whom ye were called unto the fellowship of his Son Jesus Christ our Lord.

In verse seven, the word "coming" is the same word translated as manifestation in Romans 8:19.

Read with this light, we can see that a totally different meaning can be found in 1 Corinthians 1:7, than what is normally understood or preached, and it fits perfectly with the statement in Romans 8:19.

This particular verse is not speaking about the second coming of Jesus that we are waiting for; it is actually speaking about the manifestation or the revealing of Christ working in and through our lives which we should be expecting to take place. - "waiting for" (1 Cor 1:7, and Romans 8:19 are the same Greek word) = to expect fully.

As we mature in our Christian walk, we are "enriched" by God in our speech, and in our knowledge of the things of God, through our testimonies of His Presence and Intervention in our daily affairs, which in turn conforms us to His Image and His Likeness, and enables us to walk in the Gifting that He intends for us to walk in, and we become more and more the image of Christ to those who we encounter. "ALL things work together for Good for those who love God and who are called according to His Purpose".

God has never ordained that those who confess His Name should play a waiting game of enduring the miseries of this world by being faithful attendees and tithers of some organized meeting place we erroneously call "church" until Christ's Second Coming. Where did He call you to become a member of a club or a clique?

Religious people will read as far as that last statement and may even consciously agree with it as true, but continue in their apathetic warming of the pew week in and week out, doing nothing more to further the Kingdom of God.

The purpose of assembling together in the building (episunogogue = at the synagogue - Hebrews 10:27) is to build one another up, to equip one another, and to encourage one another to continue in the Work of furthering the Kingdom of God in this world as Christ has commissioned us to. That pastor should be equipping you and sending you out into the world to further the Kingdom of God.

God created man in His Image and in His Likeness and placed him in the Garden. The garden was a particular spot in the earth, and God's intention was that man would multiply and as they multiplied, the garden would expand throughout the earth as the sons of God subdued the earth. Sin distorted man's image, and he no longer carried the Likeness of God. Man's God given authority was usurped by Satan. Man began to further Satan's kingdom rather than God's.

Long story short: Jesus came to restore that which was ordained from the foundation of the world. "Of His government there shall be no end". That work of restoration is given to those who are His. He told his disciples to preach Repent, for the Kingdom of Heaven is at hand. They were to cast out devils. In casting out devils, they furthered the Kingdom of God. They were to heal the sick. In healing the sick, they furthered the Kingdom of God. Then Jesus commissioned those twelve to go into all the world and train disciples to do the same thing they were trained to do (Matt 28:19,20). Those disciples were to operate in the Likeness of Jesus, who came to seek and to save that which was lost.

The Gospel of the Kingdom of God. That is what Jesus said would be preached in the world before the end would come (Matt 24:14). It isn't being preached in most of the buildings. That is why darkness is invading our world at such a rapid pace, because the children of Light are keeping the light effectively hid inside the "bushel" or the building. YOU are called to be the Light of the world. The world is waiting to see the light. Darkness cannot comprehend the light. You were once darkness, but now you are light. You should walk as children of light.

Another place where that word translated as "manifestation" and "coming" in our two verses above is used? In Ephesians 1:17, the word is "revelation".

Eph 1:17 That the God of our Lord Jesus Christ, the Father of glory, may give unto you the spirit of wisdom and revelation in the knowledge of him:
18 The eyes of your understanding being enlightened; that ye may know what is the hope of his calling, and what the riches of the glory of his inheritance in the saints,
19 And what is the exceeding greatness of his power to us-ward who believe, according to the working of his mighty power,
20 Which he wrought in Christ, when he raised him from the dead, and set him at his own right hand in the heavenly places,
21 Far above all principality, and power, and might, and dominion, and every name that is named, not only in this world, but also in that which is to come:
22 And hath put all things under his feet, and gave him to be the head over all things to the church,
23 Which is his body, the fulness of him that filleth all in all.

Your inheritance is now, not some time in the future. Our Lord Jesus Christ has been given ALL authority and He passes the same to us. Our understanding just has to catch up with that.

Your religious duties to a social clique erroneously referred to as a church will not suffice. You are not saved by works, but you HAVE been saved to work. Work at what? Establishing His Kingdom here on earth.

Eph 2:8 For by grace are ye saved through faith; and that not of yourselves: it is the gift of God:
9 Not of works, lest any man should boast.

10 For we are his workmanship, created in Christ Jesus unto good works, which God hath before ordained that we should walk in them.

I pray God grants you revelation of your Purpose in this life.

Have you taken the Name of God in vain, or are you accomplishing His Purpose here on earth?

The Gospel

It is important that the servant of God understands the Gospel that he or she is commissioned to preach. If a person doesn't understand what the gospel ism there is a danger of preaching a different gospel than the gospel that Christ commissioned us to preach.

What is the Gospel we are to preach?

Mat 4:23 And Jesus went about all Galilee, teaching in their synagogues, and preaching the **gospel of the kingdom**, and healing all manner of sickness and all manner of disease among the people.

Mat 24:14 And this gospel of the kingdom shall be preached in all the world for a witness unto all nations; and then shall the end come.

Mar 1:14 Now after that John was put in prison, Jesus came into Galilee, **preaching the gospel of the kingdom of God,**

Mar 1:15 And saying, The time is fulfilled, and **the kingdom of God is at hand**: repent ye, and believe **the gospel**.

The Good News (Gospel) is that Satan no longer rules unchecked in this world. Jesus came to establish His Kingdom here on earth, and we are commissioned to do the same.

Luk 9:1 Then he called his twelve disciples together, and gave them power and authority over all devils, and to cure diseases.
2 And he sent them **to preach the kingdom of God**, and to heal the sick.
3 And he said unto them, Take nothing for *your* journey, neither staves, nor scrip, neither bread, neither money; neither have two coats apiece.
4 And whatsoever house ye enter into, there abide, and thence depart.
5 And whosoever will not receive you, when ye go out of that city, shake off the very dust from your feet for a testimony against them.
6 And they departed, and went through the towns, **preaching the gospel**, and healing every where.

Luk 4:18 The Spirit of the Lord *is* upon me, because he hath anointed me to preach the **gospel** to the poor; he hath sent me to heal the brokenhearted, to preach deliverance to the captives, and recovering of sight to the blind, to set at liberty them that are bruised,

Luk 8:1 And it came to pass afterward, that he went throughout every city and village, **preaching and shewing the glad tidings of the kingdom of God:** and the twelve *were* with him,

Luk 9:11 And the people, when they knew *it,* followed him: and he received them, and spake **unto them of the kingdom of God, and healed them that had need of healing**

Luk 10:8 And into whatsoever city ye enter, and they receive you, eat such things as are set before you:
9 And heal the sick that are therein, and say unto them, **The kingdom of God is come nigh unto you.**

Luk 11:19 And if I by Beelzebub cast out devils, by whom do your sons cast *them* out? therefore shall they be your judges.
20 But if I with the finger of God cast out devils, **no doubt the kingdom of God** is come upon you.

Luk 13:18 Then said he, **Unto what is the kingdom of God like**? and whereunto shall I resemble it?
19 It is like a grain of mustard seed, which a man took, and cast into his garden; and it grew, and waxed a great tree; and the fowls of the air lodged in the branches of it.
20 And again he said, **Whereunto shall I liken the kingdom of God?**
21 It is like leaven, which a woman took and hid in three measures of meal, till the whole was leavened.

Luk 17:20 And when he was demanded of the Pharisees, **when the kingdom of God** should come, he answered them and said, The kingdom of God cometh not with observation:
21 Neither shall they say, Lo here! or, lo there! for, behold, **the kingdom of God is within you.**

The Gospel never changed. It was still about the Kingdom of God in the Book of Acts:

Act 8:12 But when they believed Philip **preaching the things concerning the kingdom of God**, and the name of Jesus Christ, they were baptized, both men and women.
13 Then Simon himself believed also: and when he was baptized, he continued with Philip, and wondered, beholding the miracles and signs which were done.

Act 14:21 And when they had **preached the gospel** to that city, and had taught many, they returned again to Lystra, and *to* Iconium, and Antioch,
22 Confirming the souls of the disciples, *and* exhorting them to continue in the faith, and that we must through much tribulation **enter into the kingdom of God.**

Act 19:6 And when Paul had laid *his* hands upon them, the Holy Ghost came on them; and they spake with tongues, and prophesied.

7 And all the men were about twelve.

8 And he went into the synagogue, and spake boldly for the space of three months, **disputing and persuading the things concerning the kingdom of God**.

Act 20:23 Save that the Holy Ghost witnesseth in every city, saying that bonds and afflictions abide me.

24 But none of these things move me, neither count I my life dear unto myself, so that I might finish my course with joy, and the ministry, which I have received of the Lord Jesus, **to testify the gospel of the grace of God**.

25 And now, behold, I know that ye all, **among whom I have gone preaching the kingdom of God**, shall see my face no more.

26 Wherefore I take you to record this day, that I *am* pure from the blood of all *men*.

Act 28:23 And when they had appointed him a day, there came many to him into *his* lodging; **to whom he expounded and testified the kingdom of God**, persuading them concerning Jesus, both out of the law of Moses, and *out of* the prophets, from morning till evening

30 And Paul dwelt two whole years in his own hired house, and received all that came in unto him,

31 **Preaching the kingdom of God,** and teaching those things which concern the Lord Jesus Christ, with all confidence, no man forbidding him.

Rom 14:16 Let not then your good be evil spoken of:

17 **For the kingdom of God is not meat and drink**; but righteousness, and peace, and joy in the Holy Ghost.

18 For he that in these things serveth Christ *is* acceptable to God, and approved of men.

19 Let us therefore follow after the things which make for peace, and things wherewith one may edify another.

1Co 6:9 Know ye not that the unrighteous shall **not inherit the kingdom of God?** Be not deceived: neither fornicators, nor idolaters, nor adulterers, nor effeminate, nor abusers of themselves with mankind,

10 Nor thieves, nor covetous, nor drunkards, nor revilers, nor extortioners, shall **inherit the kingdom of God.**

11 And such were some of you: but ye are washed, but ye are sanctified, but ye are justified in the name of the Lord Jesus, and by the Spirit of our God.

When does a person receive his or her inheritance? After they die or while they are still living? When should you expect to inherit the Kingdom of God? After you die, or while you are still living? The inheritance comes with a condition. Those who engage in the above named sins cannot walk in their inheritance. Remember when Jesus said that the Kingdom of God is within you?

Luk 17:20 And when he was demanded of the Pharisees, **when the kingdom of God** should come, he answered them and said, The kingdom of God cometh not with observation:
21 Neither shall they say, Lo here! or, lo there! for, behold, **the kingdom of God is within you.**

Jesus' teaching was that the kingdom of God isn't something you can tangibly put your hands on, or make a prediction of it's coming sometime in the future like so many prognosticators do today. In the above passage, Jesus was speaking to the Pharisees when He said "the Kingdom of God is within you". In the previous chapter Jesus said this:

Luk 16:13 No servant can serve two masters: for either he will hate the one, and love the other; or else he will hold to the one, and despise the other. Ye cannot serve God and mammon.

In Luke 16:13, Jesus was speaking of a frame of mind we are to have regarding our conduct in life. The person whose life is centered around the pursuit after material wealth cannot serve God. He follows this statement with the story of Lazarus and the rich man. The rich man had pursued his comfort while he was living, and ignored his obligations to help his fellow man. His mindset during his lifetime was that he should be served by others, instead of serving others.

Luk 16:25 But Abraham said, Son, remember that thou in thy lifetime receivedst thy good things, and likewise Lazarus evil things: but now he is comforted, and thou art tormented.

Then in chapter 17, when asked when the Kingdom of God should come, Jesus told the Pharisees that it wasn't going to come in a way that they could physically see. Instead, He said the Kingdom of God is *within* you. Jesus was talking about a mindset or a mentality that we hold concerning the things of this world or the things of the Kingdom of God. The word "Repent" literally "means to change one's mind" concerning a thing. You can't sit on a fence. You can't have the best of both worlds. Jesus said elsewhere that if we make the Kingdom of God our priority, we will have our needs taken care of.

Mat 6:31 Therefore take no thought, saying, What shall we eat? or, What shall we drink? or, Wherewithal shall we be clothed?

32 (For after all these things do the Gentiles seek:) for your heavenly Father knoweth that ye have need of all these things.
33 **But seek ye first the kingdom of God, and his righteousness**; and all these things shall be added unto you.
34 Take therefore no thought for the morrow: for the morrow shall take thought for the things of itself. Sufficient unto the day *is* the evil thereof.

A little before Jesus said to seek first the Kingdom of God, He said when we pray we are to pray like this: "Thy Kingdom come, Thy Will be done, on earth, as it is in heaven." Notice the prayer is not "thy Kingdom come sometime in the distant future". The next words say give us **this day** our *daily* bread. The invitation in the prayer for our Father's Kingdom to come is a present prayer, not a future hope. In fact Jesus said not to take thought for tomorrow. It's amazing how we overlook the details.

Righteousness and the Kingdom of God cannot be divorced from one another. They go hand in hand, just as sin and corruption walk hand in hand with this world.

Rom 14:16 Let not then your good be evil spoken of:
17 **For the kingdom of God is not meat and drink**; but righteousness, and peace, and joy in the Holy Ghost.
18 For he that in these things serveth Christ *is* acceptable to God, and approved of men.

If our affections are on the things of this world, we cannot walk in the full authority that Jesus has given us as His ambassadors in this world. 1 Corinthians 6:9-10 tells us that if I allow myself to wallow in sin, I cannot enjoy my inheritance.

1Co 6:9 Know ye not that the unrighteous shall **not inherit the kingdom of God?** Be not deceived: neither fornicators, nor idolaters, nor adulterers, nor effeminate, nor abusers of themselves with mankind,
10 Nor thieves, nor covetous, nor drunkards, nor revilers, nor extortioners, shall **inherit the kingdom of God.**
11 And such were some of you: but ye are washed, but ye are sanctified, but ye are justified in the name of the Lord Jesus, and by the Spirit of our God.
1 Corinthians 6 tells me that I am a temple of God. The Holy Spirit dwells within me. I should understand that the Holy Spirit is God, not some idea or concept.

In First John, chapter one, we are told that God is Light, and in Him there is no darkness. If we walk in darkness, we cannot have fellowship with Him. He cannot work in us and through us if we are actively walking in sin. To clarify: *we cannot walk in our inheritance if we are in sin.* You cannot serve two masters.

The Kingdom of God isn't just a New Covenant concept. In Deuteronomy 11, God laid down some conditions for His people to enjoy heaven on earth.

Deu 11:21 That your days may be multiplied, and the days of your children, in the land which the LORD sware unto your fathers to give them, as the days of heaven upon the earth.
22 For if ye shall diligently keep all these commandments which I command you, to do them, to love the LORD your God, to walk in all his ways, and to cleave unto him;
23 Then will the LORD drive out all these nations from before you, and ye shall possess greater nations and mightier than yourselves.
24 Every place whereon the soles of your feet shall tread shall be yours: from the wilderness and Lebanon, from the river, the river Euphrates, even unto the uttermost sea shall your coast be.
25 There shall no man be able to stand before you: *for* the LORD your God shall lay the fear of you and the dread of you upon all the land that ye shall tread upon, as he hath said unto you.
26 Behold, I set before you this day a blessing and a curse;
27 A blessing, if ye obey the commandments of the LORD your God, which I command you this day:
28 And a curse, if ye will not obey the commandments of the LORD your God, but turn aside out of the way which I command you this day, to go after other gods, which ye have not known.

Walking in obedience to the Will of God is a choice.

Walking in obedience to the Will of God enables us to partake of our inheritance in this life.

No devil can stand before a child of God who is walking in the Light and who is in active intimate fellowship with God. Jesus commissioned the disciples and those who would follow them to spread the Kingdom of God by proclaiming the Good News of the Kingdom of God, casting out demons and healing the sick.

The Good News is that the tyranny of sin no longer rules over a citizen of the Kingdom of God. Your inheritance as a child of God gives you great authority over the power of the enemy. As long as you walk in the Light of Christ and maintain your fellowship with Him, it is the Father's good pleasure to give to you the Kingdom.

Luk 12:32 Fear not, little flock; for **it is your Father's good pleasure to give you the kingdom.**

33 Sell that ye have, and give alms; provide yourselves bags which wax not old, a treasure in the heavens that faileth not, where no thief approacheth, neither moth corrupteth.
34 **For where your treasure is, there will your heart be also.**

Rom 14:16 Let not then your good be evil spoken of:
17 **For the kingdom of God is not meat and drink**; but righteousness, and peace, and joy in the Holy Ghost.
18 For he that in these things serveth Christ *is* acceptable to God, and approved of men.

1 Cor 6:12 All things are lawful unto me, but all things are not expedient: all things are lawful for me, but I will not be brought under the power of any.
13 Meats for the belly, and the belly for meats: but God shall destroy both it and them. Now the body *is* not for fornication, but for the Lord; and the Lord for the body.
14 And God hath both raised up the Lord, and will also raise up us by his own power.
15 Know ye not that your bodies are the members of Christ? shall I then take the members of Christ, and make *them* the members of an harlot? God forbid.
16 What? know ye not that he which is joined to an harlot is one body? for two, saith he, shall be one flesh.
17 But he that is joined unto the Lord is one spirit.
18 Flee fornication. Every sin that a man doeth is without the body; but he that committeth fornication sinneth against his own body.
19 What? know ye not that your body is the temple of the Holy Ghost *which is* in you, which ye have of God, and ye are not your own?
20 For ye are bought with a price: therefore glorify God in your body, and in your spirit, which are God's.

The Word of God tells us not to be deceived. You cannot walk in the authority that Christ has given you as an ambassador of His Kingdom if you are living in willful sin. You are no longer your own. You need to stop living like you are still your own, if you want to partake of your inheritance.

Gal 5:21 Envyings, murders, drunkenness, revellings, and such like: of the which I tell you before, as I have also told *you* in time past, that they which do such things shall not inherit the **kingdom of God.**

And Jesus, which is called Justus, who are of the circumcision. **These only *are my* fellow workers unto the kingdom of God**, which have been a comfort unto me.

2Th 1:5 *Which is* a manifest token of the righteous judgment of God, **that ye may be counted worthy of the kingdom of God**, for which ye also suffer:

By now it should be firmly established in the disciple's mind that the Gospel that must be preached is the Gospel of the Kingdom of God. When the Gospel of the Kingdom of God is preached, it will be demonstrated through the lives of those who proclaim it.

1Th 1:5 For our **gospel came not unto you in word only**, but also in power, and in the Holy Ghost, and in much assurance; as ye know what manner of men we were among you for your sake.
6 And ye became followers of us, and of the Lord, having received the word in much affliction, with joy of the Holy Ghost:
7 So that ye were ensamples to all that believe in Macedonia and Achaia.
8 For from you sounded out the word of the Lord not only in Macedonia and Achaia, but also in every place your faith to God-ward is spread abroad; so that we need not to speak any thing.
9 For they themselves shew of us what manner of entering in we had unto you, and how ye turned to God from idols to serve the living and true God;
10 And to wait for his Son from heaven, whom he raised from the dead, *even* Jesus, which delivered us from the wrath to come.

1Co 4:19 But I will come to you shortly, if the Lord will, and will know, not the speech of them which are puffed up, but the power.
20 For the **kingdom of God *is* not in word, but in power** (Dunamis)
21 What will ye? shall I come unto you with a rod, or in love, and *in* the spirit of meekness?

1Co 2:4 And my speech and my preaching *was* not with enticing words of man's wisdom, but in demonstration of the Spirit and of power:
5 That your faith should not stand in the wisdom of men, but in the power of God.

Mar 16:15 And he said unto them, Go ye into all the world, and preach the **gospel to every creature.**
16 He that believeth and is baptized shall be saved; but he that believeth not shall be damned.
17 And these signs shall follow them that believe; In my name shall they cast out devils; they shall speak with new tongues;
18 They shall take up serpents; and if they drink any deadly thing, it shall not hurt them; they shall lay hands on the sick, and they shall recover.

It is the Word of God.

Whose report will you believe? If you have read this book from the beginning to end, one of two things will have occurred. Either you will have just assimilated more information for your religious lifestyle, or you will have gone on to maturity and will accomplish that which God has Purposed for you in your life.

Now, Go. It is time to do what any grown up Christian should do:

Preach the Gospel.

Deliver the Captives.

Loose the prisoners.

Heal the sick.

Cast out demons.

The Kingdom of God is at hand!

The Church

A little bit of clarification here.

There is absolutely nothing wrong with the Church. The Saints of God who comprise the Church today are thriving and walking in the Blessings of the Promises of the Living God that they serve. Jesus said that the Gates of Hell would not prevail against the Church, and indeed, they have not and they cannot, and they will not ever prevail against the Church.

Satan is a master counterfeit. He does all he can to try to thwart God's Purpose. Like the Pharaoh's magicians who withstood Moses were able to duplicate many of the signs that God wrought through Moses, Satan also attempts to duplicate the Church of the Living God, by filling the land with his counterfeit church.

Jesus said many would come in His Name and deceive many. These deceivers have infiltrated the Church as in the parable that Jesus told with the wheat and tares, and have set up shop and called it church. Here are some of the ways Satan deceives with his counterfeit church:

Because of fear concerning the increasing wickedness in the land, the church looks to be raptured out of this mess that the world has become, while the Saints of God who comprise the Church fiercely wield the Sword of the Spirit of God, and actively engages the enemy, furthering the Kingdom of God one soul at a time.

While the Church (every member) is being discipled to go out into the world and preach the Gospel of the Kingdom of God and to make more disciples, the church makes members, and institutes its programs, it's social groups, and its' endless meetings that are erroneously called revivals designed to keep those members in the pew and entertained in the four walls. A lot of "good things" happen in the church. As a result, those who attend become content with their weekly meetings, and their scheduled routine.

Most people prefer the comfort and the familiarity of the church inside the four walls, rather than doing what the Church is called to do, forsaking all (reputation, comfort, financial security and safety) for the sake of the Kingdom of God. The church doesn't "Go into all the world" as Jesus commanded. They leave that for the Church.

The church is composed of a body of spectators who continually go to the altar in defeat, and is led by a man who is called a pastor, who rules over them, shaming them into being better members, or more faithful attendants, or better givers, regulating their dress codes, and making long sermons about the need for their tithes and offerings.

A pastor in the Church is continuously encouraging his fellowship to minister to one another and to minister to the lost. His desire is that every member of the Body of Christ that he shepherds will walk in his or her gifting and calling.

The Church gives. The Church doesn't need to be coerced, or promised to receive a hundred fold return for their generosity. It is in the Nature of the Church to give, just as the Father gave His Only Begotten Son for them.

The Church is composed of a Body of Believers who are being trained to be overcomers by Prophets, apostles, evangelists, pastors and teachers. The church is generally led by one individual or a board of individuals who control what is done in the four walls.

The church is continually sin conscious.

The Church is continually conscious of their identity in Christ, Who has saved them from their sin.

The pastor of a church is all about increasing his congregation, and building bigger buildings.

A pastor in the Church is all about the Kingdom of God, and working with other pastors and other ministers in the Church in unity with one another to further the Kingdom of God in their region.

The Church upholds its wounded, and encourages those who have fallen to get back up and to get back in the fight, and goes out to rescue those who have been taken captive by the enemy.

The church shoots it's wounded. It washes its hands of those who have fallen, and looks down its nose at those who have been taken captive.

Pharaoh's magicians couldn't duplicate some of the things that God did through Moses. The church can't duplicate the Love that is evident in the Church. Love for God that compels them to do His Will, Love for the Body of Christ (even those who are part of the church), and Love for the Lost.

The church can't duplicate the zeal of the Church for the things of the Kingdom of God. The Church doesn't need to be coerced into fulfilling the Great Commission, it is their delight to be used by God to rescue the perishing.

The church has its occasional outreaches or mission trips.

The Church is continually reaching out and their life is a mission.

The church has to set forth rules to bring its people in submission.

The Church walks in perfect liberty to serve the Living God.

Heathen see the church, and they confuse it with the Church, and don't want anything to do with it. That's Satan's grand design.

But when they meet the Church, they experience the Power of God and come out of darkness into the Light, becoming disciples who learn to Go and make disciples.

The Church is alive and well and thriving in the world. But the devil doesn't want you to know that, so he tries to get you to be a part of his church, in the hopes you won't know the difference.

But now you have read this book. Apply it to your life, and *BE* the Church.

Answer helps
Chapter 1

2) What is compassion? Compassion for others should be the motivating force that compels one to ministry, not the prospect of a means of income, or because we are *supposed* to minister to others.

If we can't see others as Jesus sees them, then what we do in the name of Christ can bring more damage to the cause of Christ than Glory to His Name.

Jesus' ministry was motivated by a compassion for those He encountered, which came as a result of genuine unconditional Love for the multitudes who were held captive by the god of this age.

A minster of God should reflect nothing less than Christ's Love and Compassion toward others.

6) Who is called to ministry? All who are in Christ.

Chapter 8

5) Jesus was a peacemaker between God **and** Man. **As such, those who are in ministry should be peacemakers between** God **and** Man.

7) What is the definition of a heretic? (pg 109)
Heresies: G139 αἵρεσις hairesis Thayer Definition:

1) act of taking, capture: e.g. storming a city
2) choosing, choice
3) that which is chosen 4) a body of men following their own tenets (sect or party)
 4a) of the Sadducees 4b) of the Pharisees 4c) of the Christians 5) dissensions arising from diversity of opinions and aims
Denominations can easily fall under this category.

8) Rom 16:17 says: Now I beseech you, brethren, mark them which cause divisions and offences contrary to the doctrine which ye have learned; and avoid them. Which doctrine is Paul referring to? The Apostle's Doctrine, which is the doctrine of Christ.

Chapter 9
The sermon on the mount is a message principally meant for Disciples

All Christians are called to Be disciples

The definition of a disciple is: A learner, pupil, disciple

A minister of the Gospel is to live his or her life as an <u>Example</u> to others.

1Ti 5:17 Let the elders that rule well be counted worthy of <u>double honor</u>, **especially they who labour in the word and doctrine.**

What does the above verse actually mean? <u>That those who teach others in the way of Christ should be supported by those who are discipled by them. At the same time, they should not be in the office of an elder if their goal is to be supported. The workman is worthy of his labor.</u>

Honor: <u></u>G5092 τιμή timē *tee-may'*
From <u>G5099</u>; a *value*, **that is,** *money* **paid, or (concretely and collectively)** *valuables*; **by analogy** *esteem* **(especially of the highest degree), or the** *dignity* **itself: - honour, precious, price, some.**

Describe the difference between leadership in the world and leadership in the Kingdom of God. <u>Those who lead in the world are in a position of self promotion and gain. Those who lead in the Kingdom of God are in a position of servitude for others.</u>

One must learn to <u>submit</u> **to** <u>authority</u> **before they can effectively exercise authority.**

Chapter 12:

Before His <u>Death, burial and resurrection</u> **the disciples ministered primarily in the** <u>authority</u> **they were given by Jesus.**

The scope of their ministry was <u>Exclusively</u> **to the people** <u>of Israel</u>

Chapter 13:

What does it mean when we are told that we are *complete* **in Him?** <u>Just as it pleased God that in Christ should all His fullness dwell, *it also pleases God that the fullness of Christ should dwell in you through His Holy Spirit.*</u>

Chapter 15:

***What* is going on to perfection, fulfilling the Will of God for your life?**
<u>Stepping into your Calling</u>

What is the difference between walking in the Authority of God as a child of God and the Gifts of the Holy Spirit? <u>We are all given authority to proclaim the Kingdom of God in the market place. The Gifts of the Holy Spirit are given to every man severally as He wills for the maintenance of the Body of Christ.</u>

Explain the Gift of Faith in contrast to going from Faith to Faith <u>The Gift of Faith is supernaturally invested through the Holy Spirit to some in the Body of Christ to in order to demonstrate to others what Faith looks like in a believer. These others will go from Faith to Faith as they are encouraged to continue by those with the Gift of Faith</u>

Who is qualified to operate in the Gifts of the Holy Spirit? <u>Every Born Again Believer who has been baptized in the Holy Spirit</u>

Who determines what your Gifting is? <u>The Holy Spirit</u>

www.ingramcontent.com/pod-product-compliance
Lightning Source LLC
Chambersburg PA
CBHW081509040426
42447CB00013B/3169